Phillis Wheatley

Phillis Wheatley

Biography of a Genius in Bondage

VINCENT CARRETTA

The University of Georgia Press

Athens and London

A Sarah Mills Hodge Fund Publication

This publication is made possible, in part, through a grant
from the Hodge Foundation in memory of its founder,
Sarah Mills Hodge, who devoted her life to the relief and
education of African Americans in Savannah, Georgia.

Published by the University of Georgia Press
Athens, Georgia 30602
www.ugapress.org
© 2011 by Vincent Carretta
All rights reserved

Designed by April Leidig-Higgins
Set in Adobe Caslon by Copperline Book Services, Inc.
Printed and bound by Thomson-Shore, Inc.

The paper in this book meets the guidelines for
permanence and durability of the Committee on
Production Guidelines for Book Longevity of the
Council on Library Resources.

Printed in the United States of America
15   14   13   12   11   C   5   4   3   2   1

Library of Congress Cataloging-in-Publication Data
Carretta, Vincent.
Phillis Wheatley : biography of a genius in bondage /
Vincent Carretta.
     p. cm.
Includes bibliographical references and index.
ISBN 978-0-8203-3338-0 (cloth : alk.paper)
     1. Wheatley, Phillis, 1753–1784.   2. African American
women poets — Biography.   3. Poets, American — Colonial
period, ca. 1600–1775 — Biography.   4. Slaves — United
States — Biography.   I. Title.
PS866.W5Z5827   2011
811'.1 — dc22
[B]   2011016374

British Library Cataloging-in-Publication Data available

To the memory of
Lillian "Maude" Carretta
(1919–2010)

Contents

Preface

. . . .

IN NOVEMBER 2005, a 174-word letter signed by Phillis Wheatley to a fellow servant of African descent in 1776 sold at auction for $253,000, well over double what it had been expected to fetch. It was reportedly the highest price ever paid for a letter by a woman of African descent. Anyone whose correspondence is worth over $1,400 a word has more than enough cultural significance to deserve an authoritative biography. The publication of *Phillis Wheatley* in 2011 coincides with the 250th anniversary of Wheatley's arrival in Boston from Africa. She was only about seven years old when she stepped off the slave ship.

Wheatley was a pioneer of American and African American literature, and her poems appear in every anthology of early American literature. Googling "Phillis Wheatley" turns up over 15,500 items. Despite opposition since the eighteenth century from those who have questioned the literary quality or the political and social implications of her writings, Wheatley has achieved iconic status in American culture. Elementary, middle, and high schools throughout the United States bear her name. A prominent statue in Boston memorializes her. Wheatley has been the subject of numerous recent stories written for children and adolescents. Her appeal is understandable: the prejudices against her race, social status, gender, and age notwithstanding, in 1773 she became the first person of African descent in the Americas to publish a book. The collection of poems she wrote in Boston while she was still a teenager first appeared in London and made her the earliest international celebrity of African descent.

DESPITE WHEATLEY'S historical significance and literary status, *Phillis Wheatley* is the first full-length biography of her. William Henry Robinson published a seventy-page biographical introduction to his *Phillis Wheatley and Her Writings* in 1984. Now long out of print, Robinson's book appeared early in the current period of historical research into all aspects of African American studies. Wheatley is a very challenging and elusive biographical subject. Her biographer must not only reconstruct the religious and political contexts within which and about which she so often wrote, but also try to fill in the significant gaps in her short life. Although Wheatley's historical and literary significance is now rarely questioned, much of her life has remained a mystery. She left no autobiography and rarely writes about her own life in the surviving documents. Her biographer must try to resist the urge to read her writings, especially her poems, as transparently autobiographical.

Where did she come from? How did Wheatley overcome the odds against her to gain transatlantic fame? How active a role did she play in the production and distribution of her writings? How was she able to establish a network of associations that included many of the most important people in North American and British military, political, religious, and social life? What more can be found about Phillis Wheatley's husband, John Peters? Did Phillis die a celebrity or in desperate obscurity? Her artistic legacy is still controversial. As a writer, was she an imitator or an innovator? Was she an overly accommodating "race traitor," as some black critics considered her during the 1960s and 1970s, or a subtly subversive defender of racial freedom and equality? *Phillis Wheatley* addresses all of these questions.

Phillis Wheatley is deeply indebted to the research of Robinson, and to the editorial labors of Julian D. Mason Jr., and John C. Shields, as well as to publications by the many scholars cited in the endnotes below. I have profited from the work of my predecessors, my own previous experience as a biographer of Olaudah Equiano, and recently available digital databases of eighteenth-century primary sources. My own discoveries include more writings by and attributed to Wheatley; new information about her origins, her upbringing in Boston, her likely role in the production and distribution of her works, the way she gained her freedom, her religious and political identities, and her marriage to John Peters, including the fact that they lived together for months before their wedding; and a plausible explanation for why she disappeared from the public record for several years during the 1780s.

Although we usually classify Wheatley today as an African American writer, she spent all but the last year of her life as the subject of Britain's George III, to whom she addressed one of her earliest poems, "To the KING's Most excellent Majesty." My biography shows when, where, how, and why she eventually chose an African American identity rather than the African-British identity available to her. Phillis Wheatley played a far more active role in establishing her African American identity than has previously been recognized. Wheatley's trip to London in 1773 transformed not only her literary identity. It offered her the opportunity to transform her legal, social, and political identities as well. For someone from such humble and unpromising beginnings, Wheatley developed a remarkable transatlantic network of friendships and affiliations that transcended race, class, status, political, religious, and geographical boundaries. *Phillis Wheatley* reconstructs that network, relocating Wheatley from the margins to the center of her eighteenth-century transatlantic world. My biography recounts the life of a woman who rose from the indignity of enslavement to earn international celebrity, only to die in obscurity and poverty a few years later. *Phillis Wheatley* restores Phillis Wheatley to the recognition and status she deserves as a heroic figure in an age of heroes.

Acknowledgments

. . . .

I AM GREATLY INDEBTED to the staffs and collections of the following institutions: the Dartmouth College Library; the Emory University Library; the Haverford College Library; the McKeldin Library of the University of Maryland; the Widener and Houghton Libraries at Harvard University; the Howard University Library; the Van Pelt Library at the University of Pennsylvania; the John Carter Brown Library; the Massachusetts Historical Society; the Connecticut Historical Society; the Historical Society of Pennsylvania; the Boston Public Library; the Rhode Island Historical Society; the Newport Historical Society; the Massachusetts Archives; the Wilmington (Massachusetts) Historical Commission; the New England Historic Genealogical Society; the American Antiquarian Society; the American Philosophical Society; the College of Physicians of Philadelphia Historical Library and Wood Institute; the Folger Shakespeare Library; the Church of Latter Day Saints' Family History Library; the Library of Congress; the British Library; the Dr. Williams's Library; the Cheshunt Foundation, Cambridge University Library; the National Archives (Kew); the London Metropolitan Archive; and the Staffordshire Record Office.

For advice, assistance, encouragement, and support in my research and writing I thank Valerie Andrews, William L. Andrews, Paula Backscheider, J. L. Bell, Anne E. Bentley, Jeffrey Bilbro, Elizabeth Bouvier, Randall K. Burkett, Patricia Carretta, Sean P. Casey, Betsy Cazden, Philander D. Chase, Patrick Collins, William W. Cook, Philip N. Cronenwett, Susan Danforth, Karen DePauw, Jeremy Dibbell, Peter Drummey, Norman Fiering, Samuel Forman, Henry Louis Gates Jr., Jordan Goffin, James N. Green, Elaine Grublin, Isobel Grundy, Ryan Hanley, Carole Holden, Andrea Houser, Maurice Jackson, Judi Jennings, Judy Lucey, Jane Kamensky, Phil Lapsansky, Bertram Lippincott III, Joseph F. Marcy Jr., Julian D. Mason, Terry McDermott, Steve Mentz, Sylvia Miller, Margot Minardi, Philip D. Morgan, Kimberly Nusco, Felicity Nussbaum, Leslie Tobias Olsen, Adele Passmore, Zachary Petrea, John Pollack, Tracy Potter, David Powell, Kim Reynolds, Anna Russo, Boyd Stanley Schlenther, Chernoh Sesay, David S. Shields, John C. Shields, Garry Shutak, Eric Slauter, Russell Stoermer, John

Wood Sweet, Kirsten Sword, Lee Teverow, Margaret Thompson, Jennifer J. Thorn, Laurel Thatcher Ulrich, Ruth Holmes Whitehead, Edward L. Widmer, Conrad E. Wright, and David L. Wykes.

For generous financial support for the research and writing of *Phillis Wheatley* I am very grateful to the University of Maryland, the National Endowment for the Humanities, the John Carter Brown Library, the Massachusetts Historical Society, the American Society for Eighteenth-Century Studies, the Library Company of Philadelphia, Queen Mary College of the University of London, and the John Simon Guggenheim Memorial Foundation. I thank my dean, James Harris, and my department chair, Kent Cartwright, for granting me leave to accept those fellowships.

My greatest debt is to Pat, my partner in all things that truly matter.

Phillis Wheatley

Chapter 1

"On Being Brought from Africa to America"

The terror the little girl must have felt when she looked out for the last time from the deck of the *Phillis* was probably mixed with relief and wonder. The child was a victim of the largest involuntary human migration in history. She had been kidnapped from her family in Africa and forced to spend up to two months crossing the Atlantic. She now faced land again at last. Although it had rained the night before, that sunny July day in 1761 revealed to her the most bustling metropolis she had ever seen.[1] Boston, Massachusetts, was home to a little over fifteen thousand people. Barely eight hundred of them were of African descent.[2] Only about twenty of the latter were not enslaved. A dozen years would pass before the child aboard the *Phillis* would gain her freedom and join that small number.

But first she had to be brought ashore and sold. Her small size and missing front teeth told potential buyers that she was only about seven years old. She was what was called a refuse slave, one whose age rendered her of little market value. To the Boston merchant John Wheatley, however, she was the gift he wanted to give his wife, Susanna. His new purchase had been stripped of her African identity to be made a commodity on the eighteenth-century global market. Her new owner renamed her after the slave ship that had brought her to America. The little girl who had been enslaved in Africa continued on her improbable journey to become the founding mother of African American literature, Phillis Wheatley.

Very few black slaves could have been exported to the Americas without the complicity of other Africans. The existence of powerful African political and military coastal states, along with the disease environment, made Europeans dependent on Africans for the maintenance of the slave trade. Societies that practice slavery traditionally enslave outsiders. For example, ancient Hebrews and eighteenth-century Muslims reserved the condition of chattel slavery for unbelievers. Defenders of slavery cited Leviticus 25: 45–46 to justify their enslavement of outsiders.[3] Europeans were able to exploit this tradition of enslaving those perceived as outsiders, aliens, or strangers in Africa because the concept of *Africa* was mainly geographic. *Africa* was not a social, political, or religious category in the way that *Europe* was in the eighteenth century. Nor was the notion of *nation* or *state* equivalent on the two continents. The indigenous peoples of Africa did not think of themselves as *African*: they were Ashanti, Fante, Yoruba, or any one of a number of other ethnic groups with differing languages, religions, and political systems. Tending to see themselves as more dissimilar than alike, the various African peoples were willing to enslave and sell to Europeans those outside their own group because they did not identify with them.

Diseases like malaria and yellow fever restricted Europeans to factories (trading posts) on the coast of Africa or to their slave ships "coasting" offshore. Extraordinarily high mortality rates affected the European slave traders as well as the enslaved Africans. Nearly half the deaths of slave ships' crewmembers occurred while they waited offshore to collect their human cargoes in the hostile disease environment. Approximately half of the Europeans who went ashore in Africa died from disease. Christian traders enslaved more than twelve million Africans bound for the Americas between 1492 and around 1870.[4] Perhaps a million of the enslaved people died before they left Africa. They perished from abuse, disease, exhaustion, and depression on their way from the African interior to the Atlantic coast or while waiting aboard ships as the European slave traders completed their human cargoes. About an equal number died from illness, suicide, rebellions, and shipwreck during the portion of the so-called Middle Passage between the African and American coasts. Phillis Wheatley was one of the approximately ten million who survived the Middle Passage across the Atlantic to arrive in the Americas.

Over six million enslaved Africans arrived in the Americas between 1700 and the legal suppression of the British and United States transatlantic slave trades in 1808. The number of Africans annually forced across the Atlantic reached around sixty thousand between 1740 and 1760, and it peaked during the 1780s at about eighty thousand a year, more than half of them on British ships based in Bristol, Liverpool, and London. Most of the Africans were taken to the European colonies in the Caribbean and South America. About 29 percent of the total number brought to the Americas went to the

British colonies. More than four out of five of the people taken from Africa by British slave traders were destined for the West Indies.

To most eighteenth-century Europeans and European Americans, the transatlantic slave trade was a necessary part of the economic system that provided them such pleasures of life as sugar and tobacco. Sugar in particular was difficult, dangerous, and expensive to grow, harvest, and process. Coerced labor was economically more attractive to planters than paid labor. On the eve of the American Revolution, of the total population of five hundred thousand people throughout the British West Indies, more than 90 percent were of African descent. Jamaica was by far the most populous, with about three hundred thousand people; Barbados had one hundred thousand. Enslaved Africans outnumbered European emigrants to the Americas by a ratio of more than three to one before the nineteenth century.[5] But because of the brutal working conditions in the most valuable British colonial possessions, enslaved Africans had a much higher mortality rate than European immigrants. As many as one-third of the imported slaves may have died during "seasoning," the period of a few months after arriving in the New World during which the enslaved Africans were supposed to become acclimated to the alien disease and harsh social environments of the Americas.[6] The high death rate, combined with the age and gender imbalance of the overwhelmingly male imported slaves, led to the negative growth rate of the overall West Indian slave population. Without the continuous importation of enslaved Africans, the Caribbean slave population probably would have declined by 2–4 percent annually.

In contrast, by the middle of the eighteenth century natural increase was expanding the much smaller population of enslaved Africans brought to Britain's North American colonies. The North American colonies were of relatively marginal economic significance to Britain compared to the West Indian plantations during the eighteenth century. Only about 3.6 percent of the people who survived the Middle Passage ended up in the colonies that later became part of the United States.[7] Of the nearly four hundred thousand enslaved Africans brought to British North America before 1808, less than 10 percent were destined to reach the colonies north of Maryland.[8] About one-fifth of the approximately two million people at mid-century in the North American Colonies were of African descent. The percentage of Africans within the overall population of these various colonies ranged from

60 percent in South Carolina to 2 percent in Massachusetts. England had around 6,500,000 people in 1771. The at-most ten to twenty thousand blacks, less than 0.2 percent of the total population, were concentrated in the slave-trading ports of Bristol, Liverpool, and especially London.

Only toward the end of the eighteenth century would people forcibly removed from Africa begin to embrace the diasporan public social and political identity of *African*. For example, some in both Britain and America began to call themselves "Sons of Africa." In a sense, *Africa* did not exist as an idea rather than a place until after the antislave trade and antislavery movements began. Survivors of the Middle Passage in effect "became African in America."[9] Of the millions of enslaved Africans taken to the British colonies and their descendants by the end of the eighteenth century, Phillis Wheatley was one of fewer than twenty whose words found their way directly into print during their lifetimes.

The future Phillis Wheatley probably never even saw the person primarily responsible for having her brought from Africa to America. Timothy Fitch (1725–90) was a wealthy merchant living in Medford, Massachusetts, today a suburb north of Boston. He also had homes in Boston, his birthplace, and Salem, Massachusetts. Fitch profited from trade in goods as well as human beings from Philadelphia to New England and across the Atlantic to the west coast of Africa. He owned several vessels, including the schooner *Pompey*. His brig, *Phillis* (also referred to variously as *The Charming Phillis*, *The Phillis*, or the *Schooner Phillis*) brought the future poet to Boston. The *Phillis* was probably a little less than seventy feet in length, about twenty feet in width, and nine feet in depth. American slave ships tended to be much smaller than the larger vessels of English slave traders, which were designed to carry hundreds of people. Luckily, sixteen letters and invoices from Timothy Fitch to his employees and associates in the transatlantic slave trade survive at the Medford Historical Society. They give us uncommon insight into the conduct of the trade, since such correspondence is extremely rare. Even more extraordinary is the fact that these documents relate directly to the original enslavement in Africa and transportation across the Atlantic of the child who would become known as Phillis Wheatley.

On 8 November 1760 Fitch ordered his employee Peter Gwinn (also spelled Gwin, or Gwynn), commander of "my Brigg Phillis," to go with his eight-man crew first to "Sinigall," on the west coast of Africa. There he was to "purchase 100 Or 110 Prime Slaves" in exchange for 2,640 gallons of rum and other goods. Fitch reminded Gwinn that he would be accompanied by "Capt: Ennes in my schooner Pompey."[10] "Sinigall" was Fitch's ironically misspelled attempt at *Senegal*, an area until recently dominated by France. The French had founded their slave-trading post, or factory, of Saint-Louis on an island at the mouth of the Senegal River in 1659. Saint-Louis fell to the British in 1758 during the Seven Years' War (1756–63), known in North America as the French and Indian War. The British quickly renamed the captured factory Fort Lewis. Fitch's "Sinigall" was the northern limit of the region of Africa that Europeans called Senegambia. It encompassed the sub-Saharan African mainland beyond the 300-mile-long coastline bordered by the Senegal River to the north and the Casamance River to the south. Senegambia (modern-day Senegal and Gambia) included the French slave-trading post on the island of Gorée, as well as the British slave-trading factory of Fort James, built in 1651 on an island at the mouth of the Gambia River.

The Senegambia region had for decades been the site of contention between Britain and France for control of the local slave trade. The Senegambia region was the primary source for the British transatlantic slave trade during the seventeenth and early eighteenth centuries because of its geographic proximity to Europe and the British American colonies. The longer the Middle Passage, the higher the mortality rate of the enslaved Africans, which averaged about 13 percent per transatlantic crossing.[11] The voyage across the Atlantic normally lasted about six to eight weeks in each direction. Furthermore, the more time a slave ship spent trying to maximize its load along the coast of Africa, "the white man's graveyard," the higher the mortality rate of both its European crewmembers and their human cargo. By the mid-eighteenth century, however, Senegambia had become relatively less significant as a source of slaves than more densely populated areas farther south and east on the African coast. Human cargoes could usually be filled more quickly off the "Windward Coast" (present-day Guinea-Bissau, Guinea, Sierra Leone, Liberia, and the Ivory Coast), the "Gold Coast" (present-day Ghana), the "Bight of Benin" (Togo, Benin, and western Nigeria), and the "Bight of Biafra" (eastern Nigeria and Cameroon).

Fitch's preference for slaves from the Senegambia region reflected widespread eighteenth-century prejudices and stereotypes about the many different groups of African peoples forced into the transatlantic slave trade.

Although American and European slave traders identified the enslaved Africans they bought with the particular coastal factory at which they purchased them, the victims often originated hundreds of miles from the coast and frequently had little or no relation to the local Africans nearer the individual factories. The stereotype of enslaved Africans purchased at Senegal, Gorée, and Fort James was relatively positive. Edward Long's assessment in 1774 reflected the view of many eighteenth-century transatlantic slave traders. Long was a racist defender of slavery, and his writings on the subject are very unpleasant to read. Discussing the alleged "bestial or fetid smell, which [all Africans] have in a greater or less degree," Long favored "those of Senegal (who are distinguished from the other herds by greater acuteness of understanding and mildness of disposition) [and who] have the least of this noxious odour." Long elsewhere remarks that "the Negroes brought from Senegal are of better understanding than the rest, and fitter for learning trades, and for menial domestic services. They are good commanders over other Negroes, having a high spirit, and a tolerable share of fidelity: but they are unfit for hard work; their bodies are not robust, nor their constitution vigorous. The delicacy of their frame, perhaps, has some effect on their minds, for they are easier disciplined than any other of the African Blacks."[12]

The Middle Passage that brought the future Phillis Wheatley to Boston on 11 July 1761 was in many ways exceptional.[13] She arrived during an interruption of a more comprehensive decline of the transatlantic slave trade to Boston since the 1740s. Due to the Seven Years' War, her Middle Passage may have been the only shipment of enslaved Africans to arrive in Boston in 1761, and one of only three slave-trading voyages from Africa to any of Britain's North American or Caribbean colonies that year.[14]

Fitch's letters to his employees in 1759, 1760, 1761, and 1762 show that he was intensely aware of the dangers a slaver faced by lingering along the African coast, especially during wartime. Caution and speed were required to avoid the French and disease. Fitch's 14 January 1759 letter to Captain William Ellery advised Ellery to bring his human cargo to South Carolina rather than the West Indies to reduce the chances of encountering a hostile French man-of-war. In his 12 January 1760 letter to Gwinn, Fitch ordered him to be careful to avoid "Any of the Enemys Vesells" on the African coast. He also told him, "You Must Spend as little Time as possible at Sinagal and than proceed down the Coast to SereLeon [Sierra Leone] & thair make the best Trade you can from place to place till you have disposed of all your Cargo & purcha[sed] your compleat Cargo of Young Slaves." Fitch warned Gwinn to leave the coast by the first of May, the beginning of the rainy season, to avoid damage to the vessel and increased mortality of the crew and cargo. Fitch commanded Gwinn on 8 November 1760, "you must do your Business with Dispatch at Sinagall, not tarry more than five or Six Days if you Can Avoid it by any means & then proceed to Seward [seaward] to such places as you may Judge most Beneficial for your Trade ———."

Fitch was greatly disappointed by the 1760–61 voyage that brought Phillis Wheatley from Africa to America. It was a relative disaster in its length, mortality rate, and cargo.[15] The previous voyage in 1760 lasted 207 days roundtrip from Boston to Africa and back.[16] Of the 95 enslaved Africans who left Africa, only 74 were still alive when the *Phillis* returned to Boston. The 1761–62 roundtrip voyage took 257 days, with 103 of the 118 enslaved Africans reaching Boston. The 1760–61 voyage that brought the child known to us as Phillis Wheatley from Africa to Boston took about 240 days. Only 75 of the 96 enslaved Africans survived to be sold in Boston, a mortality rate of nearly 25 percent. That was twice the average death rate on the Middle Passage. Gwinn was so pressed for time that he was unable to follow Fitch's orders: "[A]fter your Completely Slaved, you are to Come off, & if Early you may fall into the Southward & go into Philadelphia or [New] York or [New] Jerseys, where I hear there is no Duty on Slaves & there dispose of as many Slaves as you Can for Cash immediately." Fitch had to go directly from Africa to Boston in 1761.

Phillis Wheatley probably would not have been part of Gwinn's human cargo in 1761 if his voyage had been more successful. Normally only about 6 percent of Africans enslaved from the Senegambia region during the eighteenth century were female, and most of these were women.[17] Fitch had repeatedly reminded Gwinn to avoid buying female slaves: "be sure to bring as Fiew [few] women & Girls as possible" (12 January 1760); "and now in Regard to your purchasing Slaves, you'l Observe to get as few Girl Slaves as Possible & as many Prime Boys as you Can (8 November 1760). Fitch was so displeased with the voyage that brought Phillis Wheatley to Boston that before Gwinn's next slaving voyage to Africa Fitch admonished him on 4 September 1761:

Touching first at Sinagall, & there dispose of as much of your Cargo as you Can to Advantage for Cash or Prime Slaves & then Proceed Down the Coast to such Places as You may Judge most Likely to dispose of your Cargo, & Slave Your Vessell[.] [A]s you'l be very Early upon the Coast, you are not to take any Children & Especially Girls, if you can Avoid it by any means, & as fiew Woman as Possible, & them Likely. [B]ut as many Prime Young Men Boys as you can get from 14 to 20 Years of Age. Take no Slave on Board that has the Least Defect, or Sickly as you will be Early & have a Choice well Assorted & Good Cargo[.] [M]ake no Doubt you'l be able to Pick your Slaves. I had Rather you be Two Months Longer on the Coast then to Bring off Such a Cargo as your Last, which were very small & the meanest Cargo I Ever had Come.

The surviving evidence tells us less about where in Africa Phillis Wheatley was born and raised than about where she probably did not come from. The odds are very low that she was originally bought at either Fort Lewis or Fort James. Gwinn spent about four months along the west coast of Africa collecting his disappointing human cargo. Approximately half of the estimated 240 days of the roundtrip 1760–61 voyage were spent crossing the Atlantic. Gwinn left the coast to return to Boston with his small cargo just as the rainy season began in Africa. He left too late to be able to stop at Philadelphia or New York with a cargo he would have had great difficulty selling in either place. An experienced slaver like Gwinn was extremely unlikely to have procured the least desirable slaves as soon as he reached Senegal. He was far more likely to have ignored Fitch's orders and bought refuse slaves, particularly young girls, only as a last resort. And he most likely would have done so far down the coast of Africa from Senegal, just before he had to return to Boston. Gwinn probably acquired the future Phillis Wheatley near the end of the months he spent along the coast of Africa, either around Sierra Leone, where Fitch had ordered him to go after leaving "Sinigall," farther down the Windward Coast, or even perhaps as far southeast as near the Gold Coast. When the arrival of the *Phillis* with the future Phillis Wheatley among its human cargo was first announced in a Boston newspaper, it was described as having come "from the Windward Coast."[18]

Phillis Wheatley says virtually nothing about her native Africa in her surviving writings. Even if Gwinn bought her at "Sinigall," we should not assume that she was a native of the area surrounding the British factory. African entrepreneurs sometimes brought enslaved fellow Africans to the coast from hundreds of miles inland. Wheatley mentions a specific location in Africa only once in her known writings. She recalls a very romanticized "Gambia" in "PHILIS's [*sic*] Reply to the Answer in our last by the Gentleman in the Navy," a poem published in Boston in January 1775 in the *Royal American Magazine*.[19] Although it is impossible to identify exactly where Wheatley's journey from Africa to America began, some commentators have asserted with varying degrees of conviction that she was born in Senegal. Others say Gambia. The noted African American author Langston Hughes had no doubt that Wheatley was a native of Senegal and spoke "Senegalese."[20] Senegal commemorated her as native-born with a stamp issued in 1971. Some literary critics leap to conclusions about Phillis Wheatley's birthplace and upbringing that are unsupported by the available evidence.[21] Speculation, rather than the historical record, leaves a little girl bearing heavy cultural baggage on the Middle Passage.

The young girl's experience of the Middle Passage was probably very similar to the one her contemporary Olaudah Equiano (1745?–97) describes in his autobiography:

> when the ship we were in had got in all her cargo, they made ready with many fearful noises, and we were all put under deck, so that we could not see how they managed the vessel. But this disappointment was the least of my sorrow. The stench of the hold while we were on the coast was so intolerably loathsome, that it was dangerous to remain there for any time, and some of us had been permitted to stay on the deck for the fresh air; but now that the whole ship's cargo were confined together, it became absolutely pestilential. The closeness of the place, and the heat of the climate, added to the number in the ship, which was so crowded that each had scarcely room to turn himself, almost suffocated us. This produced copious perspirations, so that the air soon became unfit for respiration, from a variety of loathsome smells, and brought on a sickness among the slaves, of which many died, thus falling victims to the improvident avarice, as I may call it, of their purchasers. This wretched situation was again aggravated by the galling of the chains, now become insupportable; and the filth of the necessary tubs [latrines], into which the children often fell, and were almost suffocated. The shrieks of the

women, and the groans of the dying, rendered the whole a scene of horror almost inconceiveable. Happily perhaps for myself I was soon reduced so low here that it was thought necessary to keep me almost always on deck; and from my extreme youth I was not put in fetters. In this situation I expected every hour to share the fate of my companions, some of whom were almost daily brought upon deck at the point of death, which I began to hope would soon put an end to my miseries. Often did I think many of the inhabitants of the deep much more happy than myself; I envied them the freedom they enjoyed, and as often wished I could change my condition for theirs. Every circumstance I met with served only to render my state more painful, and heighten my apprehensions, and my opinion of the cruelty of the whites.[22]

Phillis Wheatley does not mention her own Middle Passage in any of her known writings. Perhaps her experience was understandably so traumatic that she was never able or willing to reimagine it. Nearly one out of four of her fellow enslaved Africans died aboard the *Phillis* on their way to Boston in 1761. She was clearly lucky to have survived. The sight of so much death around her may help to account for her subsequent attention to death in so many of her earliest poems. From contemporaneous accounts of the Middle Passage by and about other enslaved Africans we can be quite sure that as a prepubescent girl she was allowed to roam the vessel much more freely than older enslaved Africans, who might pose a physical threat to the crew. Out of concern for hygiene and security, enslaved adult Africans were usually stripped naked from the time they were initially seized in Africa. At most, they would have been allowed to cover their pubic areas. As a young child the future Phillis Wheatley was likely naked from the time she was first enslaved until she reached Boston and was put up for sale. In fact, she had probably spent her young life prior to her enslavement unclothed as well, as was customary for African children. Her very young age meant that she was far less likely than her older enslaved fellow Africans to have been raped by members of the crew.[23] But her presumed relative freedom of movement and freedom from the threat of physical abuse would not have compensated for the unimaginable fear that a young child must have felt in such a situation.

The *Phillis* reached Boston in 1761 at the peak of the annual season for selling imported slaves.[24] The town had developed on a peninsula bordered by the Charles River on the west and north, and Boston Harbor fronting the Atlantic Ocean on the east. Eighteenth-century Boston was only about two miles in length from its North End to Boston Neck, the isthmus connecting it to the mainland. No place in the town was more than half a mile from water. As by far the most populous town in Massachusetts, Boston was the political, cultural, and economic engine of the colony, and not surprisingly the center of its slave trade. Boston in 1743 had been the most populous town in British North America, with 16,382 residents, followed by Philadelphia (13,000) and New York (11,000). By the time Phillis arrived, however, Boston's population—unlike the more economically vibrant Philadelphia (23,750) and New York (18,000)—was in an extended period of stagnation, even slight decline. Boston's estimated population had decreased slightly from 15,731 in 1750 to 15,631 in 1760, and would decline further to 15,520 by 1770.

The little girl aboard the *Phillis* was about to join the more than half of Boston's population that was under the age of sixteen. White women outnumbered white men largely because of deaths during the war. And men of African descent outnumbered women of African descent by a ratio of more than five to three because slave traders preferred to import young males. Boston's slave traders sold people at taverns and other places of business throughout the town because it lacked a separate marketplace dedicated to the sale of human beings. Onshore sales of newly arrived enslaved Africans most commonly took place along or near Long Wharf, at the bottom of King Street. Others were sold aboard the vessels that had brought them from Africa, often in part to quarantine them.

Comparison of the advertisements for human cargoes that Gwinn brought to Boston for Fitch in 1760 and 1761 indicates the depth of Fitch's disappointment with the return on his investment in 1761, and the probability that the enslaved Africans were collected from various parts of Africa. The announcement in the *Boston Weekly News-Letter* on 7 August 1760 emphasizes the quality of the implicitly male "prime young Slaves from the Windward Coast." There is no indication of inferior goods being offered for sale:

Just Imported
From *Africa*
A Number of prime young
Slaves from the Windward Coast, and to
Be Sold on board the Schooner *Phillis* lying at New-Boston.

The sale of the enslaved Africans to prospective buyers on board the *Phillis* in 1760 suggests that the survivors of that Middle Passage were in relatively presentable condition when they arrived.

There has been a great deal of confusion about when and by whom the future Phillis Wheatley was first sold in Boston.[25] The advertisement for the human cargo that included the future Phillis Wheatley first appeared in the *Boston Gazette* on 13 July 1761, repeating almost verbatim the advertisement from the year before. At least initially, Fitch apparently tried to sell his cargo directly without using a broker:

> Just Imported
> From *Africa*
> A Number of prime young
> *SLAVES* from the Windward Coast, and to
> Be Sold on board Capt. *Gwin* lying at New-Boston.

The same issue included an advertisement for a different sale by a broker for slave merchants:

> To be Sold at a Store adjoining to Mr. *John Avery*'s Dwelling House at the South End near the Market; a Parcel of likely young Negroes: Inquire of said *Avery* at his House next Door to the White-Horse [tavern], or of *James Russell*, Esq. of *Charlestown*.

The *Boston Evening Post* on 3 August 1761 contained two advertisements by the slave dealer John Avery (1711–96).[26] One is the same as that which had appeared in the *Boston Gazette* on 13 July. It clearly did not include the future poet, but the other may have. That 3 August 1761 advertisement quickly undercuts its initial claim that what is being sold is "[a] Parcel of likely Negroes," that is, a cargo of strong or sturdy people of African descent. These slaves are available "cheap for Cash, or short Credit with Interest." The least desirable among them are the "small Negroes": children. The sellers were so desperate to dispose of these inferior goods that they offered to barter them for "any Negro Men, strong and hearty, tho' not of the best moral Character, which are proper Subjects for Transportation." In other words, Avery was willing to trade the children for slaves whose criminal records had made them undesirable and unsellable in Massachusetts, but who may still have resale value if transported to the West Indies:

To Be Sold.
A Parcel of likely Negroes, Imported from Africa, cheap for Cash,
or short

Credit with Interest, enquire of John Avery, at his House next Door
to the White-Horse, or at a Store adjoining to said Avery's Distill
House, at the South End, near the South Market:—Also if any Persons Have any Negro Men, strong and hearty, tho' not of The best
moral Character, which are proper Subjects For Transportation, may
have an Exchange for small Negroes.[27]

If Fitch failed to sell the future Phillis Wheatley aboard the *Phillis* and
consequently used Avery as an agent, she was one of those "small Negroes,"
indeed the only one of that human cargo we can now identify.

Other advertisements in the same 3 August 1761 issue of the *Boston Evening Post* indicate that the little girl was being forced to enter a society
in which, as a slave, she would have no legal control over her own fate, a
society in which a "Strong healthy Negro Boy, about 14 or 15 Years of Age,
that can do any Sort of Business about a House" could be "sold only for
want of Employ." To some potential buyers she would be simply one piece
of merchandise among many to be purchased: "to be sold *at private Sale*, an
elegant gilt Leather Screen, imported last Spring from London,—a Saddle
and a Chaise Horse, a Chaise & Chair, and a likely Negro Fellow, about
20 Years old, that has had the Small Pox." The reference to small pox was
intended to reassure buyers that the young man was now immune from that
disease. Slaves with no market value were disposed of as quickly as possible:
"[a] likely, hearty male Negro Child about a Month old, to be given away."[28]

The future Phillis Wheatley probably first arrived in Boston at Avery's
wharf at the end of what is now Beach Street. Avery's house was located at
the southwest corner of present-day Avery and Washington Streets. Like
most of his white contemporaries, Avery saw no contradiction between his
involvement with the slave trade and his public image as a humanitarian
and philanthropist. He served on committees responsible for the oversight
of the poor and the schools during the 1760s. He became a trustee of the
Massachusetts Humane Society in 1789. Whether the little girl was sold by
Gwinn aboard the *Phillis*, or by Avery ashore, she was bought by Susanna
(1709–74) and John Wheatley (1703–78), the parents of eighteen-year-old

twins Mary (1743–78) and Nathaniel (1743–83).[29] Their three other children, John, Susanna, and Sarah, had all died prematurely years earlier. According to Margaretta Matilda Odell, a great grandniece of Susanna Wheatley, writing in the nineteenth century, "Mrs. Wheatley wished to obtain a young negress, with the view of training her up under her own eye, that she might, by gentle usage, secure to herself a faithful domestic in her old age." She reportedly chose "[t]he poor, naked child (for she had no other covering than a quantity of dirty carpet about her like a filibeg [kilt]," who was "of a slender frame and evidently suffering from change of climate." Susanna Wheatley picked Phillis rather than one of "several robust, healthy females, exhibited at the same time" because of "the humble and modest demeanor and the interesting features of the little stranger."[30] Phillis was most likely completely naked when she arrived. Odell probably claimed otherwise out of a Victorian sense of modesty.[31] Eighteenth-century slave buyers expected to see exactly what they were buying. Too young and sickly to have much if any labor value, Phillis would have been considered a luxury good, valuable mainly as an indicator of her owners' disposable income.

A sentimental reason probably lay behind Susanna Wheatley's economically irrational choice of the little girl rather than a more obviously suitable domestic slave. Just a few weeks before the Wheatleys purchased Phillis they had observed the ninth anniversary of the death of their daughter Sarah. The unusually precise recording of her age on her gravestone in the Granary Burial Ground suggests that she had been a favorite child: "Here lyes ye Body / of Sarah Wheatley, / Daugh^{tr} of Mr John & M^{rs} / Susanna Wheatley, / Who Died may 11th / 1752, Aged 7 Years / 9 months & 18 Days."[32] Bought at almost exactly the same age Sarah had been when she died, the future Phillis Wheatley may have appealed to Susanna and John Wheatley as a surrogate for their late beloved daughter, their last-born child. Such a psychological link between Susanna and Phillis Wheatley would help to account for the extraordinary relationship that all surviving evidence indicates existed between the mistress and her slave. According to Phillis's nineteenth-century biographer, she "had a child's place in [the Wheatley's] house and in their hearts."[33] The Wheatleys renamed their little purchase Phillis, after the slave ship that had brought her on the Middle Passage from Africa to America. Being renamed was one of many acts of deracination suffered by enslaved people of African descent as whites sought to erase their African personal identities and redefine them as property.

Unlike the overwhelming majority of enslaved Africans brought to the Americas, Phillis had been brought to a *society with slaves*, where the economy was not based on slavery, rather than to a *slave society* in the West Indies or the American South, where the economy depended upon slave labor.[34] Slave owners in slave societies typically strongly resisted allowing their slaves, who were legally defined as chattel property, to be converted to Christianity during the seventeenth and eighteenth centuries. The high percentages of slaves in the populations of slave societies rendered them a constant threat to their owners and to the economic and social system built on their coerced labor. Their owners feared that access to spiritual equality would inevitably lead to demands for recognition of their personhood and consequently for legal equality, despite laws explicitly denying that baptism and conversion to Christianity conferred freedom.[35]

The legal condition of enslaved people in New England societies with slaves was quite different. There, according to Lorenzo Greene, the "slave held a position somewhere between that of a plantation slave and an indentured servant. This was due to the influence of Jewish slavery, after which the Puritans patterned their system of involuntary servitude. The New England slave was in a measure a member of his master's family and, following the Hebraic tradition, was usually referred to as 'servant,' rarely as slave. Holding this intermediate status, Negroes were considered both as property and as persons before the law."[36] Although slaves in New England were considered property that could be bought, sold, and bequeathed, they were not denied by law the rights to be baptized, to marry, and to learn to read, rights denied them by law in the slave societies to the south. But whether New England slaves were able to exercise those rights depended upon the generosity of their masters. Many slaves in slave societies had very little direct contact with their owners. In societies with slaves, however, a far higher percentage of slaves knew their owners intimately since they usually worked in the home, especially in town settings. The downside of such intimacy was the likelihood that the enslaved person was exposed to constant surveillance by his or her owner. Such intimacy also greatly increased the opportunities abusive and sadistic owners had to oppress or torment their slaves. In such situations young women slaves were particularly vulnerable to rape, and they were far more likely to be accused of infanticide than their free white counterparts.[37]

John and Susanna Wheatley took their new acquisition to their recently restored house at the corner of King Street and Mackerel Lane (now State Street and Kilby Street). The Wheatleys lived in a fashionable part of Boston. Phillis Wheatley arrived while Boston was experiencing a brief building boom following the "Great Fire" of 1760, which had destroyed nearly four hundred houses. The Wheatleys had suffered more than £300 worth of damage to their personal and real estate property in the Great Fire. The figure of £300 presumably refers to colonial paper currency, also called lawful money, rather than British money. British and colonial money were both measured in pounds, shillings, and pence.[38] Each colony issued its own local paper currency, called "lawful money." A colonial pound was worth less than a British pound sterling. The softer colonial currency was basically backed up by various forms of promissory notes, and was inferior in value to the harder British currency in the form of specie, or coin. Conversion rates for the currencies of the various colonies fluctuated throughout the eighteenth century, most wildly during the American Revolution. John Tudor (1709–95) noted in his diary on 20 March 1760: "The loss to the Sufferers in Houses, Stores, Merchandizes, Furnature & was at £100,000 Sterling."[39]

Phillis was a minor investment for Susanna and John Wheatley. John Wheatley was a substantial property owner, whose primary occupation was that of a quite successful tailor. His clientele included the eminent and very wealthy John Hancock (1737–93). But like most of his fellow businessmen in Boston, John Wheatley did not risk relying on only one source of income. He was also a merchant who bought and sold a variety of goods exchanged in the global economy. In addition, he lent money at interest. The land and property Wheatley owned included a brick warehouse on King Street.[40] Not surprisingly given his status, John Wheatley was a town official, sworn in as one of Boston's two constables in 1739. Although John Wheatley did not fully retire until the summer of 1771, by 1764 his son, Nathaniel, was effectively managing his father's business interests.[41] Like his father, Nathaniel was also a town official. In 1770 he became one of twelve "Clerks of the Market," who regulated Boston's commerce.[42]

Nathaniel Wheatley advertised in Boston newspapers products from around the world on sale at the Wheatleys' store on King Street. For example, on 6 September 1764 he offered "London Bohea Tea [from China], *West-India* and *New England* Rum, Molasses, Sugar, Coffee, Chocolate, *Philadelphia* Bar-Iron and Flour . . . Likewise a few Barrels of choice Vinegar."[43] At other times Wheatley advertised "Choice table [edible] Fish . . .

Ship Bread [hardtack, a hard unsalted biscuit], Connecticut Pork, Sperma-ceti Candles, Russia Duck [a fine white linen canvas] . . . new Rice, Glass Globe Lamps, . . . good Pot Ash [used to make soap, glass, and soil fertil-izer]," as well as "New Castle Coals, and Tin Plates."[44] We have no evidence that the Wheatleys sold slaves. But like many of their fellow Americans, they owned at least one enslaved person of African descent. And like all eighteenth-century consumers on both sides of the Atlantic, the Wheat-leys participated indirectly in the transatlantic slave trade by dealing in the products of that trade. Africans had been enslaved and brought to the West Indies to produce the sugar used to make the rum and molasses bought and sold in Boston, some of which was then brought to Africa to purchase more enslaved people to keep the commercial cycle going.

Wheatley apparently owned at least one vessel, "a Fine Sloop of 84 Tons, to be let on Freight or by the Month" that Nathaniel advertised in the *Boston Evening Post* on 1 October 1764. He conducted most of his transatlantic and intercolonial trade, however, using the three-masted schooner, the *London Packet*, commanded by Robert Calef. With its burden, or carrying capacity, of 150 tons and a ten-man crew, the *London Packet* was probably at least as large as the *Phillis*.[45] Built in 1764, the American-built *London Packet* was originally owned by "Chapman & Co.," but by 1769 its owners were Joseph Rotch (1704–84) of Nantucket, Massachusetts, as well as Alexander Cham-pion and George Wayley of London.[46] Several years later Rotch's son Joseph Jr. (1743–73) became the subject of Phillis Wheatley's poem "To a Gentle-man on His Voyage to *Great Britain* for the Recovery of His Health," first printed in her *Poems on Various Subjects, Religious and Moral* (London, 1773).

Nathaniel Wheatley wisely distributed his commercial eggs in several baskets to lessen the risk of a catastrophic loss of any one ship carrying all of his merchandise. Thus in the winter of 1769–70 Wheatley imported from London twenty-five bundles of Russia duck and a bale of cloth aboard the brigantine *Leviathan*, owned by Thomas Jenkins, Paul Bunker, and Joseph Bernard of Nantucket, as well as by Isaac Buxton and John Enderby of London.[47] In partnership with Joseph Rotch, the American co-owner of the *London Packet*, Wheatley imported a wide range of raw materials and man-ufactured goods from London on the *Betsy*, owned by Alexander Cham-pion, Thomas Dikason, and Samuel Enderby.[48] Wheatley's transatlantic connections were personal as well as commercial: Samuel Enderby (1717–97) became Nathaniel Wheatley's father-in-law in 1774. Enderby founded the

London firm of Samuel Enderby & Sons, which traded primarily in the very lucrative spermaceti wax processed from the oil found in the heads of sperm whales. Enderby purchased spermaceti from American whalers based in Massachusetts, particularly Nantucket Island, and Rhode Island. Besides being used to make high-quality candles and cosmetics, spermaceti was essential for many industrial needs later satisfied by petroleum products. Wheatley was a middleman between American whalers and London merchants. His correspondence during the 1760s and 1770s with Nicholas Brown & Company in Providence, Rhode Island, contains repeated references to "head matter" and "oil."

More information about the relative wealth of John and Nathaniel Wheatley can be gleaned from *The Massachusetts Tax Valuation List of 1771*, which includes 5,510 people in Boston qualified to be "Poll Rateable." The assessed amounts are in colonial currency. "Nathan'l Wheatly" is listed as owning one horse and one warehouse.[49] His "Annual Worth of the Whole Real Estate" is assessed as £20, and the "Value of Factorys, Commissions" as £600. John Wheatley is listed as having one "Houses and Shops Adjoining," with his "Annual Worth of the Whole Real Estate" assessed as £40. His "Value of Money lent at Interest" was £1,333, 6 shillings, 8 pence.

John Wheatley's other property in 1771 included one horse and one "Servant for Life," a New England euphemism for a slave. Odell may be correct that the Wheatley family owned several slaves in 1761, one of them a coachman named Prince, but ten years later Phillis was their only "Servant for Life."[50] The Wheatleys also had an unknown number of other, presumably free, white servants in 1771. Writing to Susanna Wheatley on 5 March 1771, a friend of the family asked her, "Please to remember me to Phillis and the rest of your Servants."[51] John Wheatley was extraordinary in owning any slaves. Of the 5,510 Bostonians evaluated in 1771, 183 owned a total of 261 "Servants for Life," about a 3.3 percent ownership rate. Like John Wheatley, most Bostonian slave owners had only one "Servant for Life": 119 owned one; 55 owned two; 4 owned three; 4 owned four; and 1 owned six.

White Bostonians were very concerned about controlling the lives of the people of African descent who lived among them, whether free or enslaved. Newspaper reports of slave insurrections during the Middle Passage, the threat individual slaves posed to their owners, and rebellions in the American South and the West Indies reminded Bostonians that their involuntary labor force of enslaved people of African descent might constitute an enemy within. The same 3 August 1761 issue of the *Boston Evening Post* that first advertised the sale of the future Phillis Wheatley informed readers:

> Three Negroes were lately condemned in Calvert County, in Maryland, for murdering Mr. Smith [*sic*], their Mistress, by poison, some Years ago; but, by some mistake in the Jury proceedings, it seems they are to have another trial. . . .
>
> By Capt. Lyell from the Coast of Africa, we have advice, that Capt. Nicoll, of this Port [New York], was not cut off by the Negroes, as was some time ago published; but that he lost 40 of his slaves by an insurrection and saved his vessel.

Boston authorities repeatedly tried to keep the enslaved people among them under control. On 12 March 1759 the Boston selectmen "voted that the Selectmen be and they hereby are desired to give Notice to all such Persons as are Licenced, either as Innholders or Retailers that if they sell Rum or any Liquors to negroes or Molatto Servants, after the Second of April next without a written Order from their respective Master or Mistresses, they will not be allowed to renew their Licences any more." On 12 August 1761 the selectmen reminded the retailers of liquor of the 1759 ban, and on 13 November 1761 the selectmen told the Constable of the Watch "to take up all Negroes Indians and Molotta Slaves, that they may be absent from their Masters Houses, after 9 oClock at Night, unless they can give a good and satisfactory Account of their business."[52] The order was repeated eight years later. Motivating the selectmen's orders was the constant fear of a slave rebellion: on 29 October 1768 "[t]he Several Constables of the Watch [were] directed by the Selectmen, to be watchful of the Negroes & to take up those of them that may be in gangs at unseasonable hours—Zachary Johnnot Esqr Messrs Nathan Spear, William Foster & others enter their Complaint with the Selectmen against John Wilson Esqr of the 59 Regiment of Foot, for practicing on their Negro servants to induce them immediately to enter into a dangerous conspiracy against their Masters promising them their freedom as a reward—whereupon Mr Justice Ruddock was desired by the Selectmen to take the several Affidavits relative to the above mentioned complaint—."[53]

Britons, and British Americans to a lesser extent, did not believe that all people of African descent should be slaves. Social status could supersede race as a defining category, as it does in the fictional accounts published in the late seventeenth century of Oronokoo by Aphra Behn (1640–89) and

Thomas Southerne (1660–1746), or in the historical cases of Job Ben Solomon, also known as Ayuba Suleiman Diallo (1701–73), and William Ansah Sessarakoo (fl. 1736–49) that found their way into print in the 1730s and 1740s. One of the cruel ironies of the "democratic" revolution in the thirteen North American colonies was that it also "democratized" slavery, making all people of African descent equally eligible for enslavement. Throughout the eighteenth century the more hierarchical Britons recognized slavery as an inappropriate status for at least some Africans. But those fortunate Africans were a precious few.

Even free people of African descent in Boston were subject to compulsory labor and discriminated against in employment. Nine of the ten "Free Negroes" included on *The Massachusetts Tax Valuation List of 1771* are unnamed. Together they owned one "Houses and Shops Adjoining" and £4 in "Annual Worth of the Whole Real Estate." Caesar, the other free black, had one "Houses and Shops Adjoining" and £4 in "Annual Worth of the Whole Real Estate." The Boston Selectmen ruled on 15 December 1762, "To Scipio and other Free Negroes residing in the Town of Boston. You are hereby severally Ordered and Required to perform so many Days work as is here under affixed to your Names, and this at the Time and Place you shall be directed to by mr John Swetser, appointed an Overseer for this purpose. It being such a proportion of Time as is adjudged to be equivalent to the service of Trainings, Watchings and other duty required of the rest of his Majestys Subjects, the benefit of which you share. Hereof fail not as you avoid the penalty of the Law in such case made and provided."[54] At their 24 June 1778 meeting "the Selectmen . . . directed Mr Peirce to call upon one—Lewis—a French Negro, who carrys on the Barbers Trade in King Street & acquainted him that if he continues to counteract the other Barbers & is guilty of a breach of the Laws he will be prosecuted to the extent of the Laws."[55]

Coerced labor took various forms in Britain and its American colonies. Scots miners, although they were not chattels (personal possessions of an owner), belonged, like feudal serfs, to the mine in which they worked. This labor system did not legally end until the middle of the eighteenth century. Since the sixteenth century, people in England convicted of petty crimes, such as vagrancy, were sentenced to involuntary servitude in workhouses called bridewells. After the Transportation Act of 1718, at least fifty thousand convicts were transported at the government's expense from Britain to the colonies to be sold as servants to work out their sentences. Before 1718, convicts like the English grandmother of Benjamin Banneker (1731–1806), Molly Welsh, frequently received pardons on the condition that they would either pay for their own passage to America, or go at the expense of merchants, who then sold them as indentured servants in the Colonies. Welsh arrived in Maryland around 1683. The legal enslavement of poor white Britons not convicted of crimes was still imaginable during the first half of the eighteenth century.[56]

Indentured white servants and apprentices signed away their freedom in Britain and its colonies for a specified amount of time in exchange for room and board and a guaranteed job or job-training. In effect, they became voluntary slaves, whose services were often sold at public auction. White indentured servants were the primary source of labor in the British Caribbean and North American colonies during the first decades of settlement. Indentured servants and apprentices differed from chattel slaves because they served for limited periods and did not pass their status on to their children. But the fact that they were in effect leased rather than owned rendered them less valuable to their masters, and consequently they were sometimes treated more harshly than slaves. Elizabeth Spriggs wrote from Maryland to her father in London to describe her indentured situation in 1755:

> What we unfortunate English people suffer here is beyond the probability of you in England to conceive. Let it suffice that I, one of the unhappy number, am toiling almost day and night, and very often in the horses' drudgery with only this comfort that: 'You bitch, you do not half enough': and then tied up and whipped to that degree that you'd not serve an animal; scarce anything but Indian corn [maize] and salt to eat, and that even begrudged. Nay, many negroes are better used.[57]

Few, if any, indentured servants, however, would have traded their status for that of chattel slavery.

Phillis was not the only unfree laborer in the Wheatley household during the 1760s. On 14 August 1766, when Phillis was about twelve years old, John Wheatley placed a runaway advertisement in the *Boston News-Letter and New-England Chronicle* for "*Abner Wade*, an indented Servant, 19 years of Age, about 5 feet 3 inches high, light Complection, brown Hair tied behind, [who] looks very young for a Person of his Age." Wheatley's advertisement promised twenty dollars plus costs to anyone who caught and returned the runaway Wade to "his Master." The items that the advertisement implies Wade stole from Wheatley offer more evidence of Wheatley's wealth: "[Wade] [h]ad on when he went away a blue Coat, with brass Buttons, light coloured Waistcoat, and a pair [of] scarlet knit Breeches[.] [H]e also took with him a light coloured Broad-cloth Coat & Jacket, dark coloured cotton velvet Breeches, blue Great coat, a Chest with a Number of other Articles." Perhaps the indentured adolescent Abner Wade felt more oppressed by the Wheatleys than the enslaved child Phillis. Or he may have been motivated by the far greater freedom of movement and employment opportunities available to a white man but denied to a woman, especially a slave. Not surprisingly, most runaway servants and slaves were male.

In practical terms, the first ten years of Phillis's life in the Wheatley household would not have been very different had she been legally free. The legal restraints Boston's selectmen imposed on the activities of adults of African descent would not have affected her. As a minor, Phillis would not have had freedom of movement, even if she had been free and white. At least initially, Phillis was too young to be of much domestic help. What we know of Phillis's early life suggests that she was probably relatively unaffected by her enslaved condition. Female domestic servants and slaves normally spent most of their time working within the owner's home, largely invisible to outsiders.[58] Phillis, however, was apparently spared the "hours devoted to washing and ironing, cooking and baking, sewing and knitting" that occupied the lives of most women, whites and blacks, in eighteenth-century colonial American towns as well as on farms.[59] Her experience of slavery was nearer that of a domestic male servant or slave in England and America, who often conducted some of his master's public business, and who usually accompanied his owners in their public activities. Male servants and slaves were consequently often visible displays of their masters' wealth, fashion, and social status.

Ample evidence indicates that Phillis was raised above her station, that is, that she was treated more like a member of the Wheatley family than as a servant, let alone as a slave. We do not know where Phillis ate and slept in the Wheatley house. Unlike most slaves she may well have been allowed to share their table. And she probably did not spend her nights in an unheated attic, as most slaves spent theirs. Her accommodations may have been similar to those of another extraordinary New England slave, whose owners permitted her and her child to sleep in a private bed in a hallway.[60] The Wheatleys gave Phillis access to a dictionary and a place to write, and

allowed her to mix socially with their politically, religiously, and socially
prominent guests.[61] At least some white Bostonians were reportedly startled
to discover that they were expected to share their tea table with Phillis.[62]

According to Odell, however, "[w]henever [Phillis] was invited to the
houses of individuals of wealth and distinction (which frequently happened)
she always declined the seat offered her at their board, and, requesting that
a side-table might be laid for her, dined modestly apart from the rest of the
company.[63] But Phillis always received preferential treatment:

> upon the occasion of one of these visits, the weather changed during
> the absence of Phillis; and her anxious mistress, fearful of the effects
> of cold and damp upon her already delicate health, ordered Prince (also
> an African and a slave) to take the chaise, and bring home her *protegee*.
> When the chaise returned, the good lady drew near the window, as
> it approached the house, and exclaimed—'Do but look at the saucy
> varlet—if he hasn't the impudence to sit upon the same seat with *my
> Phillis!*' And poor Prince received a severe reprimand for forgetting the
> dignity thus kindly, though perhaps to him unaccountably, attached to
> the sable person of 'my Phillis.'[64]

Phillis was apparently isolated during her childhood from most of her fellow enslaved people of African descent. Odell is the only known source
who comments on her personal interaction with other blacks within the
Wheatley household.

The Wheatleys' treatment of Phillis enabled them to publicize their status, piety, and charity. They also used her to display their commitment
to evangelical Christianity. They demonstrated that they could afford to
spare Phillis the drudgery one would expect to be assigned to someone
in her condition. Very few owners granted slaves the "leisure Moments"
that would allow them to write poetry.[65] The investment John and Susanna
Wheatley made in their little refuse slave had already begun to produce
interest when her fellow servant Abner Wade ran off. The religious training and extraordinary education they gave Phillis began to pay dividends
surprisingly quickly. Religion would give Phillis the motive, means, and opportunity to begin writing in 1765, and she would soon publicly demonstrate
her value as an item of conspicuous consumption. She would also soon come
to recognize that comparatively gilded though her cage may have been, her
enslavement was a cage nevertheless.

Chapter 2

"Thoughts on the Works of Providence"

S usanna Wheatley dealt with Phillis's religious education as conscientiously as she did that of her own children. As a recent editor of Phillis Wheatley's writings observes, "Susanna Wheatley was a quite active Christian . . . [e]ngaged in missions work by correspondence, encouragement, accommodating visiting ministers in her home, and (at least occasionally) donations of money."[1] Like many evangelical New England slave owners, Susanna Wheatley felt obligated to introduce Phillis to Christianity.[2] Few, if any, contemporaneous owners, however, made an equivalent investment in the religious upbringing of their slaves. Phillis Wheatley's owner clearly took a great interest in her behavior and treated her as if she were a family member, apparently without ever making her feel oppressed by that interest.

Susanna and John Wheatley had been married in the Congregationalist New South Church on 25 December 1741. All of their children were baptized there. Congregationalists were Dissenters or Nonconformists. Like Anglicans, they were Protestants who rejected the authority that the Roman Catholic Church claimed for the Pope and the teachings of medieval theologians (the "Church Fathers"). But Dissenters refused to conform to the Thirty-Nine Articles that constituted the doctrine of the Anglican Church of England. They considered Anglicanism insufficiently Protestant in its rejection of the doctrine and forms of the Roman Catholic Church. Dissenters rejected the doctrinal status both Churches accorded the apocryphal books of the Old Testament. All Dissenting sects rejected the mediating role between believers and God that the Anglican Church and the Church of Rome assigned to priests. Dissenters maintained that a believer had direct access to the word of God through the Bible. Hence they emphasized the need for literacy, or at least the ability to read. Most English Dissenters were Congregationalists, Baptists, Presbyterians, or Quakers. Of the various Dissenting sects, Congregationalists were theologically and genetically the most direct descendants of the Puritans who settled New England in the seventeenth century. Dissenters in colonial Massachusetts were so overwhelmingly Congregationalists that Congregationalism was the established religion supported by public taxes.

Congregationalism was so called because the male members of each church had the authority to choose their own minister. Unlike Episcopal churches, which were governed by bishops, or Presbyterian churches, which were administered by ministers and elected laity, each Congregational church was independent and self-governing. Congregationalists followed the doctrine of the sixteenth-century Protestant theologian John Calvin (1509–64). Calvinism holds that very few Christians are among the elect, those predestined or elected by the grace of God to be saved. Everyone else is a reprobate, doomed to eternal damnation, despite faith or acts of charity. Grace is given, not earned. As the descendants of Adam and Eve, who lapsed into evil by their own free will, all humans inherited the postlapsarian depravity of original sin. Consequently, the "*natural* state" of humanity was corrupt. Calvinism seems to offer Christians no assurance in this world of their fate in the next, and thus little encouragement to try to act on their own spiritual behalf. But Calvinism in practice offers emotional comfort to all who believe that the Spirit of Christ is working within them and that their good works are the visible fruits of their faith.

Phillis Wheatley arrived in Boston during the transatlantic Great Awakening, which stressed conversion through spiritual rebirth and acceptance of Jesus Christ as one's personal savior. The Methodist Anglicans John Wesley (1703–91), his brother Charles Wesley (1707–88), and George Whitefield (1714–70) started the evangelical Protestant movement in Britain. Methodism, so-called because its adherents sought to methodize the principles and practice of Anglicanism by establishing a routine of personal devotion and charitable acts, was the evangelical reform movement within the Church of England. The Wesley brothers, together with Whitefield, founded Methodism in the 1730s. Conservative Anglicans looked with suspicion on the "enthusiastic" Methodists, whom they considered potential Dissenting separatists from the Church. Fellow Anglicans frequently attacked and mocked John Wesley and Whitefield for their fervent preaching styles and their itinerant ministering to the lower orders of British society. Methodist preachers were often physically assaulted and assailed in print. Methodists frequently brought their extemporaneous preaching outdoors to the people, rather than insisting that the people come to church to hear a polished sermon read to them. Such ministry was particularly effective in parts of Britain and America not sufficiently served by existing parish organizations.

The Massachusetts Congregationalist Jonathan Edwards (1703–58) was one of the leading promoters of the Awakening in North America. Congregationalism in New England experienced a great schism during the religious revival of the Great Awakening from the 1730s to the 1770s, prompted by a profound disagreement over the roles of emotion and reason in the promotion and expression of faith. Many evangelicals believed in private revelations. Evangelical "New Light" Congregationalists questioned the piety of more conservative "Old Light" ministers, who appealed primarily to the minds rather than the feelings of their listeners. Conservative politicians, "Old Light" theologians, and non-Methodist Anglicans considered enthusiastic evangelicals threats to the stability of church and state. But we should be careful not to overemphasize the sectarian differences among the Protestant sects or within Congregationalism. Many Bostonians, clergymen as well as laypeople, occasionally attended more than one church. And evangelicalism often took precedence over sectarianism. Congregationalist Susanna Wheatley, for example, befriended Presbyterian and Anglican Methodist missionaries who often stayed with the Wheatleys when they preached in Boston.

Whitefield was more influential than John Wesley during the initial decades of Methodism primarily because he was considered a more powerful orator. Whitefield made seven missionary tours of North America before his death in Newburyport, Massachusetts, in 1770. He had first taken to preaching in the fields when the churchwardens in Islington, then a suburb of London, refused to allow him to use the pulpit in the parish church. Samuel Johnson (1709–84), the great literary critic, biographer, and lexicographer, observed to his biographer James Boswell (1740–95) that Whitefield "would be followed by crowds were he to wear a night-cap in the pulpit, or were he to preach from a tree." Johnson appreciated why Whitefield and other Methodist preachers were so popular: "Sir, it is owing to their expressing themselves in a plain and familiar manner, which is the only way to do good to the common people, and which clergymen of genius and learning ought to do from a principle of duty, when it is suited to their congregations; a practice, for which they would be praised by men of sense."[3] Benjamin Franklin (1706–90) was impressed by Whitefield's elocution when he heard him preach in Philadelphia: "without being interested in the Subject, one could not help being pleas'd with the Discourse."[4] Indeed, Franklin had come to hear Whitefield simply out of curiosity. He was so swayed by his oratorical powers that he made a donation.

Olaudah Equiano, the spiritual autobiographer and most significant eighteenth-century author of African descent, heard the celebrated White-field preach in Savannah, Georgia, on 10 February 1765:

> I came to a church crowded with people; the church-yard was full likewise, and a number of people were even mounted on ladders, look-ing in at the windows. I thought this a strange sight, as I had never seen churches, either in England or the West Indies, crowded in this manner before. I therefore made bold to ask some people the meaning of all this, and they told me the Rev. George Whitfield was preach-ing. I had often heard of this gentleman, and had wished to see and hear him; but I had never before had an opportunity. I now therefore resolved to gratify myself with the sight, and pressed in amidst the multitude. When I got into the church I saw this pious man exhorting the people with the greatest fervour and earnestness, and sweating as much as ever I did while in slavery on Montserrat beach. I was very much struck and impressed with this; I thought it strange I had never seen divines exert themselves in this manner before, and was no longer at a loss to account for the thin congregations they preached to.[5]

Benjamin Rush (1745–1813), a Philadelphia physician with whom Phillis Wheatley corresponded, heard Whitefield preach in Philadelphia a few months later. He was as dazzled by Whitefield's oratorical powers as Equi-ano had been:

> The Revd Mr Whi[t]efield, who returned from Georgia Sometime ago, preached yesterday morning in Our Church, & Afterwards Ad-ministred [*sic*] ye Sacrament. The words he preached from were the first six verses of the second Chapter of St John Revelation: wch words when you read would naturally lead him to address Ministers of the Gospel to whom the Epistle is more imediately [*sic*] directed. O, Sir, it was a Sight that no doubt pleased & astonished Angels to see such a number of faithfull [*sic*] zealous Ministers convened in One place, & eating & drinking around the Lords table.

Nothing could equal the Solemnity of yᵉ Day. Mʳ Whitefield when he came down from yᵉ pulpit & began to speak to the Communicants seemed as if he had come fresh from Heaven, & glowed with all the Seraphic Love of a *Gabriel*. When he spoke on the dying love of a Mediator in instituting the Feast of his Supper the night in which he was betrayed When he praised the Son of God thro' all his Sufferings, and beheld him wounded for Our Sin & bruised for Our Iniquities, his soul catched [*sic*] fire at the Thoughts, and Earth seemed scarce able to contain him. 'Twas a Heaven upon Earth I believe to many Souls, for I think I never see [*sic*] more Attention and Solemnity in a place of worship in my life before.[6]

Whitefield was a stricter Calvinist in his writings, which address the minds of his readers, than he was as a preacher speaking to the emotions of his audiences. His moderately Calvinist appeals to the emotions of his listeners enabled them to "feel in themselves the working of the Spirit of Christ." Whitefield also benefited from the organizational skills of his authoritarian patron, Selina Hastings, the Countess of Huntingdon (1707–91), who established the "Huntingdonian Connexion" of Calvinist Methodist chapels throughout Britain.

The Wesley brothers embraced a more liberal, or relatively Arminian, interpretation of the requirements for salvation. Named after Jacobus Arminius (Jakob Hermandszoon, 1560–1609), one of Calvin's earliest theological opponents, Arminianism holds that all who believe and repent of their sins can be saved. Omniscient God, of course, knows who will be saved but has not arbitrarily predetermined and restricted their number. Arminians and Calvinists agree that personal salvation requires recognition that one is a sinner undeserving of redemption. A believer may be granted grace if he or she submits to God completely. If grace is granted, the believer experiences the joy of the new birth through the assurance, or revelation, of his or her personal salvation. Providence is God acting as the designer, caretaker, and superintendent of the world and its inhabitants, especially humankind. As the derivation of the Latin term *pro-video* (to look forward) implies, events in God's creation happen by plan, not chance. And because God is benevolent, all events, no matter how apparently evil, are part of the grand design God has revealed in the Bible.

Evangelicals are committed to zealously preaching and disseminating the

Christian gospel, especially the first four Gospels of the New Testament. They see themselves as imitators of the first evangelists. Like the apostles Matthew, Mark, Luke, and John, they are missionaries spreading the message that salvation occurs by faith alone and emphasizing the authority of the Bible. Although Wesley and Whitefield were concerned with saving souls, not reforming society, eighteenth-century Methodism was perceived as far more subversive than the socially conservative Methodism of the following centuries. The early Methodists were accused of being levelers because they preached against desiring the riches of this world and because their sermons were offered to all, regardless of social status or economic class. Opponents of Methodism were especially dismayed by the emotional appeal of Methodist sermons, bothered by how suddenly conversions took place, and concerned by the use of Methodist lay ministers. Methodists were condemned for addressing the poor and the enslaved, who were often ignored by more conservative and less evangelical Anglican ministers. People of African descent were no doubt drawn to Whitefield in part because his energetic and emotive oratorical style was similar to that found in many native African religions.

Evangelical Methodists felt that all levels of society, including slaves, potentially share in salvation. Whitefield directly addressed slaves in his audiences during his seven American tours. When physical liberation from enslavement in the present seemed impossible, spiritual freedom and equality in the afterlife offered some solace. And a faith that depends on predestination for salvation rather than on spiritual rewards for good works may have been especially attractive to those whose ability to perform good works was severely limited by their social condition. Poor whites and free blacks, as well as slaves, normally lacked the means and opportunities to make charitable contributions or attend church. Evangelical Christianity offered the poor a way to try to make sense of their present misery.

To anyone who believed that the afterlife was far more important than temporal existence, what mattered most was that pagan Africans be exposed to the truth of Christianity and be humanely treated in whatever social condition they were placed. Thus slavery could even be seen as a kind of fortunate fall, whereby the discomfort of the slaves' present life was compensated by the chance given them of achieving eternal salvation. Enslavement of their bodies introduced pagans to the means to freedom for their souls through conversion to Christianity. Jacobus Elisa Joannes Capitein (c.1717–47), a native African, defends this notion of a fortunate fall in his Latin dissertation.[7] Capitein justifies slavery as having biblical precedent in the past and serving evangelical ends in the present and future. One of the most celebrated and learned eighteenth-century blacks, Capitein had been brought from present-day Ghana, where the Dutch had a slave-trading factory at Elmina, to Holland. There he studied theology from 1726 to 1742, when he was ordained. He returned to Elmina as a missionary. The fortunate fall into slavery is also the subject of one of Wheatley's earliest poems, the well-known "On Being Brought from Africa to America."

People of African descent were not drawn to Whitefield because of any antislavery beliefs on his part. Whitefield's most expansive comments on slavery are found in his widely known *Three Letters from the Reverend Mr. G. Whitefield . . . Letter III. To the Inhabitants of Maryland, Virginia, North and South-Carolina*, published by Benjamin Franklin in Philadelphia in 1740, following Whitefield's tour of the American South. Whitefield avoids the subject of emancipation in his appeal to slave owners to ameliorate the conditions of their slaves and to expose them to Christianity: "I must inform you in the Meekness and Gentleness of *Christ*, that I think God has a Quarrel with you for your Abuse and Cruelty to the poor Negroes. Whether it be lawful for Christians to buy Slaves, and thereby encourage the Nations from whom they are bought, to be at perpetual War with each other, I shall not take upon me to determine; sure I am, it is sinful, when bought, to use them as bad, nay worse, than as though they were Brutes. . . . I challenge the whole World to produce a single Instance of a Negroe's being made a thorough Christian, and thereby made a worse Servant."[8] When Whitefield decided during the 1740s to own slaves in Georgia he considered the choice an economic necessity, rather than a moral issue. Slaves produced the rice that supported his Orphan House in Bethesda, Georgia, ten miles from Savannah. When the Countess of Huntingdon inherited Whitefield's four thousand acres and fifty slaves in Georgia in 1770, she too became a slave owner. Like most evangelicals during the period, neither Whitefield nor Huntingdon saw slavery and Christianity as incompatible. Nowhere in the New Testament is slavery explicitly prohibited.

But exposure to Christianity could lead to consequences neither Whitefield nor the countess ever intended. In 1775 the countess sent David Margate, "a runaway slave," to Georgia. She had had him trained in Britain to serve as a missionary to her slaves at Bethesda. The Huntingdonian minister

Rev. William Piercy, who knew Phillis Wheatley, was initially impressed by "David the African." He wrote to the countess from Bethesda, "I love the appearance of David. He appears pious & devoted & I do hope the Lord will make him a blessing to these poor heathen around us."[9] When Piercy brought Margate to New York a few months later he discovered that the "blessing" of freedom Margate offered to his listeners posed an existential threat to his sponsors as well as to himself: "[Margate] spoke and acted so rashly that bench warrants have been issued out against him ever since; & had he not instantly returned to Georgia privately he would have been taken up & hanged by the negro Laws of the province."[10]

Margate's self-restraint was short-lived once he returned to Georgia, where, Rev. Piercy told the countess,

> the Devil put it into [Margate's] head that he was sent here to be a second Moses, & should be called to deliver his people from slavery. This shocking delusion he spoke of & told my Bro[r] that you told him so & appointed the time. . . . Nothing could have happened of a more distressing nature, we are so surrounded with blacks, or have given me greater pain as my soul so much longed for the instruction & salvation of your slaves. I don't indeed know what Judgment to form either of his words or Conduct since he has been at Bethesda; but the whole has been the most alarming & brought me into the greatest reproach as well as Censure from the Governor & all the white people. We have been under a continual apprehension of an Insurrection among the Slaves from his conduct & discourses to the negroes. And this upon such strong grounds as have almost distressed me to death both day & night.[11]

Margate was not the first person of African descent to identify himself with Moses. Forty years earlier an anonymous and very likely fictional former slave delivered "The Speech of Moses Bon Sáam" to his comrades-in-arms resisting white slave owners in Jamaica. Once the purported speaker had learned to read, he discovered "that the very Man, from whom they [slave owners] had deriv'd the *Name* they had given me, of *Moses* had been the happy *Deliverer* of a *Nation! Of* a Nation *chosen* and *belov'd* by *God!* the Deliverer of this chosen Nation, from such a *Slavery as ours!*"[12] Equiano tells us that when an old slave told him during the 1760s that he had often been cheated by whites, "This artless tale moved me much, and I could not help feeling the just cause Moses had in redressing his brother against the Egyptian. I exhorted the man to look up still to the God on the top, since there was no redress below."[13] Equiano clearly assumes that his readers will recognize that his allusion to Moses "redressing his brother" refers to Exodus 2:11–15: "One day, when Moses had grown up, he went out to his people and looked on their burdens; and he saw an Egyptian beating a Hebrew, one of his people. He looked this way and that, and seeing no one he killed the Egyptian and hid him in the sand."[14] Equiano counts on his readers to recognize the implications of his allusion: passive acceptance of oppression is not the only option available to the enslaved, and active resistance has biblical justification. Margate's perception of himself as "a second Moses" had political as well as religious implications during a period when Moses was playing an increasingly prominent role in Revolutionary anti-British rhetoric.[15]

Piercy soon heard "that the People are determined to send a party of men to Georgia & take David & should they lay hold of Him he will certainly be hanged for what he has delivered, as all the laws are against him." Piercy ordered that Margate be sent "away privately by the first ship that he might escape with his life" and return to England.[16] Margate returned from Charles Town (later Charleston), South Carolina, to England, but not before causing more trouble inspired by his exposure to Christianity. Rev. William Piercy's brother, Rev. Richard Piercy, wrote from Bethesda to his patron, the countess:

> [R]especting David [Margate,] I sincerely sympathize with your Ladyship on his Account & wish I cou'd bear a more important Part of your Ladyships continual Trials, or in some Measure be a means of alleviating them. David render'd himself so odious to the whites upon his Arrival in Charles Town, that had he not been sent to England I have not a Doubt but that he wou'd have been hanged for it. . . . [I]n his Sermon at a Friends House . . . he not only severely reflected against the Laws of the Province respecting Slaves but even against the Thing itself: he also compared their State to that of the Israelites during their Egyptian Bondage & summed up the whole with this Remark that he did not doubt but that the Lord wou'd deliver his People (meaning the Slaves) from their Taskmasters as he did the Jews. Had a White Man

said as much his Life must have gone much less a Negroe, who in these Parts are in the most abject State.[17]

Although he almost destroyed the Countess of Huntingdon's Bethesda project, Margate disappears from the historical record once he left to return to England.

Whitefield and Huntingdon linked Phillis Wheatley to the larger transatlantic network of evangelical Christians that had brought Margate to Georgia. They consequently also connected her to the earliest authors of African descent. Whitefield's American preaching tours exposed several members of the first generation of black authors to Methodism. The use of lay ministers by Methodists and other Dissenting sects gave black authors like Equiano, Briton Hammon (fl. 1760), Jupiter Hammon (1711–ca. 1800), James Albert Ukawsaw Gronniosaw (ca. 1710–75), John Marrant (1755–91), George Liele (ca. 1751–1825), David George (ca. 1743–ca. 1810), and Boston King (ca. 1760–1802) the opportunity and authority to exercise agency and influence in person and print.[18] For example, the *Boston Evening Post* reported on 29 April 1765, "We hear that the Rev. Mr. George Whitefield is expected home from America some time in March, and intends bringing over with him a Black, which [*sic*] he has converted, and who speaks the English language so well, that he has preached to crouded [*sic*] audiences several times in America."[19] Gronniosaw, Marrant, Equiano, and other people of African descent besides Wheatley gained access to the Countess of Huntingdon's literary patronage through Whitefield. Many of them turned to Christianity to resist slavery in ways more subtle and effective than Margate's open defiance.

Whitefield visited Boston during his second (1739–41), sixth (1763–65), and last (1769–70) tours of America. Susanna Wheatley greatly admired Whitefield and his patron, the Countess of Huntingdon. Although Phillis was probably already familiar with Whitefield through his publications, she could have first seen him when he came to Boston in 1764. The town officially welcomed him as a hero: "a very general Meeting of the Freeholders and other Inhabitants of this Town [Boston] . . . voted unanimously that the Thanks of the Town be given the Rev. Mr. George Whitefield, for his charitable Care and Pains in collecting a considerable Sum of Money in Great Britain, for the Benefit of the distressed Sufferers by the great Fire in Boston, 1760."[20] Whitefield initially preached in the surrounding towns because Boston was suffering one of its periodic small pox epidemics. But on 27 February 1764 the *Boston Evening Post* reported, "Last Tuesday Forenoon the Rev. Mr. Whitefield preached to a large Audience at the Old South Meeting House." And on 7 June 1764 the *Boston News-Letter and New-England Chronicle* informed readers that "the Rev. Mr. George Whitefield having preached his Farewell Sermon on Tuesday last, at the Old-South, intends setting out this Day, or Tomorrow, for the Southward." Whitefield arrived at his orphanage in Bethesda, Georgia, in December 1769, at the beginning of his last tour of North America. He had preached in Philadelphia and New York before reaching Boston in August 1770. He preached there three times in Old South, as well as once in the Congregational New North Church, whose minister was Rev. Andrew Eliot (1718–78). From Boston he proceeded farther north to Newbury-Port, Massachusetts.[21]

No known record survives of Phillis Wheatley having heard Whitefield preach at either Old South or New North. In light of Susannah Wheatley's commitment to her religious education, however, it is very likely that Phillis was given the opportunity to share the experiences described by Franklin, Equiano, and Rush. The evidence we have about Phillis's religious upbringing strongly suggests that she would not willingly have missed the chance to see and hear Whitefield in action. The earliest record we have of Phillis Wheatley's exposure to Christianity suggests that her engagement was more active than passive. She was baptized "18 August 1771 (At old South) Phillis servt of Mr Wheatly." As was customary in records of slaves, Phillis had no surname. She had probably not been baptized earlier because Congregationalists were commonly baptized at the age of eighteen, the age her owners may have assumed she reached in the summer of 1771. Rev. Samuel Cooper (1725–83), minister of the Brattle Street Church, baptized Phillis at Old South because Old South had not yet called Rev. John Bacon (1738–1820) and Rev. John Hunt (1744–75) to serve as its joint pastors. Being baptized at Old South, rather than at New South, the Wheatley family church, may have been one of Phillis Wheatley's earliest acts of independence, though she was still a slave. Old South no doubt appealed to Phillis because it accepted the Half-Way Covenant, which permitted the baptism of children whose parents were not full members of the church. Old South probably also appealed to Phillis Wheatley because during the 1760s it was the Congregationalist church in Boston most sympathetic to Whitefield's Methodist mission.

According to "A Conversation between a New York Gentleman & Phillis," which either records or (more likely) imagines an interview of Phillis Wheatley, Phillis underwent a literary and religious catechism sometime before she was baptized in 1771. This "Conversation" is probably the "dialogue" that John Andrews (1743–1822), a Boston lawyer, mentioned on 24 February 1773 to his brother-in-law, William Barrow (d. 1776), a Philadelphia merchant: "[I] have not as yet been able to procure a coppy of her dialogue with Mʳ Murry, if I do, will send it." Much of the "Conversation" sounds like a catechist's preparation or examination of a catechumen, a candidate for baptism:

Q: Was you ever Baptiz'd Phillis?

A: No Sir, I was not, & fear it is a great neglect not to be baptiz'd when I know 'twas a command of Christ.

Q: To be sure Phillis it is a great neglect not to obey it, when Christ commanded it, why don't you be baptiz'd?

A: Many Years prevent it Sir; why don't the *Friends* Baptize?

Q: It is nowhere read in the Bible that Christ baptized.

A: No Sir, yet Christ commanded his Disciples, saying, go & baptize all Nations in the name of the Father &c.

Q: Do you think if Christ had thought it necessary he wou'd not have baptiz'd?

A: I do not think if it had been unnecessary that Christ wou'd have commanded his Disciples to have done it, much less to have suffer'd it himself.

Q: But I speak with Respect to Christ himself, wou'd he not have baptiz'd had it been necessary?

A: I believe he wou'd.

Q: But it's said, I will baptize you with the holy Ghost & with Fire.

A: Sir Christ reserv'd that Baptism to himself but John baptiz'd the Baptism of Repentance, but it was all they (his Disciples) cou'd do.

Q: What do you think of the Sacrament of the Lord's Supper did you ever partake of it do you think that you are actually eating the Body & drinking the Blood of the Lord or take it only in a Spiritual manner?

A: I suppose it receiv'd in a spiritual Manner Sir

Q: But we read, "when he took the Bread, he bless'd it & brake it & gave to his Disciples & said Take, eat, This is my Body" & ought we not to take it so?

A: A Person who observes the bare Words only, may take it so, but I take it as offer'd spiritually, to commemorate his Death & Love till he appears to judge the World—[Q:]You are right Phillis.

Q: Do you imagine that we shall certainly rise from the Dead at the last Day?

A: I believe we shall Sir.

Q: With what Bodies do you think we shall rise at the last day?

A: I believe we shall rise with these Bodies at the last day, that we may receive Judgement in them according to the Works that have been done in them whether they be good or Evil.

Q: But how can this gross & mortal Body inherit eternal life?

A: It shall not then be gross & mortal, for it shall have put on immortality: it's sown a natural Body but it shall be rais'd a spiritual Body &c so then it shall not longer be a gross & mortal, but a spiritual Body.

Q: But it is said Flesh & Blood cannot inherit the Kingdom of Heaven & if we have flesh & blood at the Resurrection how shall we inherit the Kingdom of Heaven?

A: By Flesh & Blood I suppose is meant the corrupt Affections, but these separated from the Body will render it spiritual.

Q: Where do you think the Soul will be during it's separation from the Body?

A: I believe the Spirits of the just will be with God 'till the Resurrection.

Q: Do you think there will be any difference in the happiness of the just?

A: According to their Works Sir.

Q: But how will a Body dismembered & cast to distant Parts of the World be gathered together?

A: Tho' a Limb were cut off, a Hand or Foot & cast to the uttermost Parts of the World, yet the same Power that made it shall gather it to it's proper Body.

Q: Do you think that a Woman has a Soul Phillis?

A: I do Sir.

Q: What makes you think that a Woman has a Soul? Of Man it is said, when God created Man he breath'd into his Nostrils the Breath of Life, & Man became a living Soul; but nothing of all this is said of the Womans Creation, do you think it would not have been mention'd of her as well as it was of Adam & would you suppose from that, that a Woman has a soul?

A: Not from that Sir, but here's a proof that a Woman has a soul; when one came to our Lord to heal her of a Disease he said to her, Daughter thy Sins are forgiven thee. Now Sir if a Woman has no soul any more than the Brutes, why should what she does amiss be accounted Sin, more than the Crimes of the Brute Creation, & we know the Brute creation have no souls.

A very right Answer Phillis[22]

Phillis Wheatley's writings demonstrate that she was granted an education that went well beyond what was needed in order to be catechized on Christianity. Phillis was obviously precocious, and the Wheatleys offered her an extraordinary opportunity to develop her talents and interests. They may have done so as a kind of social experiment to discover what effect education might have on an African. And perhaps they, particularly Susanna, did so because they saw in Phillis the daughter, Sarah, they had lost at the same age nearly ten years earlier. Whatever the reason or combination of reasons, within just four years of arriving in Boston Phillis was literate enough in her new language to write a letter to a Presbyterian minister and to make her first attempt at composing verse, a short elegy on the death of a neighbor. Susanna Wheatley's surviving letters show that she was sufficiently literate to have taught Phillis to read and write, but Hannah Mather Crocker (1752–1829), Phillis's contemporary, recorded many years later that Mary Wheatley had been Phillis's tutor: "Mr Wheatley purchased her [Phillis] he bought her to wait on his only daughter. She was a pretty smart sprightly child. they grew very fond of her and treated her as well as if their own. her young Mrs who was Miss Mary Wheatly [sic], and was afterwards the very amiable wife of Dr John Lathrop [1740–1816]. Phillis was sent to school and educated with Miss Mary. She soon acquired the English language and made some progress in the latin She never was looked on as a slave she could work handsome [i.e., sew and do needlework skillfully], and read and write well for that day."[23] Hannah Mather Crocker was the daughter of Samuel Mather (1706–85), granddaughter of Cotton Mather (1663–1728), and niece of Thomas Hutchinson (1711–80), the last royal governor of Massachusetts. She may well have known Phillis Wheatley, since her father and the governor were among the eighteen men who attested to Wheatley's authorship in *Poems on Various Subjects, Religious and Moral* in 1773.

Basic literacy was fairly widespread in eighteenth-century Boston, especially among free adult white men, largely because Protestants emphasized the need for Christians to have direct access to the Bible. Exaggerating a bit, one of Wheatley's male contemporaries remarked, "Scarce any are to be found among us, even in the obscurest parts, who are not able to read and write with some tolerable propriety."[24] By one estimate, nearly ninety percent of practicing Christians were literate.[25] Literacy was very generously defined. The ability to read was far more common than the ability to write. One historian estimates that "only about half the white American female population in the eighteenth century may have been sufficiently literate to sign a name to a will."[26] Hannah Mather Crocker remarked that during Phillis Wheatley's lifetime "if women could even read and badly write their name it was thought enough for *them*, who by some were esteemed as only mere 'domestick animals.'"[27] Some people of African descent were allowed to learn to read in order to enable them to become Christians. But they were often discouraged from learning to write because of white fears of possible conspiratorial communication among geographically separated blacks. Only the most educated white men, and very few white women, learned Latin. Even fewer people of African descent, men or women, learned it.

Evidence of the educational experiences of individual people of African descent in eighteenth-century Boston is largely lacking. One account we have comes to us filtered through the pen of a white transcriber, or amanuensis: the life of Phillis Wheatley's contemporary Chloe Spear (1750?–1815). According to the *Memoir of Mrs. Chloe Spear, A Native of Africa*,[28] she was kidnapped in Africa and brought to Philadelphia at about the age of twelve. There "the subject of our little history, whom, she said, the sailors used to call *Pickaninny*, on account of her being the smallest of the lot, was sick; consequently she did not meet a ready sale."[29] She was eventually bought by John Bradford (d. 1784), a merchant captain, who renamed her and took her to his home in Boston's North End, where he had lived since at least 1746. Chloe reportedly "was taught nothing, comparatively, of her duty to God, nor to read the blessed Bible. She was, it is true, sent to meeting half the day on the Sabbath; but the seat assigned to herself and her associates was remote from the view of the congregation; and she confessed, that as they did not understand the preaching, they took no interest in it, and spent the time in playing, eating nuts, &c. and derived no benefit whatever, though the preaching probably was evangelical."[30] Chloe soon developed an urge to learn to read:

> when, (as she was accustomed to do,) she went to conduct the children of the family to, and from *school,* she discovered that they were obtaining something of which she remained ignorant. This excited an inclination to learn to read, and after becoming a little acquainted with the school-mistress, who, it would seem, manifested some sympathy for the enslaved youth, she ventured to express her desire.
>
> How to accomplish her object, was a question which required consideration. She was aware that it would not do to make known her wishes at home, and she could not attend at the regular school hours, both for want of time, and because the children would expose the fact to their parents. But after some reflection, an expedient was devised that promised success. "So," said Chloe, "I ask de Mistress how much she hab week to teach me such time I get when school out, and my work done? She say, *"five copper."*[31]

Chloe saved the tips she occasionally received from visitors to her master's house and bought "a Psalter, which contained the Psalms, Proverbs, and our Lord's Sermon on the mount" with her five copper coins.[32] When Bradford discovered that she was not only being taught to read but trying to learn to spell as well, "[h]e angrily forbade her going again to the schoolmistress for instruction, even under penalty of being suspended by her two thumbs, and severely whipped; he said it made negroes saucy to know how to read, &c." Despite his threats, however, she "hid her book under her pillow, and when not likely to be detected, she used to labour over it, and strive to remember what she had learned, and to find out as much as she could herself."[33] Chloe continued her education with the help of a sympathetic white neighbor, eventually won her master's approval, and after her manumission held religious meetings at her home.

Phillis Wheatley never faced the obstacles Chloe Spear encountered in her path to education. The education that Phillis Wheatley received from

Susanna and/or Mary Wheatley would have been very impressive for a white man of high social standing at the time. Mary may have attended one of the publicly funded Boston schools open to both boys and girls, or she may have been taught privately by a schoolmaster. A girl of Mary's social status and presumed aspirations was expected to acquire an education appropriate for her station, one far more advanced than that appropriate for a servant or slave. When Nicholas Brown (1729–91), Nathaniel Wheatley's wealthy business associate in Providence, Rhode Island, sought a proper education for his daughter Joanna, he sent her to live in Boston under the supervision of Rev. Samuel Stillman (1737–1807). Stillman assured Brown, "I have introduced her to one, who is thought to be one of the best masters in Boston for writing, ciphering, spelling, letter-writing &c. and whatever else is necessary to the accomplishment of a young lady in that way. . . . Master Tileston is very capable of teaching & has for years been employed by this town as a School-master. The young ladies he teaches at private hours."[34]

Phillis Wheatley's writings reveal a familiarity with Classical literature, at least in translation, as well as geography, history, politics, and English literature, unusual subjects for girls at the time. Her master reported in 1772 that she had "a great Inclination to learn the Latin Tongue, and has made some Progress in it."[35] Some modern critics have gone further than the evidence allows to claim that "she was a slave who knew Greek and read Ovid in the original Latin."[36] None of her surviving writings demonstrates a familiarity with Classical sources that could not have been gained from translations or contemporaneous dictionaries of mythology. For example, when Wheatley alludes to the beginning of Homer's *Iliad* in her opening lines to "Niobe in Distress" ("APOLLO's Wrath to man the dreadful spring / Of ills innumer'rous, tuneful goddess, sing!") she clearly echoes Alexander Pope's translation (ACHILLES' Wrath, to Greece the direful spring / Of woes unnumber'd, heav'nly goddess, sing!") rather than Homer's original Greek.

Phillis Wheatley's handwriting reflects her extraordinary education. The handwritings of eighteenth-century students taught by the same instructor were often quite similar, especially in more formal documents. William H. Robinson, a scholar and biographer of Phillis Wheatley, believes that at least a couple of business letters signed by Nathaniel Wheatley were dictated by him to Phillis and are thus in her handwriting. However, the result of comparing letters known to be in Nathaniel's hand with ones known to be in Phillis's is not as conclusive as one would hope. Given that Mary and Nathaniel Wheatley were eighteen years old when Phillis met them, she probably did not directly share their writing teacher or teachers. But if either of them taught Phillis, as seems very likely, she would have learned the same style of penmanship.

The superiority of Phillis Wheatley's education is also obvious when we compare it to that of one of her white contemporaries, Anna Green Winslow (1759–79?). Winslow's diary is a rare record of the interests and educational and social experiences available to an intelligent girl on the eve of the American Revolution.[37] In 1770 Anna Green Winslow's socially and politically prominent parents sent her from Nova Scotia to Boston to live with Sarah and John Deming, her aunt and uncle, in order to get a proper education. As a student in Boston's South Writing School, Anna Green Winslow took great pride in her penmanship, which is one of the reasons she shared her diary with her parents. She also attended a sewing school, where she learned to "work handsome," the types of sewing and needle-work that Hannah Mather Crocker says Mary Wheatley taught Phillis. The Demings lived about fifteen hundred feet southwest of the Wheatleys and knew the Lathrops. Anna dined at least once with Mary Wheatley La-throp. Although Anna never mentions Phillis in her surviving diary entries from November 1771 to the end of May 1773, she had ample opportunity to be aware of the slightly older girl. Like the Wheatleys, the Demings owned a slave, Lucinda, who, like Phillis, had been born in Africa. The Demings bought her when she was about seven years old. The same John Avery who may have sold Phillis to the Wheatleys may also have sold Lucinda to the Demings: Avery was John Deming's brother-in-law and his partner in trade with the West Indies. Phillis Wheatley's writings suggest that, with her op-portunities for education and access to information about the world beyond her Boston household, her early life was significantly more like that of Anna Green Winslow than that of Lucinda or Chloe Spear.

Anna Green Winslow was an avid reader of secular texts, especially nov-els and periodicals. She mentions enjoying John Bunyan's *Pilgrim's Prog-ress*, as well as adult works that had been abridged for "the Instruction and Amusement of all good Boys and Girls." These included Samuel Richard-son's *Sir Charles Grandison*, Jonathan Swift's *Gulliver's Travels*, and Henry Fielding's *Joseph Andrews*.[38] She also read books expressly written for chil-dren, such as *The Puzzling Cap: A Collection of Riddles*, *The Little Female*

Orators; or, Nine Evenings Entertainment, and *The History of Little Goody Two-Shoes.* Anna Green Winslow followed the public media, noting the latest fashions in imported London magazines, recording Boston obituaries, and commenting on current events in Boston newspapers. In her 21 February 1772 diary entry she proudly announces, "As I am (as we say) a daughter of liberty I chuse to wear as much of our own manufactory as pocible [*sic*]" to express solidarity with those who had been boycotting the importation of nonessential English goods to protest against the duties imposed on them by the Townsend Acts of 1767.[39] By the time Anna Green Winslow was twelve years old, she was not only transcribing in her commonplace book verse published by others, but apparently writing her own verse as well.

Religion is the most common subject in Anna Green Winslow's diary. She found it a source of pleasure as well as instruction. Her religious experiences went well beyond attending church and reading the Bible daily to her aunt.[40] Almost half the newspaper articles, books, and pamphlets available in Boston during her stay there dealt with religious subjects.[41] Sermons were a major source of entertainment for most people in earlier periods. Public theatrical performances were banned in Boston during Phillis Wheatley's lifetime. One went to church to experience drama. Anna Green Winslow often comments on the style as well as the content of the many sermons she heard by various ministers. For example, she records on 4 January 1772 hearing Rev. Charles Chauncy (1705–87) preach in the morning, and dining later that day with company that included Rev. Ebenezer Pemberton (1704–77) and Rev. Samuel Cooper.[42] On 27 February 1772 she mentions having heard Rev. Mather Byles (1707–88).[43]

Phillis Wheatley probably also attended sermons by a variety of preachers. All four of the ministers Winslow mentions are among the eighteen men who attested to the authenticity of Wheatley's *Poems on Various Subjects, Religious and Moral.* Phillis Wheatley and Anna Green Winslow heard at least some of the same sermons because Anna and the Demings attended the Old South church where Phillis was baptized in 1771. Phillis and Anna very probably saw each other at least weekly. Sermons were normally an hour long, and required services took place twice on Sundays, in the morning and again in the afternoon. Anna Green Winslow may have shared the family pew with her aunt and uncle. Phillis, however, probably sat in the section of the balcony reserved for females of African descent. When Anna Green Winslow "went to catechizing with [her] Aunt" on 13 February 1772 to hear Rev. John Bacon and Rev. John Hunt, coministers of Old South, take turns asking questions and giving answers about Christianity, she and her fellow congregant Phillis Wheatley must have been seated within sight of each other. Phillis, however, was, in effect, invisible to her younger neighbor.[44]

But Phillis's exposure to Christianity, and consequently to literacy, soon made her known to fellow believers beyond Boston, including at least one fellow native African, Obour (also spelled Abour and Arbour) Tanner (1750?–1835), in Newport, Rhode Island. Although we do not know if Phillis Wheatley and Obour Tanner ever met in person, Wheatley's surviving correspondence reveals that they developed an increasingly affectionate epistolary relationship. They may have been taken from Africa on the same vessel, as one critic suggests, but there is no evidence to support that possibility.[45] Obour initiated their correspondence in late 1771 or early 1772. She was Wheatley's only known correspondent of African descent. She may have been about three years older than Phillis: Obour was baptized and admitted in the First Congregational Church in Newport on 10 July 1768 as Obour Tanner, euphemistically identified as the "servant of James Tanner." Assuming that Obour Tanner was baptized when she was thought to have been eighteen years old, as was the usual Congregational practice, she was probably born around 1750. She and Phillis may have met because of James Tanner's link with Boston. He had been admitted to membership in the First Congregational Church in Newport on 5 March 1758 after having been dismissed from "South Church" in Boston. Rev. Samuel Hopkins (1721–1803) married Obour Tanner to Barra (also spelled Barry) Collins in the First Congregational Church in Newport on 4 November 1790. Obour died in Newport on 21 June 1835.[46]

Phillis and Obour were united in their Christian faith and their consequent belief that God's providential design included the enslavement of Africans:

> Happy were it for us if we could arrive to that evangelical Repentance, and the true holiness of heart which you mention. Inexpressibly happy Should we be could we have a due Sense of Beauties and excellence of the Crucified Saviour. In his Crucifixion may be seen marvellous displays of Grace and Love, Sufficient to draw and invite us to the rich and endless treasures of his mercy; let us rejoice in and adore the wonders

of God's infinite Love in bringing us from a land Semblant of darkness itself, and where the divine light of revelation (being obscur'd) is as darkness. Here, the knowledge of the true God and eternal life are made manifest; But there, profound ignorance overshadows the Land. Your observation is true, namely, that there was nothing in us to recommend us to God. Many of our fellow creatures are pass'd by, when the bowels of divine love expanded towards us. May this goodness & long Suffering of God lead us to unfeign'd repentance.

It gives me very great pleasure to hear of so many of my Nation, Seeking with eagerness the way to true felicity. (Phillis Wheatley to Obour Tanner, 19 May 1772)

Evangelical Christianity had already enabled Wheatley to become a published author by the time she and Obour Tanner established a private correspondence. Religion gave her her primary subject as well as the authority and power to write about it. She arrived in New England just as the first English-speaking authors of African descent were finding their way into print. The works in prose and print by the unrelated Briton Hammon and Jupiter Hammon were published in 1760. Like them, Wheatley was a beneficiary of the Great Awakening, with its Protestant emphases on the need for literacy because of the primacy of the Bible, on the need for spiritual self-reflection and self-assessment, and on the Christian duty to evangelize to white as well as black audiences. As an enslaved woman, she did not have the opportunity to preach directly, as Marrant, Liele, George, and King were authorized to do, but like both Hammons, Gronniosaw, and Equiano, Phillis Wheatley employed evangelical Christianity as both the means and the end for getting into print.[47]

(*Left*) Phillis Wheatley, from the Boston Women's Memorial, by Meredith Bergmann, 2003.

(*Below*) *Bowles's New One-Sheet Chart of the Atlantic or Western Ocean, Laid down from the Latest Discoveries, and Regulated by Numerous Astronomical Observations* (London, c. 1794), showing the boundaries of Phillis Wheatley's Atlantic world. Courtesy of the John Carter Brown Library at Brown University.

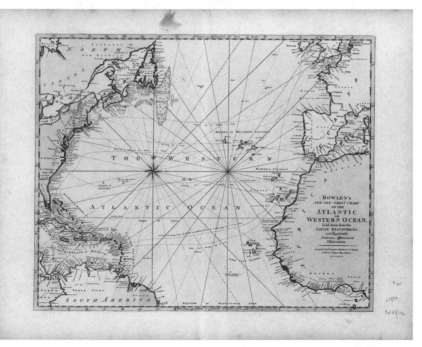

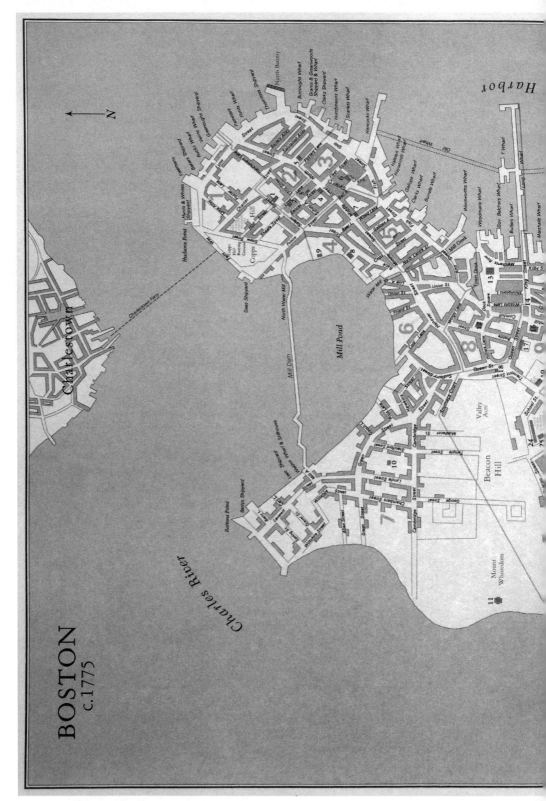

Map of Phillis Wheatley's Boston on the eve of the American Revolution. From
Lester J. Cappon, Barbara Bartz Petchenik, and John Hamilton Long, eds. *Atlas of*

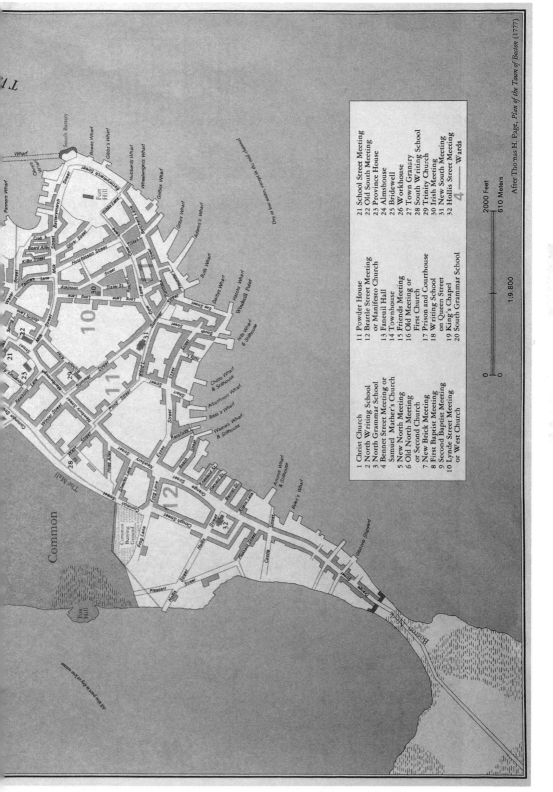

1 Christ Church
2 North Writing School
3 North Grammar School
4 Bennet Street Meeting or Samuel Mather's Church
5 New North Meeting
6 Old North Meeting or Second Church
7 New Brick Meeting
8 First Baptist Meeting
9 Second Baptist Meeting
10 Lynde Street Meeting or West Church

11 Powder House
12 Brattle Street Meeting or Manifesto Church
13 Faneuil Hall
14 Townhouse
15 Friends Meeting
16 Old Meeting or First Church
17 Prison and Courthouse
18 Writing School on Queen Street
19 King's Chapel
20 South Grammar School

21 School Street Meeting
22 Old South Meeting
23 Province House
24 Almshouse
25 Bridewell
26 Workhouse
27 Town Granary
28 South Writing School
29 Trinity Church
30 Irish Meeting
31 New South Meeting
32 Hollis Street Meeting

4 ——— Wards

After Thomas H. Page, *Plan of the Town of Boston* (1777)

0   2000 Feet
0   610 Meters

1:9,800

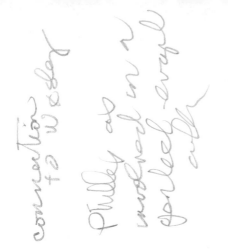

John Wesley (mezzotint, published 1770, after N. Hone). Reverend Wesley published several of Phillis Wheatley's poems in his Methodist *Arminian Magazine* in London. Library of Congress.

John Wesley M. D.
Fellow of Lincoln Colledge Oxford

The Rev.ᵈ George Whitefield. A. M.
late Chaplain to the R.ᵗ Hon.ᵇˡᵉ the
Countess of Huntingdon.
Born Dec.16.1714 O.S. Died Sep.30:1770.

George Whitefield. Phillis Wheatley's elegy on the death of Whitefield in 1770 brought her transatlantic fame and the patronage of Whitefield's patron, the Countess of Huntingdon. Wheatley probably heard him preach in Boston. Courtesy of the John Carter Brown Library at Brown University.

Olaudah Equiano (Daniel Orme's engraving is after a portrait painted by William Denton). Equiano was familiar with at least some of Phillis Wheatley's poems through the publication of Thomas Clarkson's *An Essay on the Slavery and Commerce of the Human Species* (London, 1786). Courtesy of the John Carter Brown Library at Brown University.

(*Right*) Benjamin Rush. A prominent
Philadelphia physician, Rush was
one of the earliest commentators to
praise Phillis Wheatley's poetry. Her
correspondence with him is now lost.
Library of Congress.

(*Below*) Selina Hastings, Countess
of Huntingdon (mezzotint, after
J. Russell, 1773). Huntingdon, an
evangelical Calvinist Methodist,
was the patron of Reverend George
Whitefield. Phillis Wheatley dedicated her *Poems* to Huntingdon in
1773. © National Portrait Gallery,
London.

The Right Honorable SELINA Countess Dowager of *HUNTINGDON.*

Jacobus Elisa Joannes Capitein. African-born Capitein was an ordained minister in the Dutch Reformed Church. (Andover-Harvard Theological Library, Harvard Divinity School, Harvard University)

Samuel Mather (John Greenwood). A son of Cotton Mather and cousin of Mather Byles, Samuel Mather was pastor of the Tenth Congregational Church in Boston. He signed the "Attestation" that prefaced Phillis Wheatley's *Poems* in 1773. © American Antiquarian Society.

Thomas Hutchinson
(E. Truman, oils, 1741).
The last colonial gov-
ernor of Massachusetts,
Hutchinson signed the
"Attestation" that pref-
aced Phillis Wheatley's
Poems in 1773. Courtesy
of the Massachusetts
Historical Society.

Charles Chauncy.
Chauncy was minister
of the First Unitarian
Church in Boston. He
signed the "Attestation"
that prefaced Phillis
Wheatley's *Poems* in
1773. Harvard Univer-
sity Archives, Pusey
Library.

Mather Byles Sr. (John Singleton Copley). Byles was a Congregational minister in Boston who also wrote poetry. He signed the "Attestation" that prefaced Phillis Wheatley's *Poems* in 1773. © American Antiquarian Society.

Samuel Hopkins (J. Badger, oils). Hopkins was the minister of the First Congregational Church in Newport, Rhode Island, and an early vocal opponent of slavery. Courtesy of the Massachusetts Historical Society.

The Reverend Mr. SAMSON OCCOM,

The first Indian Minister that ever was in Europe, & who accompanied the Revd. Nathanl. Whitaker D.D. in an application to Great Britain for Charities to support ye Revd. D. Wheelocks Indian Academy & Missionaries among ye Native Savages of N. America

Publish'd according to Act of Parliament, Sept: 20. 1768. by Henry Parker, at No. 82. in Cornhill, LONDON.

Samson Occom (Jonathan Spilsbury, after Mason Chamberlin mezzotint, published 1768). Occom was a Mohegan Indian who had been ordained a Presbyterian minister. He was a friend of John and Susanna Wheatley. He was also one of Phillis Wheatley's correspondents. © National Portrait Gallery, London.

EARL of DARTMOUTH.

Earl of Dartmouth (W. Evans, stipple, after T. Gainsborough). William Legge, 2nd Earl of Dartmouth, was the subject of Phillis Wheatley's 1772 panegyric celebrating his appointment as secretary of state overseeing the North American colonies, as well as his position as president of the Board of Trade and Foreign Plantations, offices he held until 1775. Dartmouth was a close friend of the Countess of Huntingdon and a strong supporter of her missionary work. Library of Congress.

Jeremy Belknap (Henry Sargent). Reverend Belknap recorded Phillis Wheatley's first known poem in his diary. Massachusetts Historical Society.

To the King's most excellent Majesty on his repealing the american Stamp act

Your Subject's hope

The crown upon your head may flourish long
And in great wars your royal arms be strong
May your Sceptre many nations sway
Resent it on them that dislike Obey
But how shall we exalt the British King
Who ruleth france Possessing every thing
The sweet remembrance of whose favours past
The meanest peasants bless the great the last
May George belov'd of all the nations round
Live and by earth and heavens blessings crown'd
May heaven protect and Guard him from on high
And at his presence every evil fly
Thus every clime with equal gladness see
When kings do smile it sets their Subjects free
When wars came on the proudest rebel fled
God thunder'd fury on their guilty head

Phillis

Phillis Wheatley, "To the King's Most Excellent Majesty" ms.
Historical Society of Pennsylvania, Gratz Collection.

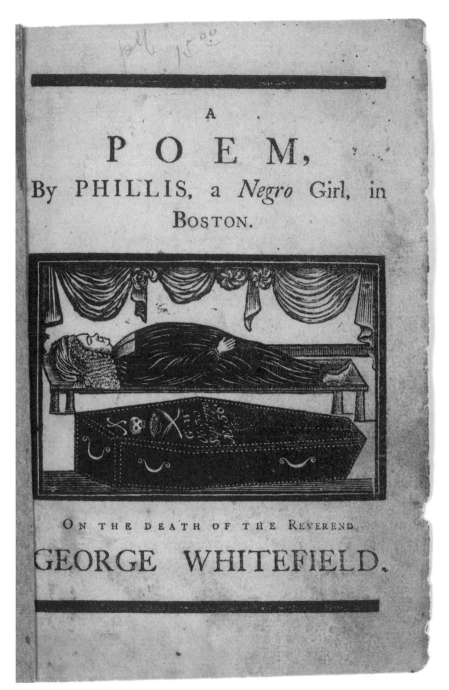

Title Page of Phillis Wheatley's 1770 elegy on the death of Reverend George Whitefield. Courtesy of the John Carter Brown Library at Brown University.

John Thornton (T. Gainsborough, oils, c.1782). Thornton, a wealthy London merchant and philanthropist, was a supporter of the Countess of Huntingdon's evangelical activities and a member of her circle. The Marine Society & Sea Cadets, London. http://www.ms-sc.org/.

Thomas Amory (John Singleton Copley). An English minister and religious author, Amory was the addressee of Phillis Wheatley's poem "To the Rev. Dr. Thomas Amory on Reading His Sermons on Daily Devotion, in Which that Duty Is Recommended and Assisted." © Museum of Fine Arts, Boston.

Job Ben Solomon and William Ansah Seesarakoo. These portraits, published in the *Gentleman's Magazine* in June 1750, are of enslaved Africans who were freed in London and repatriated to Africa because of their "noble" births. Folger Shakespeare Library.

Phillis Wheatley, *Poems* (London, 1773), frontispiece. The image of Wheatley was added to her book at the suggestion of her patron, the Countess of Huntingdon. It may have been engraved after a portrait by Scipio Moorhead, the subject of her poem "To S. M. a Young *African* Painter, on Seeing his Works." Library of Congress.

P O E M S

ON

VARIOUS SUBJECTS,

RELIGIOUS AND MORAL,

BY

PHILLIS WHEATLEY,

NEGRO SERVANT to Mr. JOHN WHEATLEY,
of BOSTON, in NEW ENGLAND.

L O N D O N:

Printed for A. BELL, Bookseller, Aldgate; and sold by
Messrs. Cox and Berry, King-Street, BOSTON.

MDCCLXXIII.

Title Page of Phillis Wheatley, *Poems* (London, 1773). Library of Congress.

John Hancock. *The honble. John Hancock of Boston in New-England, President of the American Congress —Done from an Original Picture Painted by Littleford* (London: Publish'd as the Act directs by C. Shepherd, 1775). Hancock was a very prominent Boston merchant, now best known for the size of his signature on the Declaration of Independence. He signed the "Attestation" that prefaced Phillis Wheatley's *Poems* in 1773. Library of Congress.

John Erving (John Singleton Copley). Erving was a prominent Boston merchant who signed the "Attestation" that prefaced Phillis Wheatley's *Poems* in 1773. Smith College Museum of Art, Northampton, Massachusetts.

The Hon. JAMES BOWDOIN, Efq. L. L. D.
F. R. S.

James Bowdoin. A prominent Boston merchant, Bowdoin signed the "Attestation" that prefaced Phillis Wheatley's *Poems* in 1773. Courtesy of the John Carter Brown Library at Brown University.

Joseph Green. Green was a Boston merchant and poet who owned a large library. He signed the "Attestation" that prefaced Phillis Wheatley's *Poems* in 1773. © Museum of Fine Arts, Boston.

Ignatius Sancho, *Letters of the late Ignatius Sancho, an African. To which are prefixed, memoirs of his life*. (London: Printed by J. Nichols, and sold by J. Dodsley [etc.], 1782), frontispiece. Francesco Bartolozzi engraved the portrait after a painting of the then-valet to the Duke of Montagu hastily produced by Thomas Gainsborough. Sancho was one of the earliest critics of African descent to praise Phillis Wheatley. Library of Congress.

David Wooster. A New Haven, Connecticut, merchant, Major General Wooster was mortally wounded by the British in 1777. Wooster was the subject of an elegy Phillis Wheatley sent to his widow the following year. Library of Congress.

Granville Sharp (George Dance, pencil, 1794). As a leader in the struggle in the British courts to end slavery, Sharp achieved his most significant victory with the Mansfield ruling of 1772, which declared that slaves brought to England could not legally be forced to return to enslavement in the colonies. Sharp was one of Phillis Wheatley's tour guides during her visit to London in 1773. © National Portrait Gallery, London.

George Washington. Phillis Wheatley initiated a correspondence with Washington in 1775 when she sent him a cover letter with her poem addressed to him. Courtesy of the John Carter Brown Library at Brown University.

(*Above*) John Paul Jones (J. M. Moreau the younger, portrait, 1780, copy). The Revolutionary naval hero apparently tried to initiate a correspondence with Phillis Wheatley in 1777. Library of Congress.

(*Right*) Charles Lee. Lee, the subject of Wheatley's poem "On the Capture of General Lee," challenged Washington for leadership of the American forces during the Revolution. Library of Congress.

Chapter 3

"I prefer the Verse"

Phillis Wheatley was not yet a teenager when she first began to compose verse. Her writings made her known far beyond Boston by the time she was twenty years old. A "Letter sent by the Author's Master to the Publisher," dated 14 November 1772, introduces Phillis Wheatley's *Poems on Various Subjects, Religious and Moral* (London, 1773). The letter informs her publisher and readers that "as to her Writing, her own Curiosity led her to it; and this she learnt in so short a Time, that in the Year 1765, she wrote a Letter to the Rev. Mr. Occom, the *Indian* Minister, while in *England*." Nathaniel Wheatley, the probable author of the prefatory letter, must be mistaken about the date of the now missing letter to Samson Occom (1723–92), since he and Whitaker did not reach England until 3 February 1766. Occom, an ordained Presbyterian minister, was a member of the Mohegan people in Connecticut. He had converted to Christianity at the age of seventeen during the Great Awakening. Three years later he entered a school founded by the Congregationalist minister Eleazar Wheelock (1711–79) in Lebanon, Connecticut, to study English and theology.

Occom and Nathaniel Whitaker (1732–95), a Presbyterian minister from Norwich, Connecticut, began a nearly three-year fund-raising tour of England and Scotland in 1766 to raise money for the Indian Charity School in Lebanon, Connecticut, which Wheelock founded to train Native American missionaries. Occom delivered more than three hundred sermons during their stay, and was treated as a celebrity. He met William Legge (1731–1801), 2nd Earl of Dartmouth, the Countess of Huntingdon, and even King George III (1738–1820). People of many religious persuasions welcomed Occom. For example, on 26 February 1766 Occom and Whitaker "went to See Dr. [Thomas] Gibbons [1720–85] an Independent Minister, [who] received us kindly and promised to assist us according to his Influence, in our Great Business."[1] Occom spent time in London as a sightseer, visiting the Tower of London, Parliament, and Westminster Abbey, among many other attractions. Occom and Whitaker's 1766–68 tour was so successful that they raised the astounding sum of £11,000, enabling Wheelock to move his school to Hanover, New Hampshire, and found Dartmouth College in 1769.

Phillis Wheatley probably first met Occom during Whitefield's visit to Boston in 1764. Whitefield had invited Occom to join him on his New England preaching tour. Occom subsequently corresponded with both Phillis and Susanna Wheatley. He often stayed with the Wheatleys when he visited Boston. Like Phillis Wheatley, Occom was also an author. His best-known published works are *A Sermon Preached at the Execution of Moses Paul, an Indian* (New Haven, 1772) and *A Choice Collection of Hymns and Sacred Songs* (New London, 1774). His most famous work is his unpublished "Autobiographical Narrative" composed in 1768.

Until now, Phillis Wheatley's earliest writings were thought to be the missing poem "On the Death of the Rev. Dr. *Sewell* [*sic*], when Sick, 1765," included in her 1772 "Proposals," and the missing letter she sent to Rev. Samson Occom in England. Like the letter to Occom, the missing poem is misdated in the "Proposals": Rev. Joseph Sewall (1688–1769), pastor of Old South, did not die in 1765.[2] A strong candidate for Phillis's first known piece of writing, however, is the recently discovered four-line poem written on the last page of the 1773 diary of the Congregationalist minister, Jeremy Belknap (1744–98). Belknap identifies the poem as "Phillis Wheatley's first Effort———A.D. 1765. AE II."[3] Belknap's diary is interleaved in *Bickerstaff's Boston Almanack. For the Year of Our Lord, 1773* (Boston, [1772]). Belknap transcribed the text twice, first in three lines, as if he could not decide whether it is prose or poetry. The two-word phrase "Unto Salvation" is written above the first line. A caret below the line indicates in the manuscript where the phrase should be inserted:

> Mrs Thacher's Son is gone ^{Unto} ∧^{Salvation} her Daughter too
> so I conclude
> They are both gone to be renewed

Belknap's second transcription, immediately following the first, presents the text as a four-line poem, framed in the manuscript by an opening bracket:

> Mrs Thacher's Son is gone
> Unto Salvation

Her Daughter too, so I conclude
They are both gone to be renewed

The two transcriptions were made at different times. The three-line version
is written in dark ink. The four-line poem and the "Unto Salvation" added
to the three-line version are written in a lighter-colored ink.

Mrs. Thacher (d. 30 January 1776), the former Bathsheba Doggett, was
the widow of John Kent of Boston when she married a widower, Oxenbridge
Thacher Sr. (1681–1772), in 1740. She was his second wife. The Thachers had
been one of the most distinguished Congregationalist families in Massachusetts for generations. Bathsheba's seventeen-year-old daughter, Sarah,
married Oxenbridge's twenty-one-year-old son, Oxenbridge Thacher Jr.
(1719–65), in 1741. Consequently, Oxenbridge Thacher Jr. was the "Son" of
Mrs. Oxenbridge Thacher Sr. in two senses: he was her step-son and her
son-in-law. Oxenbridge Thacher Jr. and his wife lived in central Boston,
several streets west of the home of John Wheatley and his family. Thacher
was a well-respected Boston lawyer. He was also a prominent, and promising, local politician. Like John Wheatley before him and Nathaniel Wheatley after, Thacher held various town offices. He was an early proponent of
colonial rights, and he was one of Boston's four representatives in the Massachusetts General Assembly when he died in 1765. In *Sentiments of a British
American* (1764), Thacher argued that direct taxation of the colonies by the
British Parliament was unconstitutional.

Sarah Thacher died on 4 July 1764 at her father-in-law's house in Milton,
Massachusetts. The *Boston Gazette, and Country Journal* reported on 9 July
1764 that she was a victim of the same smallpox epidemic in 1764 that caused
Whitefield to hesitate before entering Boston. Her husband was indirectly
a victim of the same epidemic the following year. The *Massachusetts Gazette and Boston News-Letter* announced on 11 July 1765 that Thacher had
died in Boston two days earlier, "after a long languishment." He had never
recovered from the side-effects of having been inoculated against the disease. John Adams (1735–1826) was also inoculated with the live smallpox
virus during the same epidemic; although inoculation was dangerous, the
mortality rate from it was significantly lower than that from contracting the
disease naturally. Phillis Wheatley luckily avoided contracting the disease
during the 1764–65 epidemic. One third of those who died from smallpox
during that outbreak were people of African descent.[4]

Premature deaths were common during the eighteenth century, and they were often discussed more directly and publicly than we are now accustomed to. Twelve-year-old Anna Green Winslow reported deaths, obituaries, and executions to her parents. She saw nothing remarkable or incongruous about mentioning in her diary a boil on her own finger immediately before dispassionately recording verses on death she found in her "grandmamma Sargent's pocket-book."[5] Her grandmother had died only six months earlier. At a time when composing verses was much more frequent than now, would-be poets often attempted to write elegies.[6] So common were elegies during the period that Philip Freneau (1752–1832), an elegist himself, noted in 1790 that "No species of poetry is more frequently attempted" than poems on death.[7] The only surviving poem by the earliest known African American author, Lucy (Terry) Prince (c. 1730–1821), is a rather crude ballad elegy. Not printed until 1855, "Bars Fight" commemorates the killing and kidnapping of white settlers by Native Americans in 1746. Lucy had been kidnapped in Africa as an infant and brought to Rhode Island to be sold. She was eventually owned by Ebenezer Wells in Deerfield, Massachusetts. Obijah Prince, a wealthy free black, bought her freedom and married her in 1760.[8] Contemporaneous satires and parodies of elegies also attested to the popularity of the genre. In 1722 Benjamin Franklin mocked the formulaic quality of elegies in one of his Silence Dogood letters. But Franklin later admitted in his *Autobiography* that his own earliest attempt at poetry was an elegy written in 1718. It has not survived.[9]

There are many reasons to accept Belknap's attribution of the verses on the deaths of Mr. and Mrs. Thacher to a young Phillis Wheatley, which would make it the first of nineteen elegies we could now assign to her (not including variants of several of those). It would also be the first of her many occasional poems—that is, her earliest poem written in response to a recent event. Belknap knew Wheatley, or at least knew of her, before 1773, because she sent him a variant manuscript version of her elegy on the death of Rev. Sewall (1688–1769), which is now at Dartmouth College. Since the Thacher elegy is not in Wheatley's hand and apparently did not come to Belknap's attention until 1773, it seems likely that it came to him through a source other than Wheatley.

That source may have been Belknap's uncle, Reverend Mather Byles (1707–88), a major published colonial poet who resided in Boston. Belknap was living in New Hampshire in 1765, when the lines on the Thachers were most likely composed, as well as in 1773, when he transcribed them. But he frequently visited Boston, his hometown, during that period. An amateur poet in his youth, Belknap imitated Byles in his own early attempts at poetry. Byles also served as a model for Wheatley, whom he encouraged as a poet. He is one of the eighteen Boston worthies who attested in print to the authenticity of her *Poems on Various Subjects, Religious and Moral*, published in London in 1773.[10] Amateur authors often circulated their writings in manuscript before, or instead of, having them printed. Pride in their slave's precocious efforts may have motivated the Wheatleys to share them with members of the Boston literati. The publication of Wheatley's *Poems* and Belknap's familiarity with at least one of her earlier elegies probably prompted him to seek more information about her in 1773. His uncle was clearly in a position to inform him about her progress as an aspiring author.

The brevity, style, genre, content, and allusions of the poem on the Thachers all point to Phillis Wheatley as its author in 1765. The succession of brief clauses, staccato rhythm, and nearly successful attempt to write couplets are typical of juvenilia, especially by someone who had been living in an English-speaking environment for only four years. As a brief occasional elegy on the death of a Boston notable, the lines in Belknap's diary anticipate the most common type of poem found among Wheatley's later works. The emphasis on private and domestic loss in the manuscript poem contrasts not surprisingly with the concentration on public and political loss found in fourteen lines titled "Written Extempore, on hearing of the Death of Oxenbridge Thacher, Esq.; on a supposed View of the Corps" that "S. Y." published in the *Boston News-Letter and New England Chronicle* on 18 July 1765. As one might expect from a young girl, the pious sentiment expressed in the piece that Belknap attributes to Wheatley concerns only the surviving mother and her late children. Although Oxenbridge Thacher Sr. was still alive when the poem was written, he is not mentioned. If Wheatley wrote the poem, she may have ignored the father because he had been living in Milton for several years and thus was unfamiliar to her. Sarah and Oxenbridge Thacher Jr. on the other hand, were members of the Old South Church, which Phillis Wheatley formally joined in 1771. Writing an elegy on their deaths effectively highlighted the spiritual community the author shared with them.

Assuming that the lines Jeremy Belknap recorded in his diary in 1773 are indeed by Phillis Wheatley and that she composed them shortly after the death of Oxenbridge Thacher Jr. in 1765, they constitute Wheatley's earliest known piece of writing of any kind. Belknap apparently accurately described the lines he recorded in 1773 as "Phillis Wheatley's first Effort." Whether or not Phillis Wheatley wrote the lines recorded in Belknap's diary, other poems that she later claimed to have composed in 1766 and 1767, as well as one we can prove was written between the beginning of October and 21 December 1767, demonstrate how extraordinarily rapidly her poetic abilities developed.

Wheatley's use of blank verse and enjambment in "On Virtue" reveals a level of skill and control that seems almost impossible for the author of the relatively clumsy verses on the deaths of the Thachers. Wheatley dates "On Virtue" 1766 in her 1772 "Proposals." It was first published in her *Poems on Various Subjects, Religious and Moral* in 1773. Some of Wheatley's improved skill and control is no doubt due to revisions and polishing she undertook between the poem's initial composition and its publication. Rather than using the simple declarative mood and excessively end-stopped final couplet found in the earlier verse, "On Virtue" is an allegorical poem whose lines flow syntactically smoothly into one another:

> O Thou bright jewel in my aim I strive
> To comprehend thee. Thine own words declare
> Wisdom is higher than a fool can reach.
> I cease to wonder, and no more attempt
> Thine height t'explore, or fathom thy profound. (ll. 1–5)

"On Virtue" is also far more profound theologically than Wheatley's lines on Thacher. Though seemingly an imitation of a Classical pagan celebration of virtue, wisdom, chastity, greatness, and goodness, "On Virtue" concludes by leading Wheatley's readers to recognize that Classical ethics are insufficient to achieve the immortality "enthron'd with Cherubs" possible only through Christianity:

> O leave me not to the false joys of time!
> But guide my steps to endless life and bliss.
> *Greatness*, or *Goodness*, say what I shall call thee,
> To give an higher appellation still,
> Teach me a better strain, a nobler lay,
> O Thou, enthron'd with Cherubs in the realms of day! (ll. 16–21)

If "A Conversation between a New York Gentleman & Phillis" is a reliable account of Phillis Wheatley's unconventional education before she was baptized, she was exposed at an early age to adult works of literature rather than to the books for children read by Anna Green Winslow at the same age. Naturally inclined to poetry, Wheatley reportedly read the translations of Homer's *Iliad* and *Odyssey* by Alexander Pope (1688–1744), as well as the canon of Classical literature—"Ovid, Horace, Virgil, &c."—all presumably also in translation. Wheatley's modern reading was rather eclectic, but apparently it was fairly limited to works published early in the eighteenth century. Pope's "Juvenile Poems" were an obvious reading choice for a young poet. Less obvious were *Rosamond. An Opera* (London, 1707) and *Cato. A Tragedy* (London, 1713), both by Joseph Addison (1672–1719). Not surprising for an aspiring poet who prefers "Religious Subjects," the Bible had the greatest influence on her developing craft:

Question. What induc'd you to write Phillis?

Ans^r. Seeing others write made me esteem it a valuable Art Sir.

Q: What put you upon writing poetry?

A: Reading Rosamond, a play which was in verse Sir.

Q: Did you ever read Cato a play?

A: I have Sir.

Q: How did you like it?

A: like it very well.

Q: What Authors have you, as Ovid, Horace, Virgil, &c.?

A: No other Sir than Pope's Homer.

Q: Did you ever read Pope's own Works?

A: I have seen the first Volume of his Works, his Juvenile Poems.

Q: How did you like them?

A: Very well Sir.

Q: But Phillis, what makes you write more upon Religious Subjects than others?

A: I prefer them Sir.

Q: How wou'd you like a Subject best, in Prose or Verse?

A: If it be a good subject 'tis all the same, but I prefer the Verse.

Q. The Verse suits you best then?

A: it does Sir.

Q: Do you read the Bible Phillis?

A: I do Sir.

Q: Which do you think the best, the old or new Testament?

A: The new Sir, however they are the same only as the old foretold what should come to pass in order to fulfill it, namely the coming of the Messiah.

Q: Do you read the new Testament more than the old?

A: I do Sir.

Q: Are you fond of reading the Bible?

A: I am Sir.

Q: Can you sing Phillis?

A: No Sir.[11]

In light of the catechetical "A Conversation between a New York Gentleman & Phillis" and the contemporaneous evangelical value placed on bearing witness to one's faith, Wheatley's emphasis on religious themes in her early poems is not surprising. Evangelical Protestantism gave people of African descent, whether free or enslaved, access to literacy to enable them to read the Bible. Short are the steps from reading the Bible to interpreting it for oneself, and from there to sharing interpretations with others in the forms of religious poems and spiritual narratives. Wheatley began writing very soon after the first works by authors of African descent appeared in 1760, inspired, authorized, and validated by the Great Awakening. The works of the first such authors concern the faith shared between author and reader, rather than the complexion and social conditions that separated the black speaker and his or her overwhelmingly white audience.

The earliest known African-British publications implicitly accept the institution of slavery: Briton Hammon's *A Narrative of the Most Uncommon Sufferings and Surprizing Deliverance of Briton Hammon, a Negro Man* (Boston, 1760); and (apparently no relation) Jupiter Hammon's *An Evening Thought. Salvation, by Christ, with Penitential Cries: Composed by Jupiter Hammon, a Negro Belonging to Mr. Lloyd* (New York, 1760). What little is known about Briton Hammon (fl. 1760) is found in his fourteen-page *Narrative*, which he may have written himself. We do not even know whether he was a free man or a slave. On Christmas Day, 1747, with the permission of his "master," Major-General John Winslow, Hammon sailed from Plymouth, Massachusetts, to Jamaica and Central America to harvest logwood for making dye. The vessel ran aground on a reef off the Florida coast on its return voyage with the harvest. Native Americans killed every one of the stranded crew except Hammon, who survived long enough to be rescued by a Spanish captain. Hammon was taken to Cuba, where he lived with the governor until he was imprisoned for more than four years for refusing to be conscripted into the Spanish navy. At the request of an American captain, Hammon was released from prison and returned to the governor's household. After living with the governor for about a year, Hammon finally escaped from Cuba on his third attempt, gaining passage on an English ship. Once in England, he joined several Royal Navy vessels as a cook. After being discharged, in London he engaged to join a slaver sailing to Guinea, but before he was to depart he overheard the conversation of a captain bound for Boston. He quickly changed his plans and signed on the voyage to Massachusetts as a cook. He learned that one of the passengers was his John Winslow, with whom he was soon reunited.[12]

Jupiter Hammon (1711–ca. 1800) was born a slave on October 17, 1711, on the Henry Lloyd plantation in Oyster Bay, Long Island, New York. Throughout his life, Hammon belonged to members of the Lloyd family, wealthy merchants whom he served as clerk and bookkeeper. He was also an occasional preacher. When the British captured Long Island in 1776, Joseph Lloyd, one of the few non-Loyalist members of the Lloyd family, took Hammon with him when he fled to Hartford, Connecticut. In addition to his poems and sermons, Hammon published *An Evening's Improvement* (Hartford, 1779), no copy of which is known to exist. His *An Address to the Negroes in the State of New York* (New York, and reprinted in Philadelphia, 1787) advises his fellow slaves to bear their own condition patiently while trying to persuade their masters to free their children. Hammon was the first person of African descent to comment in print on the poetry of Phillis Wheatley.

Both Hammons wrote about captivity, liberation, and restoration. Briton recounts being sold to the Governor of Spanish Cuba by the Caribbean Indians who captured him. The English captain, who enables him to escape from Cuba, refuses to "deliver up any *Englishman* under *English* Colours" (emphasis in original) to the pursuing Spaniards. Briton is eventually reunited with his "Master" (perhaps his employer rather than owner) in England through the providence of God. They return to Massachusetts together. Briton emphasizes his physical captivity; Jupiter focuses exclusively on his spiritual captivity by sin and his faith in liberation by Christ.

None of the later African-British authors seems to have been aware of either Hammon, probably because their works were published solely in the provinces of the British Empire and never reprinted in London. Wheatley, for example, apparently never knew that Jupiter Hammon published *An Address to Miss Phillis Wheatley, Ethiopian Poetess, in Boston, Who Came from Africa at Eight Years of Age, and Soon Became Acquainted with the Gospel of Jesus Christ* (Hartford, Connecticut, 1778). The Hammons used the two primary forms employed by almost every one of the later writers: the autobiographical prose narrative with varying degrees of religious implications, and the religious poem. Briton and Jupiter Hammon each identified himself in his title as "a Negro." Nothing else in either of their works published in 1760 indicates that they were of African descent. But the simple ethnic tag of "Negro" may have been intended to reassure rebellious European-Americans that the people of African descent around them were not necessarily a clandestine fifth column.

The much younger Phillis Wheatley lacked the maturity and experience of Briton or Jupiter Hammon. And her gender and position as a domestic slave limited her activity and mobility. Nonetheless, she emphasized her African ethnicity and moral authority more overtly in some of her earliest surviving poems than either Hammon had done. Two of these early poems exist only in various manuscript versions, enabling us to follow Wheatley's developing craft. Her "An Address to the Atheist, by P. Wheatley at the Age of 14 Years—1767—" is a revision of an earlier draft entitled "Atheism." Versions of the poem circulated in manuscript during Wheatley's lifetime, bringing her to the attention of other women beyond Boston. The circulation of manuscripts, especially of works by women, was common during the eighteenth century, as was the reading of an author's own writings in domestic circles.[13] The Quaker poet Hannah Griffitts (1727–1817) in Philadelphia included a "rough Copy" of an abbreviated variant of Wheatley's "Atheism" titled "On Atheism" among her own undated manuscripts. It is attributed to "Africania."[14]

In "An Address to the Atheist, by P. Wheatley at the Age of 14 Years—1767—" Wheatley employs the poetic convention of invoking the Classical muse to open her poem ("Muse! Where shall I begin the spacious feild [*sic*] / To tell what curses unbelief doth yield?") as well as the equally conventional assertion of poetic inadequacy ("The endless scene too far for me to tread / Too great to utter from so weak a head") only to have the poem itself undermine the conventions. For a fourteen-year-old girl to try her hand at what was considered the most serious possible subject was a remarkable expression of poetic authority. The poem's sophisticated combination of evidence from design and biblical authority to create an argument in support of theism is an impressive advance from the simple expression of faith found in her verses on the deaths of Oxenbridge and Sarah Thacher, written only two years earlier.

Wheatley's argument in "An Address" is not original. It reveals her familiarity with orthodox Congregationalist theology. She bases her argument on the belief that God is the author of two books, the book of nature and the book of revelation, which when "read," or interpreted, together correctly demonstrate the benevolence and omnipotence of the Christian God. The book of nature purportedly displays an argument from design that proves the existence of a creator, or *a* god, to any reasonable observer, including non-Christians:

> If there's no God[,] from whom did all things Spring[?]
> He made the *greatest* and *minutest* Thing.
> Angelic ranks no less his Power display
> Than the least mite scarce visible to Day[.]
> With vast astonishment my soul is struck[.]
> Have Reason'g powers thy darken'd breast forsook? (ll. 7–12)

More important, the existence and nature of the Christian God is revealed through faith in the sacred book of the Bible, particularly the New Testament:

> The Laws deep Graven by the hand of God,
> Seal'd with Immanuel's all-redeeming blood:
> This second point thy folly dares deny
> On thy devoted head for vengeance cry—
> Turn then I pray thee from the dangerous road
> Rise from the dust and seek the mighty God. (ll. 13–18)

Although Wheatley begins her poem with a conventional invocation of the Classical "Muse" and includes a reference to the "Sol" worshipped by contemporaneous pagans, she concludes by carefully rejecting Classical gods. They are merely poetic ornaments, and the sun's circuit is significant only as part of a transcendent plan:

> To whom dost thou bring
> Thy grateful tribute? Adoration pay
> To heathen Gods? Can wise *Apollo* say
> Tis I that saves thee from the deepest hell;
> *Minerva* teach thee all thy days to tell?
> Doth *Pluto* tell thee thou Shalt see the shade
> Of fell perdition for transgression made?
> Doth *Cupid* in thy breast that warmth inspire
> To love thy Brother, which is God's desire?
> Atheist! behold the wide extended skies
> And wisdom infinite shall strike thine eyes
> Mark rising Sol when far he spreads his Ray
> And his Commission read—To rule the Day
> At night behold that silver Regent bright
> And her command to lead the train of Night
> Lo! how the Stars all vocal in his praise
> Witness his Essence in celestial lays! (ll. 40–56)[15]

Two versions of another of Wheatley's unpublished early poems, "Deism" and "An Address to the Deist—1767—," are at least as sophisticated as "An Address to the Atheist." Eighteenth-century deists generally believed in a discrete (unitarian) rational God who was bound by the same laws of nature that applied to the world He had created. Deists were consequently dubious about the orthodox belief that the Bible was of supernatural origin. They also questioned biblical accounts of miraculous events, as well as the postbiblical doctrine formulated in the fourth century of the mystery of the Trinity of three beings (Father, Son, and Holy Ghost) in one God. Wheatley's poems on atheism and deism are in effect testaments to her faith. To an orthodox Trinitarian Calvinist, a deist was little better than an atheist, and orthodox Christians often equated them during the period. Hence, the theological position Wheatley embraces in "An Address to the Deist" was not extraordinary for her day:

> I ask O unbeliever, Satan's child
> Hath not thy Saviour been too much revil'd
> Th' auspicious rays that round his temples shine
> Do still declare him to be Christ divine
> Doth not the great *Eternal* call him Son

Is he not pleas'd with his beloved One—?
How canst thou thus divide the Trinity—
The blest the Holy the eternal three
Tis Satan's Snares are fluttering in the wind
Whereby he doth insnare thy foolish mind
God, the Eternal Orders this to be
Sees thy vain arg'ments to divide the three
Cans't thou not see the Consequence in store? (ll. 3–15)

What is extraordinary is the rhetorical position Wheatley assumes in the poem in relation to the imaginary deist she addresses in it and to the external reader of the poem. She significantly begins the poem, "Must Ethiopians be employ'd for you? / Much I rejoice if any good I do." Like authors before her, most notably Alexander Pope, she transforms a defect into a virtue. Pope used his status as a politically disenfranchised Roman Catholic and his appearance—he was mocked as a hunch-backed dwarf—to place himself rhetorically at the margin of his society. Doing so enabled him to speak as a disinterested observer and critic of a society he was in but not of. Wheatley, too, presents herself as a stranger in a strange land. But appropriating the term "Ethiopians" does much more than simply reveal Wheatley's complexion, ethnicity, and probable status to her readers. By calling herself an Ethiopian rather than an African or a black in a religious poem, she claims an identity that grants her biblical authority to speak to her readers. Wheatley surely expected her readers to recall that Moses had married an Ethiopian (Numbers 12:1), and that Psalms 68:31 predicts that "Ethiopia shall soon stretch out her hands unto God."

Nearly a century earlier, George Fox (1624–91), the founder of the Society of Friends, or Quakers, invoked Ethiopia to prove the equalitarian essence of Christianity based on the orthodox conviction that all humans were direct descendants of Adam and Eve. Commanding masters in *Gospel Family-Order* to treat their slaves benevolently, Fox writes,

> now consider, do not slight them, to wit the *Ethyopians*; the *Blacks*, now, neither any Man or Woman upon the Face of the Earth in that *Christ* dyed for all, both *Turks*, *Barbarians*, *Tartarians* and *Ethyopians*; he dyed for the *Tawnies*, and for the *Blacks*, as well as for you that are called *Whites*; therefore you may see in Acts 8:27 how the Lord commanded *Philip* to go toward the South, and he arose and went, *and*

behold a Man of Ethyopia. . . . And therefore now you should preach Christ to your *Ethyopians* that are in your Families, so they be free Men indeed, and be tender of and to them, and walk in Love . . . being (as the Scripture affirms) all of one Blood & of one Mold, to dwell upon the Face of the Earth; *for Christ* (I say) *shed his Blood for them, as well as for you, and hath enlightened them, as well as he hath enlightened you, and his Grace hath appeared unto them, as well as for yours* . . . and so let every Master and Governour of a Family inform them, as well as others in his Family . . . that so they may come to know Christ.[16]

In 1700 Samuel Sewall (1652–1730), Chief Justice of Massachusetts, made a similar appeal in *The Selling of Joseph*: "these *Ethiopians*, as black as they are; seeing they are the Sons and Daughters of the first Adam, the Brethren and Sisters of the Last ADAM [i.e., Christ], and the Offspring of GOD; They ought to be treated with a Respect agreeable."[17] Sewall's tract apparently had little effect. Like many of his contemporaries, Sewall had no trouble reconciling his principles with his practice. In later life he advertised slaves for sale at his house. Sewall's son Joseph (1688–1769) was the subject of one of Wheatley's earliest elegies, "On the Death of the Rev. Dr. Sewell [*sic*]. 1769," which circulated in several manuscript copies before being first published in her *Poems on Various Subjects, Religious and Moral* in 1773. In it she acknowledges Joseph Sewell as her spiritual "monitor."

Although the question with which Wheatley opens "An Address to the Deist"—"Must Ethiopians be employ'd for you?"—may initially challenge her enslaved status, the following line—"Much I rejoice if any good I do"—appears to reassure her readers that she accepts her socially and legally inferior position. But she ironically does so by implying that what pleases her is her moral superiority to them, which enables her to be their instructor. Wheatley moves in "An Address to the Deist" from differentiating herself from her readers through her use of the first-person "I" and the second-person "you" to her ultimate lesson that Ethiopians shared with her white readers a common humanity and a Trinitarian God, who "came to Save us from our Sins," as Fox and Sewall had said earlier on biblical authority.

In her subsequent poems on public events, Wheatley appropriates the persona of authority or power normally associated with men and her social superiors. "To the University of Cambridge, in New-England," first composed when she was about fifteen years old, is essentially a commencement address. Like a teacher to students, or a minister to his flock, Wheatley speaks to the young men of what was to become Harvard University, many of whom were being trained there to become ministers. Confident that "the muses" will "assist my pen," she asserts her authority as one who has "left my native shore / The land of errors, and *Egyptian* gloom" and "those dark abodes." She has known "sin, that baneful evil to the soul," and rejected it to embrace the "Father of mercy." From a position of moral superiority gained through experience she speaks as an "*Ethiop*" to warn her implicitly complacent students—"Ye pupils"—to "Improve your privileges while they stay." Audaciously, the teenaged, enslaved, self-educated, female, and formerly pagan poet of African descent assumes a voice that transcends the "privileges" of those who are reputedly her superiors in age, status, abilities, authority, race, and gender.

Comparison of the initial verse paragraph in "To the University of Cambridge, Wrote in 1767—" to the corresponding paragraph in the later "To the University of Cambridge, in New-England," quoted from *Poems on Various Subjects, Religious and Moral*, shows how carefully and rapidly Wheatley improved her craft. The differences in versification, diction, concision, and specificity of metaphors are striking:

"To the University of Cambridge, wrote in 1767—"

While an intrinsic ardor bids me write
The muse doth promise to assist my pen.
'Twas but e'en now I left my native Shore
The sable Land of error's darkest night
There, sacred Nine! for you no place was found,
Parent of mercy, 'twas thy Powerfull hand
Brought me in Safety from the dark abode. (ll. 1–7)

"To the University of CAMBRIDGE, in NEW-ENGLAND."

      WHILE an intrinsic ardor prompts to write,
The muses promise to assist my pen;
'Twas not long since I left my native shore
The land of errors, and *Egyptian* gloom:
Father of mercy, 'twas thy gracious hand
Brought me in safety from those dark abodes. (ll. 1–6)

Perhaps the most significant change Wheatley made between the manuscript and print versions is the revision of line four of the former—"The sable Land of error's darkest night"—to read "The land of errors, and *Egyptian* gloom" in the version published in 1773. Wheatley's substitution of "*Egyptian* gloom" to refer to her spiritual condition in Africa associates her and her fellow Africans with God's chosen people, the Israelites, before their Exodus from Egypt. Like anyone with faith in an omnipotent, omniscient, and benevolent God, Wheatley believes that the evil of enslavement that caused her exodus from Africa has to serve an ultimately positive purpose that may as yet be unknowable to humankind. Hence, she can say without irony, "Father of mercy, 'twas thy gracious hand / Brought me in safety from those dark abodes."

The same belief that good will providentially and paradoxically come out of apparent evil underlies what has become Wheatley's most notorious poem:

On being brought from AFRICA to AMERICA.

  'TWAS mercy brought me from my *Pagan* land,
Taught my benighted soul to understand
That there's a God, that there's a *Saviour* too:
Once I redemption neither sought nor knew.
Some view our sable race with scornful eye,
"Their colour is a diabolic die."
Remember, *Christians*, *Negros*, black as *Cain*,
May be refin'd, and join th' angelic train. (ll. 1–8)

"On Being Brought from Africa to America," which according to Wheatley's 1772 "Proposals" was written in 1768, has been called "the most reviled poem in African American literature."[18] The poem's notoriety understandably but unfairly derives from Wheatley's apparent acceptance of contemporaneous justifications for the transatlantic slave trade. Her poem is so close in sentiment to that expressed by her contemporary and admirer Jane Dunlap (fl. 1765–71) in "The Ethiopians Shall Stretch out their Hands to God, or a Call to the Ethiopians," published in 1771, that one wonders if Dunlap had seen Wheatley's poem in manuscript:

Poor Negroes flee [see?], you'l welcome be,
Your colour's no exception;

But fly to Christ, he's paid the price,
Meet for your Souls redemption.
And though your souls made black with sin,
The Lord can make them white;
And cloath'd in his pure righteousness,
They'l shine transparent bright.[19]

Modern critics have accused Wheatley, or at least the primary voice in her poem, of rejecting her African heritage and engaging in racial self-hatred.[20] But such critics confuse accommodation with appropriation. Like many authors of African descent who followed her, Wheatley repeatedly appropriates the values of Christianity to judge and find wanting hypocritical self-styled Christians of European descent. Theologically, Wheatley perceives her capture in Africa as leading to a fortunate fall that allows her formerly "benighted soul" to rise to embrace Christianity. Placed in Wheatley's 1773 *Poems* after "On Virtue" and "To the University of Cambridge, in New England," the "mercy" acknowledged in "On Being Brought from Africa to America" is granted not only to the speaker of the latter poem. The "Father of mercy," through her poetry, also grants it to her readers, who must choose between being among the "Some [who] view our sable race with scornful eye" and those who embrace the truth and "Remember [that], *Christians*, *Negros*, black as *Cain*, / May be refin'd, and join th' angelic train."[21]

Wheatley's position is completely consistent with belief in an omniscient and benevolent deity, but it does not necessarily imply that she either accepts or endorses slavery. Physical slavery paradoxically leads to the spiritual freedom offered to the servants, or slaves, of Christ. Daniel Bliss (1740–1806) expressed a very similar position in a poem published anonymously in the *Boston Gazette, and Country Journal* on 9 October 1775:

God
Wills us free
Man Wills us slaves.
God's will be done.
Here lies the body of John Jack,
Native of Africa, who died March 1773
Aged about sixty years.
Tho' born in a land of slaves
He was born free.

> Tho' he lived in a land of liberty
> He lived a slave,
> 'Till by his honest tho' stolen labour
> He acquired the source of slavery
> Which gave him his freedom:
> Tho' not long before
> Death the grand tyrant
> Gave him his final emancipation,
> And put him on a footing with kings.
> Tho' a slave to vice
> He practiced those virtues
> Without which kings are but slaves.[22]

Wheatley's contemporary Quobna Ottobah Cugoano (ca. 1757–ca. 1791), the most radical eighteenth-century author of African descent, has never been accused of being an accommodationist. He advised that "if there is no other way to deliver a man from slavery, but by enslaving his master, it would be lawful for him to do so if he was able, for this would be doing justice to himself, and be justice as the law requires, to chastise his master for enslaving of him wrongfully."[23] But even though as a free man living in England Cugoano had the social and political advantage over Wheatley when he wrote these words, he too considered his enslavement as having been a theologically fortunate fall:

> thanks be to God for his good providence towards me; I have both ob-
> tained liberty, and acquired the great advantages of some little learn-
> ing, in being able to read and write, and, what is still infinitely of
> greater advantage, I trust, to know something of HIM *who is that God
> whose providence rules over all, and who is the only Potent One that rules in
> the nations over the children of men. It is unto Him, who is the Prince of the
> Kings of the earth,*[24] *that I would give all thanks.* And, in some manner, I
> may say with Joseph, as he did with respect to the evil intention of his
> brethren, when they sold him into Egypt, that whatever evil intentions
> and bad motives those insidious robbers had in carrying me away from
> my native country and friends, I trust, was what the Lord intended for
> my good.[25] In this respect, I am highly indebted to many of the good
> people of England for learning and principles unknown to the people
> of my native country. But, above all, what I have obtained from the

Lord God of Hosts, the God of the Christians! in that divine revelation of the only true God, and the Saviour of men, what a treasure of wisdom and blessings are involved?[26]

In "On Being Brought from Africa to America" Wheatley also seems to share with Dunlap the common eighteenth-century equation of darkness with evil and sin, an equation whose origins probably lie in primordial human fears of nocturnal creatures, a fear that continues to be exploited in horror fiction and film. But by the eighteenth century, the equation had taken on racist implications.[27] Seeking a religious justification for their own economic self-interest despite the absence of any biblical foundation whatsoever for their claim, defenders of the enslavement of Africans since the middle of the fifteenth century increasingly embraced the notion that in Genesis 4:1–16 and 20–27 God cursed the descendants of Cain and/or Ham with black skin. Defenders of slavery argued that sub-Saharan Africans, as the alleged descendants of Cain and/or Ham, were cursed with a dark complexion and destined to slavery. Hence, by the late eighteenth century blackness and slavery were often synonymous in proslavery discourse.

Others during the period complicated the conventional opposition between blackness and whiteness. Wheatley was not the first person of African descent to argue that complexion was morally inconsequential. In 1758 Francis Williams (ca. 1697–1762), a free-born, wealthy, slave-owning Jamaican black, wrote a panegyric addressed to Jamaica's new governor on the occasion of his arrival on the island. Williams anticipated Wheatley's use of the relationship between blackness and whiteness, going so far as to darken his "Muse":

> Yet may you deign accept this humble song,
> Tho' wrapt in gloom, and from a falt'ring tongue;
> Tho' dark the stream on which the tribute flows,
> Not from the *skin*, but from the *heart* it rose.
> To all of human kind, benignant heaven
> (Since nought forbids) one common soul has given.
> This rule was 'stablish'd by th'Eternal Mind;
> Nor virtue's self, nor prudence are confin'd
> To *colour*; none imbues the honest heart;
> To science none belongs, and none to art.
> Oh! *Muse*, of blackest tint, why shrinks thy breast,

Why fears t'approach the *Caesar* of the *West*!
Dispel thy doubts, with confidence ascend
The regal dome, and hail him for thy friend:
Nor blush, altho' in garb funereal drest,
Thy body's white, tho' clad in sable vest.[28] (ll. 53–68)

Wheatley may be subverting conventional equations of blackness with evil and whiteness with good. The imperative "Remember" may not be addressed solely to Christians. Perhaps we should not read the final couplet as "Remember, *Christians*, [that] *Negros*, black as *Cain*, / May be refin'd, and join th' angelic train." It may also be read very differently as "Remember, [that] *Christians*, *Negros*, black as *Cain*, / May be refin'd, and join th' angelic train." In the second reading blackness would still be associated with sin, but it would more clearly be used metaphorically rather than physically. Cugoano most fully expresses the metaphorical use of blackness that can be refined away:

> by these extreme differences of colour, it was intended to point out and shew to the white man, that there is a sinful blackness in his own nature, which he can no more change, than the external blackness which he sees in another can be rendered otherwise; and it likewise holds out to the black man, that the sinful blackness of his own nature is such, that he can no more alter, than the outward appearance of his colour can be brought to that of another. And this is imported by it, that there is an inherent evil in every man, contrary to that which is good; and that all men are like Ethiopians (even God's elect)[29] in a state of nature and unregeneracy, they are black with original sin, and spotted with actual transgression, which they cannot reverse. But to this truth, asserted of blackness, I must add another glorious one. All thanks and eternal praise be to God! His infinite wisdom and goodness has found out a way of renovation, and has opened a fountain through the blood of Jesus, for sin and for uncleanness, wherein all the stains and blackest dyes of sin and pollution can be washed away for ever, and the darkest sinner be made to shine as the brightest angel in heaven.[30]

Wheatley was probably sitting near Anna Green Winslow in Old South when Rev. Bacon alluded to the "whited sepulchers" of Matthew 23:27 in his sermon on 17 November 1771. Winslow recorded his words in her diary the following day:

> He said he would lastly address himself to the young people: My dear young friends, you are pleased with beauty, & like to be tho't beautifull—but let me tell ye, you'l never be truly beautifull till you are like the King's daughter, all glorious within, all the orniments you can put on while your souls are unholy make you the more like white sepulchers garnish'd without, but full of deformity within. You think me very unpolite no doubt to address you in this manner, but I must go a little further and tell you, how cource soever it may sound to your delicacy, that while you are without holiness, your beauty is deformity —you are all over black & defil'd, ugly and loathsome to all holy be-ings, the wrath of th' great God lie's upon you, & if you die in this condition, you will be turn'd into hell, with ugly devils, to eternity.[31]

Bacon was clearly using blackness metaphorically rather than referring to skin color to describe sin. He did not equate African descent with damnation. People of European descent could be as black with sin as anyone else.[32]

Phillis Wheatley's first published work, the poem "On Messrs. Hussey and Coffin," appeared in the 14–21 December 1767 issue of the *Newport Mercury*, no doubt through the support and contacts of Susanna Wheatley.[33] The most likely contact was Sarah Haggar Wheaton Osborn (1714–96), a member of the First Congregational Church in Newport who was instrumental in the evangelical Newport revival of 1766–67. She and Susanna Wheatley were acquainted with each other and shared a mutual correspondent in Rev. Occom. The preaching of Whitefield and the Presbyterian evangelical Gilbert Tennent (1703–64) inspired Osborn to help create a female prayer society that met in her home weekly from the 1740s until her death. She also held ecumenical meetings attended by a wide spectrum of society. More than three hundred people attended her meetings in July 1766. The number reached 525 by January 1767. Osborn played a major role in having Phillis Wheatley's future correspondent, Rev. Samuel Hopkins, installed as pastor of the First Congregational Church in Newport in 1770. Wheatley probably heard Hopkins when he preached at Old South Church in Boston in 1769. From the late 1750s, Osborn ran a boarding school in her home that enrolled nearly seventy students, rich and poor, male and female, black and white. From 1766 an "Ethiopian Society," probably composed of free people of African descent, attended revival meetings at her house to sing, pray, read, and discuss religious issues. They were joined by as many as forty-two slaves, who attended with the permission of their masters.

The headnote for "On Messrs. Hussey and Coffin," addressed "To the Printer" of the *Newport Mercury*, notes the occasion for the poem: "Please to insert the following Lines, composed by a Negro Girl (belonging to one Mr. Wheatley of Boston) on the following Occasion, viz. Messrs Hussey and Coffin, as undermentioned, belonging to Nantucket, being bound from thence to Boston, narrowly escaped being cast away on Cape-Cod, in one of the late Storms; upon their Arrival, being at Mr. Wheatley's, and, while at Dinner, told of their narrow Escape, this Negro Girl at the same Time 'tending Table, heard the Relation, from which she composed the following Verses." Nathaniel Coffin (1725–80) was an Anglican Boston merchant and a slave owner. One of his slaves was a girl named Sapho.[34] Hussey was probably one of several sons of George Hussey (1694–1782), a Quaker merchant in Nantucket who owned whaling vessels and shares in Nantucket wharves. Captain Coffin's schooner, with its cargo of whale oil, was one of several vessels cast ashore during the most "terrible Gale" ever experienced by "the oldest Seamen."[35]

"On Messrs. Hussey and Coffin" is undoubtedly a version of the poem "On two friends, who were cast away" that was promised and misdated 1766 in Wheatley's 1772 "Proposals." It was not published again during Wheatley's life after its appearance in the *Newport Mercury*. The poem's combination of Christian piety and Classical allusions anticipates the themes and expression found in many of her poems. Wheatley's Calvinism is reflected in her address to a benevolent God that closes a poem acknowledging the uncertainty of the ultimate fate that would have befallen Hussey and Coffin, had they not survived the storm. Unlike the polished verse of "On Virtue," which Wheatley had years to revise before publication, the heavily end-stopped couplets in "On Messrs. Hussey and Coffin" reflect the author's youth and inexperience:

> Did Fear and Danger so perplex your Mind,
> As made you fearful of the Whistling Wind?
> Was it not Boreas knit his angry Brow
> Against you? or did Consideration bow?

To lend you Aid, did not his Winds combine?
To stop your passage with a churlish Line,
Did haughty Eolus with Contempt look down
With Aspect windy, and a study'd Frown?
Regard them not;—the Great Supreme, the Wise,
Intends for something hidden from our Eyes.
Suppose the groundless Gulph had snatch'd away
Hussey and Coffin to the raging Sea;
Where wou'd they go? where wou'd be their Abode?
With the supreme and independent God,
Or made their Beds down in the Shades below,
Where neither Pleasure nor Content can flow.
To Heaven their Souls with eager Raptures soar,
Enjoy the Bliss of him they wou'd adore.
Had the soft gliding Streams of Grace been near,
Some favourite Hope their fainting hearts to cheer,
Doubtless the Fear of Danger far had fled:
No more repeated Victory crown their Heads. (ll. 1–22)

Had I the Tongue of a Seraphim, how would I exalt thy Praise; thy Name as Incense to the Heavens should fly, and the Remembrance of thy Goodness to the shoreless Ocean of Beatitude!—Then should the Earth glow with seraphick Ardour.

Blest Soul, which sees the Day while Light doth shine,
To guide his Steps to trace the Mark divine.

Phillis Wheatley

Phillis was already commenting on transatlantic economic and political subjects by the time she was about fifteen years old. The teenaged poet was in effect laying claim to being a protonational American muse. Two surviving poems demonstrate Wheatley's interest in being recognized as the poetic voice of America responding to the growing tensions between Britain and its North American colonies during the 1760s.[36] The Seven Years' War, arguably the first worldwide war, ended in 1763 with Britain's victory against France, Spain, and Holland. But the price of victory was an increase in Britain's national debt from just over £72 million in 1755 to nearly £130 million in 1764. Britain incurred much of the debt by defending its colonies. Tax rates in Britain to support the war had risen so high that they led to protests and fears of revolt there. To try to help retire the national debt and cover at least some of the costs of defending the new borders of Britain's North American interests, the politicians appointed by George III passed a number of acts in Parliament to raise money in America to be spent on its defense.

Many colonists saw the Revenue Act (the "Sugar Act") of 1764 and subsequent legislation as unprecedented attempts to exert Parliament's authority over the thirteen colonies, which had their own legislatures but no representatives in Parliament. Colonists saw the new acts intended to raise revenue as different in kind from previous acts of Parliament aimed at regulating colonial commerce. The most significant of these new acts was the Stamp Act passed by Parliament and signed by King George III in March 1765 to go into effect in November 1765. The act imposed varying stamp duties on "every skin or piece of vellum or parchment, or sheet or piece of paper, on which shall be engrossed, written, or printed" virtually any document in the colonies, as well as on every newspaper and pamphlet published in the colonies, and even on "every pack of playing cards, and all dice, which shall be sold or used within the said colonies and plantations."[37] To the shock of Parliament and the King, colonists resisted the new act so vigorously that some newspapers suspended publication, the agents hired to collect the duties resigned, and government officials in Boston were hanged in effigy. A Stamp Act Congress convened in New York City in October 1765 to formally protest imposition of the duties, marking the first joint colonial response to the British government and a major step in the development of a national identity announced in the Declaration of Independence on 4 July 1776. Colonists boycotted imported British goods to avoid paying the taxes. Colonial resistance was so strong that a new ministry proposed, and the King agreed, to repeal the Stamp Act in March 1766. Even as it repealed the Stamp Act, however, Parliament declared its authority to impose such revenue-raising taxes on the colonies.

The growing tension between Britain and its colonies occasioned several poetic responses from Wheatley, only one of which was ever published during her lifetime. Wheatley commemorated the Stamp Act crisis with "To the King's Most Excellent Majesty on His Repealing the American Stamp Act 1768," a draft of her "On the King" listed in the 1772 "Proposals." It was ultimately published in *Poems on Various Subjects, Religious and Moral* as "To the King's Most Excellent Majesty. 1768." The occasion of the poem, significantly dated 1768, was Parliament's passage in 1767 of the so-called Townshend Acts taxing the colonists. Colonial resistance led to the occupation of Boston by British troops in 1768. Even more than Wheatley's draft, the published version of her poem celebrates the King as a parental figure who freed his children from the tyranny of Parliament and the politicians in his ministry during the earlier crisis, and it implicitly calls on him to act on their behalf again. Coming from an enslaved person of African descent, the last line is also a not-so-subtle reminder that not only taxed colonists should be set free:

> But how shall we the *British* king reward!
> Rule thou in peace, our father, and our lord!
> Midst the remembrance of thy favours past,
> The meanest peasants most admire the last.*
> May *George*, belov'd by all the nations round,
> Live with heav'ns choicest constant blessings crown'd!
> Great God, direct, and guard him from on high,
> And from his head let ev'ry evil fly!
> And may each clime with equal gladness see
> A monarch's smile can set his subjects free! (ll. 6–15)

*The Repeal of the Stamp Act. [Wheatley's note]

Wheatley's reference to a familial relationship between Britain and America underscores the alleged unnaturalness of the treatment America received and the natural link between the colonies and their mother country. Her choice of the domestic metaphor may have been influenced by Oxenbridge Thacher's earlier use of it in his pamphlet *Sentiments of a British American* (Boston, 1764), published in opposition to the Sugar Act. For a remarkable length of time—until about 1775—Americans generally prided themselves on being good subjects of their king. The question Stephen Hopkins (1707–85) asked in 1764 was intended to be rhetorical: "Are not the people in the colonies as loyal and dutiful subjects as any age or nation ever produced,—and are they not as useful to the kingdom, in this remote quarter of the world, as their fellow subjects are who dwell in *Britain*?"[38] As it became clearer to everyone that measures unpopular in America had support in Parliament as well as in the ministry, colonists clung to the belief (despite evidence to the contrary) that George III was their potential, if not their actual, ally against what they saw as threats to the British constitution and its guarantees of freedom.

Wheatley's argument and choice of imagery indicate that she was very familiar with contemporaneous political rhetoric. The same sort of rhetorical appeal occurs in the Stamp Act satire *The Times: A Poem. By an American*, attributed to Benjamin Church (1734–78) and published in Boston in 1765:

> GEORGE! Parent! King! Our Guardian, Glory, Pride,
> And thou fair REGENT! Blooming by his side!
> Thy offspring pleads a parent's fostering care,
> Reject not, frown not, but in mercy spare;
> Besprent with dust, the lowly suppliant lies,
> A helpless, guiltless, injured sacrifice. (p. 8)

Another of Wheatley's surviving poems on the Stamp Act crisis and Britain's other efforts to tax the colonies is more subversive than her published work. "America" is no doubt a draft version of "On America, 1768," listed in her 1772 "Proposals" but never published. "America" is a brief allegorical history of New England from its founding to the crisis of relations between "A certain lady" (i.e., Britannia) and her "only son" (i.e., America):

> A certain lady had an only son
> He grew up daily virtuous as he grew
> Fearing his Strength which she undoubted knew
> She laid some taxes on her darling son (ll. 8–11)

The poem calls for reconciliation between the mother and son before the child grows strong enough to be able to overpower his parent. Wheatley's references to "Scourges" (l. 15) and "rebel" (l. 23) emphasize the subtext of chattel slavery in a poem in which "[America] weeps afresh to feel this Iron chain" (l. 31). The poem's speaker implies that the "Liberty" that white Americans seek from metaphorical slavery also empowers black people suffering under actual enslavement: "Thy Power, O Liberty, makes strong the weak / And (wond'rous instinct) Ethiopians speak" (ll. 5–6). Under the pseudonym "Humphry Ploughjogger" in the *Boston Gazette* on 14 October 1765, John Adams also employed the image of slavery to protest British economic policies: "we won't be their negroes. Providence never designed us for negroes, I know, for if it had it wou'd have given us black hides, and thick lips, and flat noses, and short wooly hair, which it han't done, and therefore never intended us for slaves." Wheatley implies that black Americans have even more reason to call for "Liberty" and protest against restraints than their white owners, who suffer only metaphorical "Scourges" and chains. Wheatley subtly anticipates in her unpublished poem the question Samuel Johnson (1709–84) would later sarcastically ask in *Taxation No Tyranny* (London, 1775): "How is it we hear the loudest yelps for liberty among the drivers of Negroes?"[39]

The continuing unrest in Boston led the British government in 1768 to send Royal Governor Thomas Hutchinson the four thousand troops he requested to try to keep the peace. Their presence had the opposite effect, since there were so many of them that the citizens of Boston were forced to house them in their homes. The occupation appeared to confirm fears of a design to impose tyrannical rule on the colonies. The formation of the self-described "Sons of Liberty" and subsequent acts of resistance in turn appeared to confirm British fears of a colonial rebellion. Harassment of the occupying forces soon led to the death of eleven-year-old Christopher Snider (Seider).[40] He was only about two years younger than Wheatley when she commemorated him as the "the first martyr for the [colonial] cause" (l. 2) in her never-published "On the Death of Mr. Snider Murder'd by Richardson." Although Wheatley uses her poetic license to elevate young Snider to the status of a potential "Achilles" cut down "in his mid career" (l. 6), he may have simply been at the wrong place at the wrong time. Saying that he would rather be governed by one tyrant than by many, Boston merchant Theophilus Lillie refused to participate in the boycott of British goods. In response, some self-styled patriots erected an effigy of him in front of his store to warn others to avoid doing business with him. When Ebenezer Richardson, a loyalist like Lillie, tried to remove the effigy on 22 February 1770, he was confronted by a rock-throwing crowd composed mainly of boys who chased him back to his own house. Richardson fired randomly into the crowd from his window to keep them from breaking into his house. Portrayed by Wheatley as satanic, Richardson, "The grand Usurpers bravely vaunted Heir" (l. 22), killed Snider and wounded several others. Only the intervention of British soldiers who had heard the shots saved Richardson from the crowd when they arrested him. Richardson was tried and convicted for the murder of Snider, but served only two years in jail before being pardoned by Governor Hutchinson. Speeches denouncing tyranny and calling for Richardson's execution accompanied the massive burial parade for the boy Wheatley calls "their young champion" (l. 10) and "this young martial genius" (l. 15). Wheatley considers Snider a political martyr. His murder was "in heaven's eternal court . . . decreed" (l. 1) as part of God's providential design. Snider's death would probably be far better known today had it not been quickly overshadowed by the Boston Massacre on 5 March 1770, when British soldiers killed five civilians, including Crispus Attucks (1723–70), "the first martyr for the cause" of African descent. The Boston Massacre was the subject of Wheatley's now-lost "On the Affray in King-Street, on the Evening of the 5th of March," advertised in her 1772 "Proposals."[41]

Wheatley also continued to write nonpolitical occasional poems: "On the Death of a Young Lady of Five Years of Age" is dated 1770 in Wheatley's 1772 "Proposals" and was probably circulated in manuscript before being first published in her 1773 *Poems*. Wheatley's conflation of religious and political themes in her unpublished elegies on Rev. Joseph Sewall in 1769 and on the little-known Snider in 1770 anticipated the first poem she published in Boston, the poem that arguably eventually led to her eventual freedom. The announcement in October 1770 of Wheatley's illustrated broadside poem occasioned by the recent death of George Whitefield was more appropriate for an established poet than for a seventeen-year-old enslaved girl. The full title and headnote for the poem indicate the great expectations Phillis and her owner had for its reception:

> AN ELEGIAC POEM, On the DEATH of that celebrated Divine, and eminent Servant of JESUS CHRIST, the late Reverend, and pious GEORGE WHITEFIELD, Chaplain to the Right Honourable the Countess of Huntingdon, &c &c. Who made his Exit from this transitory State, to dwell in the celestial Realms of Bliss, on LORD'S-DAY, 30th of September, 1770, when he was seiz'd with a Fit of the Asthma, at NEWBURY-PORT, near BOSTON, in NEW-ENGLAND. In which is a Condolatory Address to His truly noble Benefactress the worthy and pious Lady HUNTINGDON,—and the Orphan-Children in GEORGIA; who, with many Thousands, are left, by the Death of this great Man, to lament the Loss of a Father, Friend, and Benefactor.
>
> By PHILLIS, a Servant Girl of 17 Years of Age, belonging to MR. J. WHEATLEY, of Boston:—And has been but 9 Years in this Country from Africa.

Wheatley's poem was one of two elegies about Whitefield advertised in the *Boston News-Letter* on 11 October 1770. Many others soon appeared. In the eleven days immediately following Whitefield's death, Wheatley had written the poem and (presumably) her owners had arranged to have it printed and sold by Ezekiel Russell (1743–96), in Queen-Street, and John Boyles, in Marlboro-Street, for "7 Coppers." It was "Embellished with a Plate, representing the Posture, in which Mr. Whitefield lay, before and after his Interment at Newbury-Port." The speed with which Wheatley produced the elegy, as well as its content and quality, indicate the astounding progress she had made as a poet since the elegy on the Thachers, as well as how familiar she was with Whitefield's cultural significance as a religious and political figure.

Wheatley opens her elegy by acknowledging Whitefield's popularity, eloquence, and exemplary piety. Whitefield's beliefs and practices allowed Wheatley to represent him as a religious figure who transcended narrow sectarianism. Claiming the "whole world" as his parish, Whitefield preached to non-Anglican as well as Anglican congregations.[42] And he promoted an ecumenical ideal of a universal Christianity: "It is very remarkable, there are but two sorts of people mentioned in Scripture: it does not say the Baptists and Independents, nor the Methodists and Presbyterians, no Jesus Christ divides the whole world into but two classes, sheep and goats."[43] Wheatley's choice of "Glow'd," "inflame," and "captivate" emphasizes Whitefield's successful use of emotional appeals in his preaching:

> Hail happy Saint on thy immortal throne!
> To thee complaints of grievance are unknown;
> We hear no more the music of thy tongue,
> Thy wonted auditories cease to throng.
> Thy lessons in unequal'd accents flow'd!
> While emulation in each bosom glow'd;
> Thou didst, in strains of eloquence refin'd,
> Inflame the soul, and captivate the mind. (ll. 1–8)

Wheatley's Whitefield transcends narrow national as well as sectarian religious identities. Wheatley reflects the widespread conviction in the colonies that Whitefield was as concerned about the liberties of Americans as he was about their souls. There was ample reason for such conviction. As he was concluding his visit in April 1764 to Portsmouth, New Hampshire, Whitefield warned two Congregationalist ministers, "I can't in conscience leave the town without acquainting you with a secret. My heart bleeds for *America*. O poor *New England*! There is a deep laid plot against both your civil and religious liberties. Your golden days are at an end. You have nothing but troubles before you. My information comes from the best authority in *Great Britain*. I was allowed to speak of the affair in general, but enjoined not to mention particulars."[44] He was as concerned about British plans to tax the American colonies as he was with an attempt to impose an Anglican bishop on them. According to Samuel Adams (1722–1803), Whitefield assured New Englanders that he would "serve our civil as well as religious Interests."[45] Colonial politics made strange bedfellows: Whitefield and the Congregationalist Rev. Charles Chauncy, his theological antagonist since the 1740s, joined forces to oppose the plan to assign an Anglican bishop to America. When the Stamp Act was repealed in 1766, Whitefield exclaimed, "Stamp Act repealed, Gloria Deo."[46] Just before leaving London for his final American tour he preached against "the great mischiefs the poor pious people [of Boston] suffered lately through the town's being disturbed by the [British] soldiers."[47] And in the last letter Whitefield wrote before his death, he expressed his sympathy for the people of Massachusetts, whose charter the British government sought to retract: "Poor *New-England* is much to be pitied; *Boston* people most of all. How falsely misrepresented! What a mercy, that our *Christian charter* cannot be dissolved!"[48] Poets depicted the late Whitefield as America's friend and defender.[49]

Wheatley represents Whitefield as a heroic transatlantic figure who resists alleged British attempts to impose tyranny on a protonational American community:

> When his AMERICANS were burden'd sore,
> When streets were crimson'd with their guiltless gore!
> Unrival'd friendship in his breast now strove:
> The fruit thereof was charity and love
> Towards *America*—couldst thou do more
> Than leave thy native home, the *British* shore,
> To cross the great Atlantic's wat'ry road,
> To see *America's* distress'd abode?
> Thy prayers, great Saint, and thy incessant cries,

Have pierc'd the bosom of thy native skies!
Thou moon hast seen, and yᵉ bright stars of light
Have witness been of his requests by night!
He pray'd that grace in every heart might dwell:
He long'd to see *America* excel. (ll. 15–28)

Wheatley goes far beyond Whitefield in imagining the capaciousness of an American community.[50] Wheatley's Whitefield addresses his message of salvation through Christ to two separate audiences in her poem: "'my dear AMERICANS'" (l. 39) and "ye *Africans*" (l. 41).[51] Prominently identified in the poem's headnote as being of African descent, Wheatley's consistent use of the first-person plural *we* renders people of both European and African descent equally American. Although Wheatley may never have read Whitefield's undated "A Prayer for a poor Negroe," in which he creates a contented slave, her writings through 1770 offer an interesting gloss on it. Wheatley shared some of the desires expressed by Whitefield's fictional "Negroe":

> Blessed be thy name [Lord], for bringing me over into a Christian country. . . . Have mercy on poor countrymen: Lord, suffer them no longer to sit in darkness, and in the shadow of death. . . . Lighten our darkness, we beseech thee, O Lord, and let us know the truth as it is in Jesus. Grant I may be truly converted myself, and then if it be thy blessed will, enable me, O lord, to strengthen my poor brethren. O take us poor negroes for thine inheritance, and bless all those who endeavour to teach us thy will.

But more significantly, by writing and publishing Wheatley repeatedly refuses to join Whitefield's "Negroe," who prays, "Lord, keep the door of my lips, that I may not offend with my tongue." Her elegy effectively rejects Whitefield's endorsement of passive acceptance of slavery by the enslaved. His "Negroe" prays,

> Make me contented with my condition, knowing, O Lord, that thou hast placed me in it. Let me never be tempted to rebel against my master or mistress; and enable me to be obedient not only to the good and gentle, but also to the forward. Lord, keep the door of my lips, that I may not offend with my tongue. Keep my hands from picking and

stealing, and suffer me not to behave unseemly on the Lord's-day. Bless my master and mistress, and my labours for their sake.[52]

Wheatley opens the closing paragraph of her eulogy on Whitefield with a direct address to Whitefield's patron, as if she is bidding for her patronage as well:

> Great COUNTESS! we *Americans* revere
> Thy name, and thus condole thy grief sincere:
> We mourn with thee, that TOMB obscurely plac'd,
> In which thy Chaplain undisturb'd doth rest. (ll. 45–48)

Wheatley's elegy brought her continental and transatlantic fame. On 19 October 1770 the *New-Hampshire Gazette, and Historical Chronicle* advertised the poem and recommended that "[t]his excellent Piece ought to be preserved . . . on Account of its being [written] by a Native of Africa, and yet would have done Honor to a Pope or Shakespere [*sic*]."

Two weeks after Wheatley's elegy on Whitefield was advertised in the *Boston News-Letter* she sent a much more direct appeal to the countess with a copy of her poem.[53] Wheatley may have corresponded with the countess earlier. Among the Countess of Huntingdon's papers is a manuscript copy of Wheatley's elegy on Rev. Joseph Sewall, who had died in June 1769. Wheatley certainly knew that both her poem on Whitefield and her accompanying letter obviously contradicted her self-deprecating reference to herself as "an untutor'd African." She also knew that the significance of ending her letter "With great humility your Ladiship's most Obedient Humble Servant" was mostly formulaic:[54]

To the Rt. Hon'ble the Countess of Huntingdon

Most noble Lady,

The Occasion of my addressing your Ladiship will, I hope, Apologize for this my boldness in doing it: it is to enclose a few lines on the decease of your worthy Chaplain, the Rev'd Mr. Whitefield, in the loss of whom I Sincerely sympathize with your Ladiship; but your great loss which is his Greater gain, will, I hope, meet with infinite reparation, in the presence of God, the Divine Benefactor whose image you bear by filial imitation.

The Tongues of the Learned are insufficient, much less the pen of an untutor'd African, to paint in lively characters, the excellencies of this Citizen of Zion! I beg an Interest in your Ladiship's Prayers and Am,

> With great humility
> your Ladiship's most
> Obedient Humble Servant
> Phillis Wheatley
> [Boston 25 October 1770]

Although determining the amount of agency, or control, Wheatley exercised in the publication and distribution of her poems while she was a slave is impossible, they could never have been produced without her active cooperation. For an adolescent slave to conduct an apparently unsolicited correspondence with a noblewoman was indeed the act of "boldness" Wheatley acknowledges.

Chapter 4

"A WONDER of the Age indeed!"

Wheatley's elegy on Whitefield brought her almost instant intercolonial and transatlantic fame after it appeared on 11 October 1770. At a time when a voyage across the Atlantic normally took at least five weeks, the *Gazeteer and New Daily Advertiser* in London advertised a version of the elegy on 16 November 1770 as "An Ode of Verses, composed in America by a Negro Girl seventeen years of age, and sent over to a gentleman of character in London. Now made public for the benefit of a family that has lately been reduced by fire, near Shoreditch church." By the end of 1770, Wheatley's poem was republished as a broadside with minor changes in New York, Philadelphia, and Newport, Rhode Island, as well as four more times in Boston. It was republished in London in 1771 with a funeral sermon for Whitefield by Rev. Ebenezer Pemberton (1705–77), minister of Boston's Congregationalist New Brick Church.[1]

Wheatley's elegy expanded her community of women supporters beyond her American and English patrons to include her fellow Bostonian poet, Jane Dunlap. In her *Poems Upon Several Sermons Preached by the Rev'd and Renowned George Whitefield While in Boston. . . . A New Year's Gift* (Boston, 1771), Dunlap styles herself "a Daughter of Liberty and Lover of Truth," who sees the publication of Wheatley's poem as an incentive for her own. Dunlap in effect acknowledges Wheatley as her muse:

> Shall his due praises be so loudly sung
> By a young Afric damsel's virgin tongue?
> And I be silent! And no mention make
> Of his blest name, who did so often speak. (ll. 17–20)[2]

The publication, distribution, and reception of Wheatley's Whitefield elegy inaugurated the most productive period of her life. She quickly wrote more poems on the deaths of locally eminent people and members of their families. Her *To Mrs. Leonard, on the Death of her Husband* was published in Boston as a broadside sometime after the death of Dr. Thomas Leonard (1744–71) on 21 June 1771. His widow, to whom he had been married for less than nine months, was Thankfull Leonard (1745–72), daughter of Thomas Hubbard (1702–73). She would become the subject of Wheatley's Boston broadside *To the Hon'ble Thomas Hubbard, Esq; On the Death of Mrs. Thankfull Leonard* at the beginning of 1773. Phillis knew the Hubbard family because they were neighbors of the Wheatleys on King Street. Thomas Hubbard was a wealthy and eminent merchant, who for many years had been a deacon of Old South Church and treasurer of Harvard College. He was one of the subscribers to Wheatley's 1773 *Poems*. Like John Avery, Hubbard was paradoxically a slave-trading philanthropist. At his death he left a substantial sum to be distributed to the poor.

Samuel Marshall, one of Susanna Wheatley's relatives, was the subject of another elegy Phillis published in 1771. Phillis may have known him through his wife, the former Lucy Tyler, whom she names in the poem, as well as through Susanna. Lucy Tyler Marshall and Phillis joined the Old South Church on the same day, 18 August 1771. Phillis's "On the Death of Doctor SAMUEL MARSHALL" appeared unsigned in the *Boston Evening-Post* on 7 October 1771. He had died on 29 September, one week before the anniversary of his marriage in 1765. Marshall (1735–71) was a prominent physician who returned to Boston in 1764 from London, where he had studied medicine after graduating from Harvard in 1754. His obituary in the *Boston Evening-Post* and the *Boston Post-Boy* on 30 September reports that he had been "suddenly seized with an Apoplectic Fit and died in a few minutes." The obituary describes him as having been "a very skillful Physician, Surgeon, and Man Midwife," possessed of "many social Virtues, and [an] agreeable, obliging Disposition," which "rendered him peculiarly endearing." To Phillis Wheatley he was "the universal Friend":

> And *Boston* too, for her Physician mourns.
> When sickness call'd for *Marshall's* kindly hand,
> Lo! how with pity would his heart expand!
> The sire, the friend, in him we oft have found,
> With gen'rous friendship did his soul abound.
> Could Esculapius then no longer stay?
> To bring his ling'ring infant into day!
> The babe unborn, in dark confines is toss'd
> And seems in anguish for it's father lost. (ll. 14–22)

Phillis Wheatley had written so many poems by the beginning of 1772 that she and her owners confidently announced in the *Boston Censor* on 29 February, 14 March, and 18 April her "Proposals for Printing by Subscription" a rather expensive book. They probably turned to Ezekiel Russell to produce the book because he had been one of the publishers of her elegy on the death of Whitefield in 1770. We do not know who wrote the "Proposals," but as one of the editors of Wheatley's writings observes, she was very likely responsible for it: "Certainly she cooperated in [its] conception and contents."[3]

The *Boston Censor*'s readers were accustomed to seeing people of African descent mentioned in print, usually unnamed, in advertisements for selling them, in advertisements for runaway slaves, or in accounts of domestic and foreign resistance to slavery. But they must have been startled by the elaborate appeal published on Wheatley's behalf:

A Collection of POEMS, wrote at several times, and upon various occasions, by PHILLIS, a Negro Girl, from the strength of her own Genius, it being but a few Years since she came to this Town an uncultivated Barbarian from *Africa*. The Poems having been seen and read by the best Judges, who think them well worthy of the Publick View; and upon critical examination, they find that the declared Author was capable of writing them. The Order in which they were penned, together with the Occasion, are as follows;

[1] On the Death of the Rev. Dr. *Sewell*, when sick, 1765—;
[2] On Virtue, [17]66—;
[3] On two Friends, who were cast away, d[itt]o.—;
[4] To the University of Cambridge, 1767—;
[5] An Address to the Atheist, do.—;
[6] An Address to the Deist, do.—;
[7] On America, 1768—;
[8] On the King, do.—;
[9] On Friendship, do.—;
[10] Thoughts on being brought from Africa to America, do.—;
[11] On the Nuptials of Mr. *Spence* to Miss *Hooper*, do.—;
[12] On the Hon. Commodore Hood, on his pardoning a Deserter, 1769—;
[13] On the Death of Reverend Dr. *Sewell*, do.—;

[14] On the Death of Master *Seider*, who was killed by *Ebenezer Richardson*, 1770.—;

[15] On the Death of the Rev. *George Whitefield*, do.—;

[16] On the Death of a young Miss, aged 5 years, do—;

[17] On the Arrival of the Ships of War, and landing of the Troops. [undated]—;

[18] On the Affray in King-Street, on the Evening of the 5th of March. [undated]—;

[19] On the death of a young Gentleman. [undated]—;

[20] To *Samuel Quincy*, Esq; a Panegyrick. [undated]—,

[21] To a Lady on her coming to America for her Health. [undated]—,

[22] To Mrs. *Leonard*, on the Death of her Husband. [undated]—;

[23] To Mrs. Boylston and Children on the Death of her Son and their Brother. [undated]—;

[24] To a Gentleman and Lady on the Death of their Son, aged 9 Months. [undated]—;

[25] To a Lady on her remarkable Deliverance in a Hurricane. [undated]—;

[26] To *James Sullivan*, Esq; and Lady on the Death of her Brother and Sister, and a child *Avis*, aged 12 Months. [undated]—;

[27] *Goliah* [*sic* for Goliath] of Gath. [undated]—;

[28] On the Death of Dr. *Samuel* Marshall. [undated]—;

It is supposed they will make one small Octavo Volume, and will contain about 200 Pages.

They will be printed on Demy [a size of paper] Paper, and beautiful Types.

The Price to Subscribers, handsomely bound and lettered, will be Four Shillings.—Stitched in blue, Three Shillings.

It is hoped Encouragement will be given to this Publication, as a reward to a very uncommon Genius, at present a Slave.

This Work will be put to the Press as soon as three Hundred Copies are subscribed for, and shall be published with all Speed.

Subscriptions are taken in by E[zekiel]. Russell, in Marlborough Street.

Like aspiring twenty-first-century writers, eighteenth-century authors faced many obstacles in trying to get a book into print. But to have a book to sell, an author needed to acquire funding to enable her to produce and distribute it. During the eighteenth century the term *bookseller* was used to describe publishers as well as wholesale dealers and retail sellers of books, whose functions often overlapped in practice. No one involved in the book trade was normally keen to invest in an unknown author's first attempt at publication. If the aspiring author had sufficient means, she could of course risk investing in herself. If not, she had to find other sources of venture capital.

Authors traditionally acquired the necessary capital by either finding a wealthy and influential patron or selling the proposed book to subscribers, who committed in advance to purchase copies of the book when it appeared. Booksellers would effectively act as the aspiring author's agents in accepting subscriptions, normally receiving a commission for doing so. Subscribers were typically promised the book for a lower price than the one asked for in retail sales. A colonial author would ideally publish her book in England, where she could protect her copyright under British law, which did not apply to colonial publications. With a list of subscribers as proof of a guaranteed market, the author sought a bookseller-publisher who would produce the book, paying the costs of publication plus a small sum to the author for its copyright. If an author was able to get subscribers to pay at least part of the book's price in advance, she subsequently paid the production costs, found bookseller-agents to distribute the work, and normally sold her copyright. If her book proved to have a market beyond its subscribers, the self-published author could negotiate a premium price for the copyright. With the sale of her copyright, the author also sold her right to profits, or royalties, from any future sales of the book. The publisher of course could agree to share profits with the author as part of the deal to buy her copyright. Just as important, by giving up her copyright an author lost control of the content as well as production of her text. The author would no longer have the legal power to revise her own text in subsequent editions; nor would she have the authority to choose what, if any, illustrations or other supplementary materials her published book might include. In the colonies, however, without the protection of copyright, an author surrendered legal control of the content, distribution, and profits of her book as soon as she delivered it to her publisher.

First-time authors in the English-speaking Atlantic world had published by subscription since the early seventeenth century. By the end of the eighteenth, however, the practice had become very uncommon because it was so susceptible to abuse. Too many would-be buyers had been disappointed by people who never produced the promised books. Publication by subscription was liable to far greater abuse if either the author or bookseller required payment in advance from subscribers. They rarely did so.[4] The British bookseller John Murray noted in 1775 that requiring payment in advance of publication "(which formerly was fashionable) is so much disliked now that the bare attempt is sufficient to throw discredit upon the performance."[5] Of the 1,063 works Murray is known to have produced between 1768 and 1795, only about twenty-five were published by subscription. Subscription was probably the only source of independent financial support available to Phillis Wheatley. Any publishers and retailers that she, or more likely Susanna Wheatley, approached would have been understandably reluctant to risk investing in a relatively inexperienced author.

Wheatley and Russell hoped to profit from the growing interest in temporally, geographically, socially, and ethnically exotic origins of literary works, such as the Ossianic forgeries of ancient oral Gaelic epics (1762) by James Macpherson (1736–96)), or the poems of the uneducated "Journeyman Shoemaker" John Bennet published in 1774, of the milkwoman Ann Yearsley (c. 1753–1806) published in 1785, and of the supposedly unlettered Scot Robert Burns (1759–96) published in 1786. References in the "Proposals" to Wheatley—"a Negro Girl," until recently "an uncultivated Barbarian from *Africa*," who has produced poetry "from the strength of her own Genius"—were clearly intended to appeal to this interest in exotic authors.

Wheatley and Russell knew that potential buyers needed to be reassured that an enslaved woman of African descent was capable of producing the promised work. They anticipated concern about the authenticity of Wheatley's poetry: "The Poems have been seen and read by the best judges, who think them well worthy of the Publick View; and upon critical examination, they find that the declared Author was capable of writing them." Similar attestations of authenticity also commonly prefaced contemporaneous works by improbable authors of European descent. Wheatley's "Proposals" is noteworthy, however, because it was the first in what would soon become a tradition of having white commentators or editors attest to the authenticity of works by people of African descent.[6]

Publication of the "Proposals" in the *Boston Censor* was apparently part of a sophisticated transatlantic publicity campaign. The "Poetical Essays" section in the March 1772 issue of the prestigious *London Magazine: Or,*

Gentleman's Monthly Intelligencer included Wheatley's most belletristic, or literary, poem to date. The poem, which would be titled "On Recollection" when it was republished in her *Poems* in 1773, was prefaced in the *London Magazine* by an exchange of letters between an unidentified "L" and Phillis. Besides reminding readers of Wheatley's elegy on Whitefield, "L" assures readers that Wheatley "discovers [reveals] a most surprising genius." Readers also learn from "L" that in the Wheatley household Phillis has the status of "a compleat sempstress," an occupation much more respectable and far less arduous than that of a charwoman or washerwoman. She is worthy of "being in company with some young ladies of family." The exchange serves the same function as the attestation in the "Proposals" in the *Boston Censor*:

To the AUTHOR of the LONDON MAGAZINE [March 1772].
Boston, in New-England, Jan. 1, 1772.

SIR,

As your Magazine is a proper repository for any thing valuable or curious, I hope you will excuse the communicating the following by one of your subscribers.

There is in this town a young *Negro woman*, who left *her* country at ten years of age, and has been in *this* eight years. She is a compleat sempstress, an accomplished mistress of her pen, and discovers a most surprising genius. Some of her productions have seen the light, among which is a poem on the death of the Rev. Mr. George Whitefield.— The following was occasioned by her being in company with some young ladies of family, when one of them said she did not remember, among all the poetical pieces she had seen, ever to have met with a poem upon RECOLLECTION. The *African* (so let me call her, for so in fact she is) took the hint, went home to her master's, and soon sent what follows.

"MADAM,

Agreeable to your proposing *Recollection* as a subject proper for me to write upon, I enclose these few thoughts upon it; and, as you was the first person who mentioned it, I thought none more proper to dedicate it to; and, if it meets with your approbation, the poem is honoured, and the authoress satisfied. I am, Madam,

Your very humble servant, PHILLIS."

The accompanying poem is a striking departure from Wheatley's previously published works. All of those had been occasional pieces written in response to contemporaneous events, such as Whitefield's death, as "L" cleverly reminds readers. Commissioned as a performance piece, "Recollection" is clearly intended to demonstrate the aesthetic value of Wheatley's poetry more openly than she had tried to do in her earlier work. The initial invocation of "Mneme" (or Mnemosyne) as her muse, references to "Maro" (Virgil) and "Menellian strains," and the absence of an overtly Christian context all serve to assert the claim of the "vent'rous *Afric*" to a place in the secular poetic tradition derived from the classical examples of the ancient Greeks and Romans. Critics have pointed out that Wheatley ironically forgets that Mneme was not a *god*, but a *goddess*, an error she would correct in her revised version of the poem published the following year in her *Poems*.[7]

Despite the seemingly coordinated transatlantic effort to elicit support, Wheatley failed to obtain the three hundred subscribers Russell thought he needed to make the risk of publishing her book of poems worth taking. One she did get was John Andrews (1743–1822), a Boston lawyer. Andrews complained on 29 May 1772 to his brother-in-law, William Barrell, a merchant in Philadelphia, "Its above two months since I subscribed for Phillis's poems, which I expected to have sent you long ago, but the want of Spirit to carry on any thing of the kind here has prevented it, as they are not yet publish'd."[8]

Phillis's ill health during the winter of 1771–72 and the spring of 1772 no doubt aggravated her disappointment at not being able to publish her collected poems. Identifying specific ailments in the past is difficult, since eighteenth-century physicians were little better at recognizing symptoms than they were at either establishing causes of diseases or curing them. Their fear that Phillis might be in "danger of a consumpsion" suggests the early signs of a pulmonary problem. On 21 April 1772 Wheatley wrote to John Thornton (1720–90) in London. He was a wealthy English merchant and philanthropist, an evangelical Anglican supporter of the Countess of Huntingdon's missionary activities, and a member of her circle. The Reverend Samson Occom had been his guest during his 1766–68 fundraising visit to England. Thornton sent money to John and Susanna Wheatley for Indian missions, and they kept him informed of their progress. Phillis Wheatley had apparently initiated a correspondence with him to request his guidance in religious matters. She expresses surprise that he has responded to her letter by "recommending the Bible to be my chief Study" and tells him,

> It has pleasd God to lay me on a bed of Sickness, and I knew not but my deathbed, but he has been graciously pleas'd to restore me in a great measure. I beg your prayers, that I may be made thankful for his paternal corrections, and that I may make proper use of them to the glory of his grace. I am Still very weak & the Physicians, seem to think there is danger of a consumpsion. And O that when my flesh and my heart fail me God would be my strength and portion for ever, that I might put my whole trust and Confidence in him, who has promis'd never to forsake those who Seek him with the whole heart. You could not, I am sure have express [*sic*] greater tenderness and affection for me, than by being a welwisher to my Soul, the friends of Souls bear Some resemblance to the father of Spirits and are made partakers of his divine Nature.

Wheatley's illness "this winter past" was also to blame for her failure to respond to Obour Tanner sooner than 19 May 1772. When Wheatley learned that her letter never reached Tanner, she wrote her again on 19 July to tell her that "I have been in a very poor state of health all the past winter and spring, and now reside in the country for the benefit of its more wholesome air. I came to town this morning to spend the Sabbath with my master and mistress." Regrettably, none of Obour Tanner's letters to Phillis Wheatley is known to exist.

Wheatley had vindicated the belief in a benevolent God, whose providential design renders apparent evil ultimately good, in her "On Being Brought from Africa to America" and in her letters to Obour Tanner; that same belief underlies two occasional poems on Christian consolation that she wrote in the summer of 1772. In both elegies Wheatley assumes a position of moral and religious authority more insistently than she had ever done before in her published works. In "To the University of Cambridge," written five years earlier, she had audaciously called on "the muses" to "assist" her in warning and advising prospective ministers. In *To the Rev. Mr. Pitkin, on the DEATH of his LADY*, published as a broadside on 16 June 1772, Wheatley adopts the persona of "the Muse" to counsel Rev. Timothy Pitkin (1727–1812), the son of the governor of Connecticut, William Pitkin (1694–1769). Timothy Pitkin was a wealthy and learned Congregationalist minister in Farmington, Connecticut, with close ties to Yale. From 1769 to 1773 he was also a trustee of Dartmouth College. Wheatley may have known him through Rev. Occom, one of several Native American Christian missionaries Pitkin worked with. By 1779 Pitkin had become one of Wheatley's correspondents. In 1752 Pitkin married Temperance Clap, the daughter of Rev. Thomas Clap (1703–67), a Congregationalist minister and president of Yale. Her sister was Mary Clap Wooster (1729–1807), to whom Wheatley would address an elegy on the death of her husband, David, in 1778. The occasion of Wheatley's poem in 1772 was the death of Temperance Clap Pitkin during childbirth on 19 May 1772. Wheatley closes her elegy by commanding Rev. Pitkin to remember the consolation his Christian faith offers him after his wife's death:

> Let Grief no longer damp the sacred Fire,
> But rise sublime, to equal Bliss aspire;
> Thy Sighs no more be wafted by the Wind,
> Complain no more, but be to Heav'n resign'd.
> 'Twas thine to shew those Treasures all divine,
> To sooth our Woes, the Task was also thine.
> Now Sorrow is recumbent on thy Heart,
> Permit the Muse that healing to impart,
> Nor can the World, a pitying tear refuse,
> They weep, and with them, ev'ry heavenly Muse. (ll. 41–50)

Consolation is also the theme of "A Poem on the Death of *Charles Eliot*, Aged 12 Months," which Wheatley sent to the child's father, Samuel Eliot, on 1 September 1772. The poem was distributed in manuscript before it was revised and published in Wheatley's *Poems* the following year. One of the copies reached John Andrews by the end of September, no doubt because the mother of the dead child was his sister-in-law. On 22 September 1772 Andrews sent a copy of the poem to Barrell, brother of the dead child's mother. Andrews described it to Barrell as "a masterly performance" marked by "Flowry Language that runs through yᵉ whole of it."⁹ Wheatley reminds Charles's parents that they should celebrate their late son's joy in the afterlife rather than selfishly and short-sightedly mourn their loss:

> Say, parents! why this unavailing moan?
> Why heave your bosoms with the rising groan?

To CHARLES, the happy subject of my song,
A happier world, and nobler strains belong.
Say, would you tear him from the realms above?
Or make less happy, frantic in your love?
Doth his beatitude increase your pain,
Or could you welcome to this earth again
The son of bliss? (ll. 27–35)

Poems that Wheatley had written earlier also continued to circulate in manuscript before being published. On 30 January 1773 Elizabeth Wallcut (1721–1811) wrote to the youngest of her three sons, Thomas (1758–1840), who was attending Dartmouth College: "according to your Desire I have Sent you Dʳ Sewalls picture and the Verses on his Death Composd by phillis wheetly which with a piece She made on our Colledg ["To the University of Cambridge"] She Sends as a present to you."[10] Thomas was five years younger than Phillis, who corresponded with him initially through his mother, and soon directly. He was one of the earliest (and youngest) admirers of Wheatley's poetry, and she actively promoted his education. The relationship between Phillis Wheatley and Thomas Wallcut is a rare instance of a woman of African descent who, when she was enslaved as well as free, was a mentor to a white youth. On 26 March 1774 she gave him the copy of Rev. Thomas Amory's *Daily Devotion Assisted and Recommended, in Four Sermons* that Rev. Charles Chauncy had given her on 14 October 1772, as well as a copy of Rev. John Lathrop's *The Importance of Early Piety*.[11]

Phillis, virtually a member of the extended Wheatley family, knew Elizabeth Wallcut, Susanna Wheatley's niece, and her family well. According to Elizabeth Wallcut's grandnephew, Elizabeth "was a sister of Colonel Thomas Marshall, who was actively engaged in the Revolutionary struggle. . . . She was a woman of very decided character. She and her family,—respectable trades-people, of but moderate means, and not highly educated,—by force of character, entered with self-sacrificing energy upon whatever movements were started for doing good. The same characteristic, later in life, she carried into her school for little ones, which for years was known as Ma'am Wallcut's Dame School, where children, some of prominent families, received their earliest training."[12]

More occasions for consolatory poems on premature deaths ended the year 1772 and began the next. Twenty-seven-year-old Mrs. Thankfull Hubbard Leonard died on 29 December 1772. Wheatley published the broadside *To the Hon'ble Thomas Hubbard, Esq.; On the Death of Mrs. Thankfull Leonard*, addressed to Mrs. Leonard's father, on 2 January 1773, offering the familiar admonition:

> Ah! cease, no more her unknown bliss bemoan!
> Suspend the sigh, and check the rising groan.
>
> . . . .
>
> To heav'n's high mandate chearfully resign'd
> She mounts, she flies, and leaves the rolling Globe behind.
> She who late sigh'd for LEONARD to return
> Has ceas'd to languish, and forgot to mourn. (ll. 9–10, 27–30)

Wheatley's published poems brought her continental attention. Benjamin Rush (1745–1813) refers to her in a footnote on the second page of his *An Address to the Inhabitants of the British Settlements in America, on the Slavery of Negroes in America*, which he published anonymously in Philadelphia in February 1773. Rush, a prominent Philadelphia physician, uses Wheatley, whom he never identifies by name, to prove that "We have [as] many well-attested anecdotes of as sublime and disinterested virtue among [Negroes] as ever adorned a Roman or a Christian character."[13] Wheatley is the only individual enslaved African Rush refers to in his argument against slavery. He apparently knew of her only through her writings, and those perhaps at second hand. Rush may have learned of Wheatley through his wife, Julia Stockton Rush (1759–1848), who apparently owned at least one of her manuscript poems.[14] Rush mistakes Wheatley's legal status and the length of time she has been "in the country": "There is now in the town of Boston a Free Negro Girl, about 18 years of age, who has been but 9 years in the country, whose singular genius and accomplishments are such as not only do honor to her sex, but to human nature. Several of her poems have been printed, and read with pleasure by the public."[15] Among the justifications of slavery that Rush refutes is the assertion that enslavement was for people of African descent a fortunate fall into Christianity:

> Nor let it be said, in the present Age, that their black color (as it is commonly called), either subjects them to, or qualifies them for slav-

ery. The vulgar notion of their being descended from Cain, who was supposed to have been marked with this color, is too absurd to need a refutation. . . .

There are some amongst us who . . . plead as a motive for importing and keeping slaves, that they become acquainted with the principles of our country.—this is like justifying a highway robbery because part of the money acquired in this manner was appropriated to some religious use,—Christianity will never be propagated by any other methods than those employed by Christ and his Apostles. Slavery is an engine as little fitted for that purpose as Fire or the Sword. A Christian slave is a contradiction in terms. (3–4, 15–16)

Rush's book was advertised initially in the *New-York Gazette, and Weekly Mercury* on 22 February 1773 and subsequently in the *Massachusetts Spy Or, Thomas's Boston Journal* (1 April 1773), the *Boston Gazette, and Country Journal* (5 April 1773), and the *Connecticut Journal* (14 May 1773). The recognition Rush gave Wheatley in his *Address* probably caused her to initiate a correspondence with him: her 1779 "Proposals" for a never-published second book includes a letter from her to him. That letter has not yet been discovered. Ironically, Rush was a slave owner himself in 1773, and would remain one for many years afterwards.

Not all the attention Wheatley's early works received was positive. A defender of slavery quickly disputed Rush's citation of her as evidence for the equality of people of African descent. By the beginning of September 1773 Richard Nisbet published *Slavery not Forbidden by Scripture* anonymously in Philadelphia. The *Boston Evening Post* began advertising it for sale in February 1774. Nisbet acknowledges that "A few instances may be found, of African negroes possessing virtues and becoming ingenious," but immediately dismisses Phillis Wheatley in a footnote without naming her: "The Author of the Address gives a single example of a negro girl writing a few silly poems, to prove that the blacks are not deficient to us in understanding."[16] Nisbet implicitly links Wheatley's poetic achievement with that of Francis Williams, whom the philosopher David Hume (1711–76) notoriously dismisses in a passage Nisbet quotes: "In Jamaica, indeed, they talk of one negro, as a man of parts and learning; but it is likely he is admired for very slender accomplishments, like a parrot, who speaks a few words plainly."[17]

Rush deleted his reference to Wheatley in all editions of his *Address* after the first, perhaps in response to Nisbet's counterattack.[18]

Phillis Wheatley continued to distribute her work privately in manuscript as well as publicly in print. "To His Honour the Lieutenant-Governor, on the Death of his Lady. *March 24, 1773*" made its public appearance in her *Poems* in 1773, but Wheatley probably gave a copy of it privately to Andrew Oliver (1706–74), lieutenant governor of Massachusetts, shortly after the death of his wife, Mary Sanford Oliver, on 17 March 1773. A Harvard graduate, Oliver had been appointed provincial secretary of Massachusetts in 1756 and became lieutenant governor in 1771. Wheatley poignantly reminds Oliver in a footnote that he had previously suffered the loss of "Three amiable Daughters who died when just arrived to Womens Estate," most recently that of Margaret Oliver Spooner barely a month earlier.[19] Wheatley paradoxically assumes a voice of humble assertiveness in addressing the man she refers to as "great Sir" (l. 37):

> *Virtue's* rewards can mortal pencil paint?
> No—all descriptive arts, and eloquence are faint;
> Nor canst thou, *Oliver*, assent refuse
> To heav'nly tidings from the *Afric* muse.
>
> . . . .
>
> Forgive the muse, forgive th'advent'rous lays,
> That fain thy soul to heav'nly scenes would raise. (ll. 25–28, 43–44)

Like Thomas Hubbard, Andrew Oliver was sufficiently impressed by Wheatley's poem on the death of his loved one to later publicly vouch for the authenticity of her poetry.

By the end of 1772 Wheatley had been ill for months, she had failed to find a publisher, and she still had not heard back from the Countess of Huntingdon directly since she had sent her the elegy on Whitefield in 1770. Wheatley knew through intermediaries, however, that the countess had received the letter and copy of the poem she had sent her. The countess was so intrigued by what she had read that she turned to members of what was commonly called her Huntingdonian Connexion to try to learn more about the young poet's Christian piety and authenticity as an author. Richard Cary (1717–90), who lived in Charlestown, just north of Boston, reported to the countess on 25 May 1772 that "The Negro Girl of Mʳˢ Wheatley's, by her

Virtuous Behaviour and Conversation in Life, gives Reason to believe, she's a Subject of Divine Grace—remarkable for her Piety, of an extraordinary Genius, and in full Communion with one of the Churches, the Family, & Girl, was affected at the kind enquiry Your Ladiship made after her."[20] Cary's account was soon corroborated by another of the countess's American correspondents. On 19 March 1773, Bernard Page wrote her:

> I have dined at Mr Wheatley's and seen Phillis; whose Presence and Conversation demonstrate the written Performances, with her Signature, to be hers. M^r & Mrs Wheatley's due respects, together with this desire, wait on your Ladyship, That if you'll honor them with any of the itinerant Ministers taking up their abode at their house when in Boston, every thing to such, shall be equally agreeable with the most desirable home & further commissioned me to add That they beg an interest in your Ladyship's Prayers at the Throne of Grace. Mrs Wheatley I verily believe is a real Child of God and a better house in Boston, in all other respects, a Gospel Minister can't desire.
>
> Phillis heartily desires, That her Duty together with her Request, whether Mr Whitefield's Elegy hath been duly received, might be humbly presented to your Ladyship. . . .
>
> Since I wrote thus far, I have again seen Phillis, who showed me a letter from a Minister to her and her Answer to the same. And I myself saw her write several lines and then took the opportunity to watch her narrowly; by which, I found she wrote a good & expeditious hand. She frequently made use of a quarto Dictionary: and well *she* deserves the use thereof: for I'll delineate her in few words: Her aspect, humble serene & graceful; her Thoughts, luminous & sepulchral, ethereal & evangelical and her Performances most excellent, yea almost inimitable. A WONDER of the Age indeed![21]

Shortly after Page wrote to the countess, Susanna Wheatley informed Rev. Occom that the process of finding a publisher and patron in London had already been set in motion. Robert Calef sailed for London on 15 November 1772, arriving at the mouth of the Thames River on 17 December.[22] On 29 March Susanna Wheatley sent Occom a copy of a 5 January letter she had received from Captain Calef, who had brought Phillis's manuscript with him to London. Acting as her literary agent, Calef had enlisted Archibald Bell to publish her book if a patron could be found. Susanna told

Occom that Bell's mission as a go-between to gain Phillis her patron had been successful. Calef had informed Susanna:

> Mr Bell (the printer) Acquaints me that about 5 weeks ago he waited upon the Countess of Huntingdon with the Poems, who was greatly pleas'd with them, and pray'd him to Read them, and often would break in upon him and say, 'is not this, or that, very fine! do read another,' and then expressd herself, She found her heart to knit with her and Questiond him much, whether She was real without a deception? He then Convinc'd her by bringing my Name [Calef] in question. She is expected in Town in a Short time when we are both to wait upon her. I had like to forget to mention to you She is fond of having the Book dedicated to her; but one thing She desir'd which She said She hardly tho't would be denied her, that was to have Phillis' picture in the frontispiece. So that, if you ~~can~~ would get it done it can be Engrav'd here. I do imagine it can be Easily done, and think would contribute greatly to the Sale of the Book. I am impatient to hear what the Old Countess Says upon the Occasion, & shall take the Earliest Opp^y of waiting upon her when She comes to Town.[23]

Although Archibald Bell was a relatively minor London bookseller he was an appropriate choice to approach the Countess of Huntingdon. He specialized in evangelical religious works that appealed to her. For example, in 1771 he published William Mason's *The Best Improvement of the Much Lamented Death of that Eminent and Faithful Minister of the Gospel, The Rev^d Mr. George Whitefield, Chaplain to the Countess of Huntingdon.* And Bell would include advertisements for other religious works on the last page of his edition of Wheatley's *Poems* in 1773: *The Memoirs of Miss Williams. A History Founded on Facts. In Two Volumes. By A.B.*, as well as *The Church-Member's Directory, or Every Christian's Companion.*

News of the efforts in London on Phillis's behalf had been spreading privately in the colonies by the time Occom received Susanna Wheatley's 29 March letter. John Andrews was overly optimistic about the publication date of Phillis's book, and he probably exaggerated the price its copyright would command when he described the status of her book to his brother-in-law William Barrell on 24 February 1773. Andrews's phrasing indicates that Phillis played a very active role in getting her poems into print by gathering signatures of Boston dignitaries attesting to her authenticity. His phrasing also suggests that she and her supporters were not completely disappointed by the failure to find a Boston publisher. The capital of the British Empire was a far more prestigious venue for publication than a colonial town. And works published in London were very likely to be distributed throughout Britain and its colonies:

> In regard to Phillis's poems they will originate from a London press, as *she was blam'd by her friends for prinᵗˢ them here* & made to expect a large emolument if she sent yᵉ copy home [i.e., London] which induced her to remand it of yᵉ printers & also of Capt Calef who could not sell it by reason of their not crediting yᵉ performance to be by a Negro, since which *she has had a paper Drawn up & signed by the Gov. Councils, Ministers & most of yᵉ people of note in this place, certifying the authenticity of it*, which Capt Calef carried last fall, therfore [*sic*] we may expect it in print by the spring ships, it is supposed the Coppy [*sic*] will sell for £100 Ster[lin]ᵍ: have not as yet been able to procure a coppy of her dialogue with Mʳ Murry, if I do, will send it. [emphases added]²⁴

Phillis Wheatley and her owners had clearly learned from the earlier failed attempt to find a publisher in Boston. For the London market they anticipated questions about the authenticity of Phillis's poetry. They mounted a sophisticated publicity campaign on both sides of the Atlantic. Solicitations for subscribers to the forthcoming London edition of Phillis Wheatley's book soon appeared in Boston and London newspapers while Phillis was still in Boston. The advertisements in the *Boston News-Letter* (16, 22 April 1773) and *Boston Post Boy* (19 April) required each subscriber to make a down payment of one shilling toward the cost of two shillings for a printed copy "sewed" or two shillings and six pence for one "neatly bound." The difference in price between the proposed London edition of 1773 and the unsuccessful Boston subscription proposal of the year before reflects the difference in value between, respectively, sterling and colonial currency. Whereas the 1772 proposal identified Phillis as "at present a Slave," the 1773 proposal more appropriately describes her for a primarily London market as "A Negro Servant to Mr. Wheatley of *Boston*." Potential buyers are told that the 1773 book would be "Dedicated by Permission" to the Countess of Huntingdon and "adorned with an elegant Frontispiece, representing the Author."

Subscriptions in Boston were received by the booksellers Edward Cox and Edward Berry, who had recently moved there from London. In 1766 they opened a shop opposite Rev. Samuel Cooper's Brattle Street Church to sell lace, stationery, jewelry, and books. By May 1771 they had moved to a shop two doors away from the British Coffee House on King Street, where Wheatley lived.[25] The advertisements in the London *Morning Post and Daily Advertiser* on 21 April and 1 May 1773 included the same information as that found in the Boston newspapers but were much more elaborate. They included the address to the public, the attestation, and the letter from John Wheatley that would appear in the published book. Subscriptions were accepted by booksellers from one end of greater London to the other: in the City of London in the east by Archibald Bell, Leonard Urquhart (d. 1789), William Richardson (d. 1811), and Edward Johnson, as well as at the New England Coffee House; in the west by Samuel Leacroft and Robert Davis (d. 1780).

Susanna and John Wheatley, and presumably Phillis, decided that Phillis should go to London to promote the forthcoming publication of her collected poems. Concern about her health rather than a desire for publicity, however, was given as the primary motive for having her go. Nathaniel Wheatley would accompany her. He had business to conduct and a marriage to arrange for himself in London. Phillis was also to take two letters with her. One, dated 30 April 1773, was from Susanna Wheatley to the Countess of Huntingdon, asking the latter to help keep Phillis in her place by not allowing her to take on airs in the big city:

> Phillis being in a poor State of Health, the Physicians advise to the Sea Air. And as my Son is coming to Engalnd upon Som [*sic*] Business, and as so good an opportunity presented I thot it my duty to send her, & as your Ladiship has condescended to take so much notice of my dear Phillis as to permit her Book to [be] Dedicated to you, and desiring her Picture in the Frontispiece: I flatter'd my Self that your good advice and Counsel will not be wanting. I tell Phillis to act wholly under the direction of your Ladiship. I did not think it worth while nor did the time permit to fit her out with Cloathes: but I have given her money to Buy what you think most proper for her. I like She should be dress'd plain. [I] Must beg the favour of your Ladiship to advise my Son to Some Christian House for Phillis to board at.[26]

Events would show that Phillis may have had an even more powerful motive for going to London than to promote her book.

The other letter Phillis brought to London was from Richard Cary to the countess, written on 3 May. Cary assured the countess yet again of the piety and promise of "the Christian Poetess" she expected to meet within a few weeks: "This will be deliver'd Your Ladiship by Phillis the Christian Poetess, whose behavior in England I Wish may be as Exemplary, as its been in Boston. This appears remarkable for her Humility, Modesty and Spiritual Mindedness. [I] hope she will continue an ornament to the Christian Name and Profession, as she grows older and has more experience. I doubt not her Writings will run more in an Evangelicall Strain. I think your Ladiship will be pleas'd with her."[27]

Phillis and Nathaniel Wheatley sailed from Boston with Robert Calef on the *London Packet* on 8 May 1773. She was probably too excited, and perhaps frightened, by the prospect of what lay ahead to notice how cloudy the weather was.[28] Perhaps she was even too excited to compare this transatlantic voyage to the Middle Passage she had been forced to endure a dozen years earlier. Everything related to Wheatley's time in London suggests that a marketing mastermind lay behind its preparation and execution. Phillis's owners were making an extraordinary investment in her celebrity and taking a considerable risk that her health and the ship would survive an always dangerous transatlantic voyage. Colonial newspapers announced her imminent and eventual departure. The *Boston News-Letter* told its readers on 3 May that the "extraordinary Negro Poet" was about to leave, and the *New York Gazette and Weekly Mercury* mentioned on 17 May that she was on her way to London.[29] Henry Hulton (1732–91), the commissioner of customs in Boston from 1767 to 1776, wrote on 10 May 1773 to a merchant friend in Liverpool, England: "There is a Negro Girl born in Africa going from hence to England by desire of Lady Huntington [*sic*]: she has shewn a great genius for Poetry & her works are to be published in London. She is certainly an extraordinary instance of natural genius. She has only been 8 or 9 years from Guinea. I have not seen her, but I am told she has read some of the best English books and translations from the antients, & that she converses upon them with great propriety."[30] To ensure that potential colonial readers remained aware of Phillis, new poems continued to be published in North America during her absence. The *Boston Post-Boy* published on 10 May "To the Empire of America, Beneath the Western Hemisphere. Farewell to America. To Mrs. S. W.," dated 7 May 1773. Other colonial newspapers republished it in the following weeks.[31]

Phillis Wheatley arrived in London on 17 June 1773. The most recent advertisement of the "Proposals" had appeared in the *Morning Post and Daily Advertiser* two days earlier. Phillis wrote to the Countess of Huntingdon ten days after she reached England. Huntingdon was recovering at her home in Wales from an illness she had contracted before Wheatley's arrival. Wheatley's letter is a model of tact, politeness, and flattery, for which she should be given full credit: "I should think my self very happy in Seeing your Ladyship, and if you was So desirous of the Image of the Author as to propose it for a Frontispiece I flatter myself that you would accept the Reality." It must have been written after she arrived, so neither Susanna nor Mary Wheatley could have played a role in its composition. Less than three weeks later, on 17 July, Wheatley wrote to the countess again to express her regret at not having been able to meet her patron. Since her arrival in England she learned of the countess's patronage of another African, Gronniosaw.[32] Her second letter, too, demonstrates how well Wheatley understood the rhetoric of the patron-client relationship: "It gives me very great satisfaction to hear of an African so worthy to be honour'd with your Ladiship's approbation & Friendship as him whom you call your Brother. I rejoice with your Ladiship in that Fund of Mental Felicity which you cannot but be possessed of, in the consideration of your exceeding great reward. My great opinion of your Ladiship's goodness, leads [me] to believe, I have an interest in your most happy hours of communion, with your most indulgent Father and our great and common Benefactor."

The timing of Phillis's return voyage had probably been planned before she left Boston rather than in response to "a message that Mrs. Wheatley was seriously ill."[33] The brevity of her stay in London made it unlikely that she could have received a letter from Boston while she was there. Calef's primary purpose in sailing to London was not to see the publication of Phillis Wheatley's *Poems*, but rather to acquire goods as soon as possible for the Boston market and to set sail for home as quickly as he could. He no doubt was keen to leave before the onset of the hurricane season would force him to delay his departure for months.

The prepublication marketing Phillis participated in during her stay in London continued after she left England. *The Morning Post and Daily Advertiser* published advertisements for her forthcoming book on 15 June and 6 and 11 August. Archibald Bell registered Wheatley's *Poems* with the Stationers' Company on 10 September to protect his copyright on the first book by an English-speaking author of African descent. The first advertisement of the book itself had appeared in the *London Chronicle or Universal Evening Post* the day before:

Dedicated, by Permission, to the Right Hon. the
Countess of Huntingdon.
This Day was published,
Price 2s. sewed, or 2s. 6d. adorned with an elegant engraved like-ness of the Author.
A Volume of POEMS, on various Subjects,
RELIGIOUS and MORAL. By PHILLIS WHEATLEY,
Negro Servant to Mr. John Wheatley, of Boston.
London: Printed for A. Bell, Bookseller, Aldgate; and at Boston, for Messrs. Cox and Berry, in King Street.
To the PUBLIC.

The Book here proposed for publication displays perhaps one of the greatest instances of pure, unassisted genius, that the world ever produced. The Author is a native of Africa, and left not that dark part of the habitable system, till she was eight years old. She is now no more than nineteen, and many of the Poems were penned before she arrived at near that age.

They were wrote upon a variety of interesting subjects, and in a stile rather to have been expected from those who, a native genius, have had the happiness of a liberal education, than from one born in the wilds of Africa.

The writer while in England a few weeks since, was conversed with by many of the principal Nobility and Gentry of this Country, who have been signally distinguished for their learning and abilities, among whom was the Earl of Dartmouth, the late Lord Lyttelton, and others who unanimously expressed their amazement at the gifts with which infinite Wisdom has furnished her.

But the Publisher means not, in this advertisement, to deliver any peculiar eulogiums on the present publication; he rather desires to submit the striking beauties of its contents to the unabashed candour of the impartial public.[34]

Archibald Bell knew how to market a book when he had one as promising as Wheatley's to sell. The advertisement immediately informs prospective buyers that the work enjoys the patronage of the powerful and influential Countess of Huntingdon. This information takes precedence over even the identities of the book's title and author. It serves to assure readers that the book is deemed worthy of being dedicated to someone so eminent. Similarly, Bell invokes "the Earl of Dartmouth, the late Lord Lyttelton, and others" to demonstrate that Wheatley has passed the most demanding social and literary tests before having her poetry presented to the public. Bell appeals to the late-eighteenth-century fascination with "pure, unassisted genius" by emphasizing that Wheatley was "born in the wilds of Africa," and that she wrote all of the poems in her book before becoming an adult and without the benefit of a formal education. The advertisement avoids any reference to Wheatley's status as a slave, perhaps out of deference to attitudes toward slavery in England following the Mansfield decision the preceding year. Mansfield had ruled that no slave brought to England from the colonies could legally be forced to return to the colonies. Bell ends the advertisement with the transparently disingenuous and self-contradictory assertion that he does not intend "to deliver any peculiar eulogiums on the present publication; he rather desires to submit the striking beauties of its contents to the unabashed candour [fairness] of the impartial public." Bell's inclusion of the book's Boston distributors indicates that he anticipated a transatlantic audience.

Phillis Wheatley's publisher included the extraordinary "elegant engraved like-ness of the Author" at the urging of the Countess of Huntingdon. Eighteenth-century books rarely included frontispiece-portraits of the author, especially not during the author's lifetime. Frontispieces were in effect status claims for authors as well as for the readers who could afford them. They reflected the expectation that buyers would be willing to pay extra for them. Colonial portraits were particularly rare: "less than 1 percent of the population of this period was represented in portraits." Although "the number of portraits painted did increase, almost doubling in the third quarter of the century. . . . Most sitters in this period were merchants or landowners and their families. Others were professional men, including lawyers and ministers. The sitter would also have been part of a social or intellectual world that saw the role of a portrait as a statement of status."[35]

Frontispiece portraits of living women authors, such as those of Margaret Cavendish, Duchess of Newcastle-upon-Tyne (1623–73), Elizabeth Singer Rowe (1674–1737), and Eliza Haywood (1693–1756), were known in England before Wheatley's appeared in 1773; however, likenesses of identifiable eighteenth-century individuals of African descent in Britain and its colonies were very unusual.[36] Eighteenth-century visual representations of "blacks generally appear with whites in double or group portraits . . . in which the white sitters are the central subjects of the painting."[37]

Two striking exceptions, however, appeared in an illustration in the June 1750 issue of the *Gentleman's Magazine*. Job Ben Solomon and William Ansah Sessarakoo were enslaved in Africa and taken, respectively, to Maryland and the West Indies. When their fates became known in London, the Royal African Company redeemed Ben Solomon, and the British government bought Sessarakoo's freedom. Both men, who had owned and traded slaves in their native lands, were repatriated to Africa to maintain good relations between the buyers and sellers in the transatlantic slave trade. The illustration reflects the belief that Sessarakoo (on the right) was considered too well-born and well-bred to be a slave. Ben Solomon (on the left), who recorded the Arabic Koran from memory while in England in 1734, was considered too well-educated to be enslaved.[38] The book he wears around his neck is presumably either his transcription of the Koran or the Arabic translation of the New Testament that he was given while in England. The book also indicates his literacy. A frontispiece portrait of a woman of Wheatley's status and ethnicity was unprecedented. Phillis Wheatley was "the first colonial American woman of any race to have her portrait printed alongside her writings."[39] Wheatley was, moreover, the first woman of sub-Saharan African descent to sit for an individualized portrait.

Wheatley's frontispiece may have been designed in Boston, perhaps by Scipio Moorhead, a black artist to whom Wheatley apparently addressed one of the poems in her book.[40] Moorhead may have been the artist who advertised in the *Boston News-Letter* on 7 January 1773: "At Mr. McLeans', Watch-Maker, near the Town Hall, is a Negro man whose extraordinary Genius has been assisted by one of the best Masters in London; he takes Faces at the lowest Rates." The frontispiece engraved in London identifies the sitter as "Phillis Wheatley Negro Servant to Mr. John Wheatley, of Boston." As in New England, the term *servant* was used in England to describe both free and unfree workers, but the latter would have been extremely rare in England in 1773. Humbly dressed as a servant or domestic slave, the contemplative poet looks upward, as if seeking inspiration for the pen she holds. By doing so, as with most eighteenth-century representations of slaves or servants, she also deferentially avoids looking directly at the viewer. Wheatley is significantly shown with a book, perhaps intended to represent her own *Poems* to express her extraordinary talents, the Bible to reflect her piety, or as a more general indication that she is an educated as well as an inspired "native genius."

A frontispiece depicting an eighteenth-century black woman capable of writing poetry had revolutionary implications. Several elements in the frontispiece, however, seem designed to limit those implications. The artistic quality of Wheatley's frontispiece is as modest as her social status.[41] The frontispiece emphasizes Wheatley's African heritage and her inferior social status by containing her likeness within an oval whose framing words appear to restrict the extent of her gaze. The Countess of Huntingdon obviously had no objection to Susanna Wheatley's request that Phillis "should be dress'd plain," as befit her condition. The dark string around Wheatley's neck subtly reminded viewers of her enslaved colonial status. Slaves in earlier paintings were conventionally depicted wearing collars "to signifie whose Servant" they were.[42] The string also recalls the common association during the period of favored slaves and collared pets.[43]

The text of Wheatley's *Poems* opens with a series of documents intended to authorize and authenticate her achievement: a preface, a letter from John Wheatley to the publisher, an address "To the Publick," and an "Attestation" by New England dignitaries. The preface conventionally describes Wheatley as an author who did not write for publication and who has agreed to have her poems printed "at the Importunity of many of her best, and most generous Friends." New authors traditionally denied writing for publication and often claimed that they agreed to allow their work to be published only at the urging or insistence of friends. In the dedication of her *Letters on the Improvement of the Mind*, Hester Mulso Chapone (1727–1801) tells Elizabeth [Robinson] Montagu (1720–1800) that she "never entertained a thought of appearing in public" until encouraged by Montagu's "partiality of friendship."[44] Mary [Whateley] Darwall (1738–1825) dedicated her *Original Poems on Several Occasions* to Lady Mary Leveson Gower Wrottesley (1717–78). She assures her patron that "The following Poems (if they may be called such) were the Amusements of Youth, Leisure, and Solitude; written without any Intention of being made public."[45]

The full title of Wheatley's book would have indicated to prospective buyers that it was her first.[46] Wheatley's title also signaled to her readers that the volume contained juvenilia—works composed before she became an adult—that critics should judge leniently. Authors and publishers were occasionally even more direct than Wheatley and Bell in seeking readers' generosity in judging a book's contents. The preface to Joseph Brown Ladd's (1764–86) *Poems of Arouet* (Charleston, South Carolina, 1786) makes the conventional disclaimer explicit: "Many things in this collection are *Juvenilia*—They appear to have been hastily written, and destitute of Limae labour [laborious literary polish]."[47] Wheatley was well aware of the convention and consequently knew how useful a distinguished patron could be for a new author. She wrote to the Countess of Huntingdon on 27 July 1773, "I conclude with thanking your Ladyship for permitting the Dedication of my Poems to you; and am not insensible, that, under the patronage of your Ladyship, not more eminent in the Station of Life than in your exemplary Piety and Virtue, my feeble efforts will be Shielded from the Severe trials of unpitying Criticism and, being encourage'd by your Ladyship's Indulgence, I the more freely resign to the world these Juvenile productions." Wheatley's poems were indeed "Juvenile productions," on which her subsequent reputation largely rests: she wrote all of the works in her *Poems on Various Subjects, Religious and Moral* while she was still an adolescent. Perhaps only Alexander Pope and John Keats (1795–1821) would still be considered major poets if judged by their juvenilia alone.

Archibald Bell used the address "To the Publick" that prefaces Wheatley's *Poems* in his London newspaper advertisements for her book during September 1773. The book added the attestation of Boston worthies. The honourable ("The Hon.") names on the list were members of the governing council of the colony of Massachusetts, followed by the gentlemen ("Esq;"), ministers who were doctors of divinity ("D.D."), and other clergymen. In retrospect, the signers seem to represent an improbable combination of religious denominations, political positions, and views on slavery. But in 1772 those categories had not yet become as divisive as they soon would be. Many of them were related to each other by blood or marriage. It is very unlikely that the attesters made Wheatley undergo an oral examination to convince them that she was capable of writing the poems to be published under her name.[48] Such an examination would have been unnecessary. Most of the men named in the "Attestation" had demonstrable direct as well as indirect ties to Phillis Wheatley herself. They already had ample evidence of her abilities. By 1773 many of them were also the recipients, addressees, or subjects of her writings. Phillis Wheatley was the nexus linking these disparate men to each other.

The "Attestation" included the politically and socially most powerful and eminent men in the colony. Thomas Hutchinson was governor of Massachusetts from 1771 to 1774, when he fled to England in the face of rising colonial opposition. Lieutenant-Governor Andrew Oliver was Hutchinson's brother-in-law. Wheatley wrote a poem on the death of Oliver's wife in March 1773. She had also earlier written poems on the deaths of Thomas Hubbard's son-in-law and daughter. John Erving (1728–1816) was a prominent Boston merchant, whose daughter married James Bowdoin (1726–90), a politician and statesman (he became governor of Massachusetts in 1785, and Bowdoin College would be named after him). Bowdoin was probably the author of "A REBUS. BY I.B.," the only poem by an author other than Wheatley that she included in her *Poems*. Wheatley would later address her unpublished "On the Capture of General Lee" to Bowdoin. Bowdoin's sister was married to James Pitts (1710–76). Harrison Gray (1711?–94), an important merchant, was actively opposed to slavery. Another important merchant, and one of Boston's major slave owners, John Hancock is most famous for his signature on the Declaration of Independence. Richard Cary wrote letters to the Countess of Huntingdon on 25 May 1772 and on 3 April and 3 May 1773, praising Phillis Wheatley. Wheatley carried a letter from him to the countess on her trip to England. Joseph Green (1705?–80) was a merchant (distiller) as well as a poet who owned one of the largest personal libraries in Boston.

The most popular and influential clergymen in Boston, representing a range of denominations, also signed the "Attestation."[49] Mather Byles, a Congregational minister, was also well known as a wit and poet. He and Joseph Green were good friends. Charles Chauncy, the minister of the First Unitarian Church and a writer on religious subjects, opposed the emotional style of Whitefield's preaching. Ebenezer Pemberton was minister of the Congregational New Brick Church in the North End. When he published his sermon in London in 1771 on the death of Whitefield, Pemberton appended to it Wheatley's previously published elegy. Andrew Eliot, minister of the Congregational New North Church, was an outspoken opponent of slavery. Samuel Cooper had baptized Wheatley in 1771, and she would publish an elegy on his death in 1784. Samuel Mather was Cotton Mather's son, Governor Hutchinson's son-in-law, Mather Byles's cousin, and Hannah Mather Crocker's father. Mather was the minister of the Tenth Congregational Church. John Moorhead (1703–73), minister of the Federal Street Presbyterian Church, was either the owner or employer of Scipio Moorhead. John Moorhead's wife, Sarah (1712–74), was a well-known Boston art teacher, who may have instructed Scipio Moorhead. Wheatley would publish an elegy addressed to Reverend Moorhead's daughter on the death of her father in December 1773.

The production of Wheatley's *Poems* was carefully planned. Several of the arguably anti-British poems advertised in the 1772 subscription proposal are not included in the 1773 volume, which was published against a background of rapidly growing tensions between Britain and its North American colonies. Many of the occasional poems advertised in 1772 were given more general titles in 1773, better suited to a London audience unfamiliar with the particular Bostonians addressed or mentioned in them. Changes in the titles of the elegies emphasized more strongly than before that the subject of the poems was the theological insignificance of mortality rather than the social significance of the particular persons who had died. As one critic notes, the changes made between the 1772 "Proposals" and the 1773 book, particularly the addition of poems on classical topics, were apparently intended to transform "[t]he local prodigy of Boston" into "an accomplished woman of letters" who deserved to be published in London.[50]

The title of Wheatley's book was appropriate for a work intended to display a new poet's talents in various forms of verse, including hymns, elegies, translations, philosophical poems, tales, and epyllions (short epics). The range of forms allowed her to display both her familiarity with tradition and her unique contribution to it. For example, Wheatley's inclusion of the epyllion "Goliath of Gath" in her *Poems* acknowledges epic poetry as the most esteemed and challenging poetic genre and the Bible as the most prestigious source of narrative subjects. Wheatley's title, however, masks the epyllion's true hero, David. As an enslaved black woman poet entering the commercial publishing market, Wheatley was understandably drawn to a story that revealed true strength underlying apparent weakness and demonstrated confidence beneath professed diffidence. Unlike the overly masculine "monster" Goliath, "[o]f fierce Deportment, and gigantic frame," who mistakenly relies on his own physical strength, David is a relatively feminized hero, a "stripling," "in youthful bloom," who has "left the flow'ry meads, / And soft recesses of the sylvan shades," and who relies on faith in God for his moral strength. Wheatley may even have been consciously writing within the tradition of associating powerful women with David, traceable to the Renaissance iconography surrounding Queen Elizabeth.[51]

Wheatley balanced biblical subjects with classical ones.[52] Almost exactly equal in length to "Goliath of Gath" is "Niobe in Distress for Her Children slain by Apollo, from *Ovid*'s Metamorphoses, Book VI. and from a view of the Painting of Mr. *Richard Wilson.*" Richard Wilson (1714–82), best known for his landscapes, based at least three paintings on the tale of Niobe and her children. Wheatley probably saw one of Wilson's paintings — perhaps *The Destruction of Niobe's Children* — or more likely an engraving after it while she was in England.[53] Ovid (43 B.C.–17 A.D.) composed his unconventional fifteen-book epic, *Metamorphoses*, around 8 A.D. Characteristically assuming a humble persona—"Muse! Lend thy aid, nor let me sue in vain, / Tho' last and meanest of the rhyming train! (ll. 7–8)—Wheatley imitates Ovid's tale of an arrogant mother whose "love too vehement hastens to destroy / Each blooming maid, and each celestial boy" (ll. 35–36). Doing so allows her to contrast God's providence demonstrated in "Goliath of Gath" and the consolations of Christianity found in her elegies with the arbitrariness of pagan deities.[54]

Many of the works in Wheatley's *Poems* that were apparently written after she published her 1772 "Proposals" deal with philosophical and belletristic subjects that would appeal to a general audience: "Thoughts on the Works of Providence," "An Hymn to the Morning," "An Hymn to the Evening," "On Recollection," "On Imagination," and "An Hymn to Humanity."[55] Most of these poems significantly contain theistic but not specifically Christian elements, allowing Wheatley to include classical allusions in poems designed to appeal philosophically and aesthetically to the widest possible readership. Wheatley's references in these works to her ethnicity and enslaved status are subdued and indirect. For example, the speaker in "On Recollection" refers to herself as a "vent'rous *Afric*" (l. 2) without further comment on her origin. Readers of "On Imagination" are presumably expected to note the contrast between the "silken fetters" (l. 11) and "soft captivity" (l. 12) imposed by "roving *Fancy*" (l. 9) and the harsh reality of chattel slavery.[56] Not surprisingly, these were the works most often cited and quoted by the earliest reviewers of Wheatley's *Poems on Various Subjects, Religious and Moral*.[57]

The volume's introductory poem, "To Maecenas," appropriately thanks her patron for his support, loosely imitating works by the Roman poets Horace (65–8 B.C.) and Virgil (70–19 B.C.). Horace begins his *Odes, Epodes, Satires,* and *Epistles* with poems addressed to Maecenas (d.8 B.C.), an extremely wealthy and politically powerful friend and patron of Virgil as well as Horace. Maecenas is also the dedicatee of Virgil's *Georgics*. Maecenas had long been proverbial as the greatest patron of poets. John Wheatley and Mather Byles have been suggested as Wheatley's patron, "Maecenas." The reference to *"Thames"* in the stanza's opening line, however, clearly suggests that the dedicatee is English. A more appropriate and likely candidate for "Maecenas," despite being a woman, is the dedicatee of Wheatley's *Poems*: the Countess of Huntingdon. Only in the poem's concluding stanza is "Maecenas" explicitly gendered male when the poem's speaker addresses him as "great Sir" and solicits "paternal rays" of protection. The closing request that "Maecenas" "defend my lays" echoes the hope Wheatley expressed in her 27 July 1773 letter to the countess that through her patronage "my feeble efforts will be shielded from the severe trials of unpitying Criticism." As an aristocratic widow, Huntingdon had virtually all the authority and power of a man. With no classical models of female patrons available to her, Wheatley's decision to address the countess in the guise of a male would be understandable and a fitting way for her to assert the proper places of her own and Huntingdon's individual talents as a poet and her patron in male-dominated traditions.

"Maecenas" enables Wheatley to claim a place in the Western literary tradition, which has included Africans since its beginning. Wheatley notes that the classical Roman playwright Terence (195/185–159 B.C.) had been born in Africa:

> The happier *Terence** all the choir inspir'd,
> His soul replenish'd, and his bosom fir'd;
> But say, ye *muses*, why this partial grace,

To one alone of *Afric*'s sable race;
From age to age transmitting thus his name
With the first glory in the rolls of fame? (ll. 37–42)

*He was an *African* by birth. [Wheatley's note]

Wheatley's footnote implies that Terence was of sub-Saharan birth. Doing so allows her to implicitly draw further parallels between his life and hers. Although Terence's ethnonym, Afer, indicates that he had been born in Africa, his birthplace was probably in North Africa, most likely in the area of either modern-day Tunisia or Libya. Terence was brought as a slave to Rome, where his owner had him educated and was so impressed by his talents that he set him free. Thomas Jefferson (1743–1826) recognized that a sub-Saharan Terence would disprove the proslavery argument that black people lacked intellectual abilities. Hence, although Jefferson acknowledged that Terence was a slave, he insisted that he was "of the race of whites."[58] The speaker in Wheatley's poem challenges the assumption that "partial [i.e., biased] grace" granted poetic inspiration to Terence "alone of *Afric*'s sable race."

Wheatley's invocation of her African predecessor marks a turning point in the poem. Humility in the face of the epic achievements of Homer and Virgil had earlier rendered the speaker mute:

But here I sit, and mourn a grov'ling mind,
That fain would mount, and ride upon the wind

. . . .

But I less happy, cannot raise the song,
The fault'ring music dies upon my tongue. (ll. 29–30, 35–36)

The speakers in other Wheatley poems repeatedly and quite conventionally characterize themselves as "[t]he languid muse in low degree" ("An Hymn to Humanity," l. 26) or the "last [newest] and meanest [lowest in social rank] of the rhyming train" ("Niobe in Distress for Her Children," l. 8). But such characterizations are belied by Wheatley's assumption of the role of *"Afric's* muse" (l. 31) in the former poem, by the publication of her *Poems*, and by her efforts to sell the book in America. The precedent set by the African Terence inspires the African speaker in "To Maecenas" to "snatch a laurel" (l. 46) as well.

Wheatley returned to Boston before she had the chance to savor the excitement of the publication and reception of her book. No doubt in part because of Huntingdon's patronage and protection, Wheatley's *Poems* was quickly, widely, and generally favorably (although usually somewhat patronizingly) reviewed in nine British periodicals. Many of the reviews included exemplary poems from the collection. Before reproducing the text of "To Maecenas," the anonymous writer in the *Critical Review* notes that "[t]he Negroes of Africa are generally treated as a dull, ignorant, and ignoble race of men, fit only to be slaves, and incapable of any considerable attainments in the liberal arts and sciences." Wheatley is a "literary phaenomenon" because "[t]here are several lines in this piece, which would be no discredit to an English poet. The whole is indeed extraordinary, considered as the production of a young Negro, who was, but a few years since, an illiterate barbarian."[59] The anonymous critic in the *London Magazine* included Wheatley's "Hymn to the Morning" to vindicate his assessment that "These poems display no astonishing power of genius; but when we consider them as the productions of a young untutored African . . . we cannot suppress our admiration of talents so vigorous and lively. We are the more surprised too, as we find her verses interspersed with the poetical names of the ancients, which she has in every instance used with strict propriety."[60]

Political considerations also affected literary judgments. In the *Gentleman's Magazine*, Richard Gough (1735–1809) reprinted "On Recollection" and laments that "Youth, innocence, and piety, united with genius, have not yet been able to restore her to the condition and character with which she was invested by the Great Author of her being. So powerful is custom in rendering the heart insensible to the rights of nature, and the claims of excellence."[61] Although the anonymous commentator in the *Monthly Review* acknowledges that Wheatley "has written many good lines, and now and then one of superior character," his judgment of her works as a whole is harsh: "The poems written by this young negro bear no endemial [endemic] marks of solar fire or spirit" because "[t]hey are merely imitative; and, indeed, most of those people have a turn for imitation, though they have little or none for invention." He is nonetheless "much concerned to find that this ingenious young woman is yet a slave. The people of Boston boast themselves chiefly on their principles of liberty. One such act as the purchase of her freedom, would, in our opinion, have done them more honour than hanging a thousand trees with ribbons and emblems."[62] By the time Phillis Wheatley was able to read the reviews and see a copy of the book itself, she was free.

Chapter 5

"A Farewell to America"

Wheatley went to England with her master's son ostensibly to recover her health and to find a British publisher for her collected poems. She may have had another reason as well, one she was not likely to have shared with her owners. Wheatley reached London on the eve of the first anniversary of a landmark legal decision against colonial slave owners. In 1771 Granville Sharp (1735–1813) had brought the *Somerset* case before the King's Bench, the highest common law court in England. Lord Chief Justice William Murray (1705–93), 1st Earl of Mansfield, ruled in June 1772 that a slave brought to England from the colonies could not legally be forced to return to the colonies as a slave. Mansfield's ruling made London a very dangerous place for any colonial slave owner to bring his human property.

Greater London was the cultural and economic, as well as political capital of the transatlantic British empire. It was by far the largest and most important city in the Western Hemisphere. Although Anglo-American populations can only be roughly estimated before the official decennial censuses began in the United States (in 1790) and in Britain (in 1801), the relative size of London was undeniable. Its mid-eighteenth-century population of around 675,000 grew to approximately 900,000 by the first census. The next-largest European city, Paris, had about 500,000 people in 1750. The English towns of Manchester, Liverpool, and Birmingham each had less than 10 percent of London's population. The largest city in British North America, Philadelphia, had around twenty thousand inhabitants at mid-century. For generations, observers had likened the relationship of London to England to an oversized head on the national body. Between 1750 and 1801 London was home to over 10 percent of the total population of England and Wales, which grew from nearly six to almost nine million. By one authoritative calculation, more than one in six eighteenth-century English people spent at least part of his or her life in London.[1] Most of the population lived and worked in Greater, or outer, London. The City of London, the "City within the walls," had a population in the late eighteenth century of around seventy thousand relatively wealthy residents living in a one-mile-square area. "The City" still refers to the small area bounded by the Thames River on the south, the Tower of London on the east, the Inns of Court on the west, and the London Wall (roughly the present-day Barbican) on the north. Most of Greater London was in the county of Middlesex, which surrounded the City of London. With its own Lord Mayor and local government, the City was the financial and commercial center of Greater London; Westminster was the administrative center of Great Britain. Samuel Johnson was not the only Englishman who believed that "when a man is tired of London, he is tired of life; for there is in London all that life can afford."[2] Works published in London were likely to be distributed throughout the empire.

For Americans visiting London for the first time the experience was usually a combination of excitement, wonder, danger, and confusion. Rev. Occom recorded some of his first impressions in his journal on 10 February 1766: "last Sabbath Evening I walk'd . . . to Cary a letter to my Lord Dartmouth and Saw Such Confusion as I never Dreamt of—there was Some at Churches Singing & Preaching, in the Streets some Cursing, Swaring & Damning one another, others was hollowing, Whestling, talking giggling, & laughing, & Coaches and footmen passing and repassing, Crossing and Cross-Crossing, and the poor Begars Praying, Crying, and Beging upon their knees."[3] Ebenezer Hazard (1744–1817) described London to his friend Benjamin Rush back in Philadelphia on 10 November 1770:

London is "a wonderful Place" indeed, it is "of itself a little World." I wish I could communicate to you my Feelings on my first Arrival. . . . Next Morning, after putting on my best Bib & Apron, I was so confused that I scarcely knew how to proceed or what to do; I felt as I had never felt before, but recollecting myself a little, I enquired the way to Leaden-Hall Street, & having rec^d the necessary Information, went to seek my Fortune. You would have laughed to see me walk the Streets of London: I walked as I had used to do at New York, but was soon convinced I was in an Error, for half a dozen busy Mortals on whose Brow sat Care, & in whose Face was Eagerness, had like to run over me: I quickened my Pace, & was very near being knocked on the Head by a Porter with a heavy Load; in short I met with many Difficulties: at last, however, I got safe to Leaden Hall Street.

Hazard's London, however, was also "this Sink of Sin": "I had not the least Idea of any human Being so absolutely void of all Sense of Modesty & Shame, & so entirely addicted to the *Lust of the Flesh*, as the '*Ladies of the Strand*.' They are the greatest Monsters I ever saw & devilishly impudent. The Street is lined with them every night from Charing Cross to St. Paul's: it is absolutely dangerous for a Man to walk through Fleet Street, after 10 OClock."[4]

When Wheatley arrived in Hazard's "Sink of Sin" she joined the thousands of blacks already resident in England.[5] The estimated number of people of African descent living in England during the last quarter of the eighteenth century ranges from five to twenty thousand.[6] Eighteenth-century terminology complicates any attempt at precision. Since *black* referred to complexion and hair color, as well as to geographical origin, people from the Indian subcontinent as well as North American Indians were often called black. The social and legal status of many of the various peoples called black in eighteenth-century England is also murky. As in New England, domestic workers in Britain were referred to as servants, whether paid or not, so identifying the slaves among them is often impossible now. The condition of many blacks in Britain was somewhere between enslaved and free, earning them "neither wages nor the whip," as one historian puts it.[7] Another classifies them as "slave-servants" to reflect their ambiguous status.[8]

The exact number of people of African descent living in eighteenth-century England will never be known, since ethnicity was not systematically recorded during the period. Records of infant baptisms rarely indicated color or ethnic origins, though records of noninfant baptisms often did. Eighteenth-century marriage records frequently are silent on ethnicity. The record of the marriage of Ignatius (1729?–80) and Anne (1733–1817) Sancho does not say that they were both of African descent. We know that fact from external sources. Nor could we tell Sancho's ethnicity from the votes he cast as a property owner in two Westminster elections for members of Parliament.

During the seventeenth century, black servants were often relatively expensive signs of conspicuous consumption and imperial connections. They were exotic products from the colonies that only the wealthy could afford at first. Black boys and men were especially desired as butlers and valets in wealthy and socially pretentious households because those roles brought them into frequent contact with the public. Black servants retained their appeal as status symbols through the eighteenth century: Equiano's first English owner bought him as a present for his cousins; Ignatius Sancho was the butler of the Duke of Montagu (1690–1749); Quobna Ottobah Cugoano was the servant of Richard Cosway (1742–1821), Principal Painter to the Prince of Wales. In 1772 the former Jamaica magistrate and legislator Edward Long complained that black servants in Britain were "more for ostentation than any *laudable* use."[9] Like other originally luxurious colonial products, such as coffee, tea, and tobacco, black people were also found in much humbler situations by the end of the eighteenth century. The prints of William Hogarth (1697–1764) and others show that by the middle third of the century blacks were found at all levels of society, including among the poor. Many of the people of African descent living in England before the 1780s had arrived there as seamen from North America and the Caribbean. Black seamen were discharged in England along with their white shipmates after service with the Royal Navy, or after having worked as sailors on merchant vessels. Equiano and his fellow black writers Briton Hammon, James Albert Ukawsaw Gronniosaw, and John Marrant are the best-known examples of former seamen of African descent. Blacks were conspicuous at every level of society because of their complexion.

The far greater demand for black male servants than for black female servants, as well as the number of black seamen, led to a gender imbalance in the black community in England. Consequently, black male/white female couples were more common than the reverse. Such couples were occasionally noted, but only very rarely condemned. There is no evidence, for example, that Equiano's marriage in 1792 to an Englishwoman led to any discrimination against him, his wife, or their two daughters.

The legal status of slavery in England was disputed throughout the eighteenth century. Slaves brought to England from the colonies took advantage of the uncertain status of slavery there even before the Mansfield ruling. The magistrate Sir John Fielding (1721–80) complained in 1768 that slaves brought to London from the West Indies

> no sooner arrive here, than they put themselves on a Footing with other Servants, become intoxicated with Liberty, grow refractory, and either by Persuasion of others, or from their own Inclinations, begin

to expect Wages according to their own Opinion of their Merits. . . . [T]here are already a great Number of black Men and Women who have made themselves so troublesome and dangerous to the Families who brought them over as to get themselves discharged; they enter into Societies, and make it their Business to corrupt and dissatisfy the Mind of every fresh black Servant that comes to *England*; first, by getting them christened or married, which they inform them makes them free (tho' it has been adjudged by our most able Lawyers, that neither of these Circumstances alter the Master's Property in a Slave). However it so far answers their Purpose, that it gets the Mob on their Side, and makes it not only difficult but dangerous to the Proprietor of these Slaves to recover the Possession of them, when once they are spirited away.[10]

Cugoano mentions that when his owner brought him to England from the West Indies at the end of 1772, after Mansfield rendered his ruling, "I was advised by some good people to get myself baptized that I might not be carried away and sold again" (7). Any slave coming from the colonies to England in 1773 would understandably be "intoxicated with Liberty" to discover a society without the colonial laws and curfews discriminating against people of African descent, and one in which a slave could in effect free herself by running away from her owner and refusing to return to the colonies.

Phillis Wheatley's own experience in England astonished her. A little more than a month after she returned to Boston she wrote to David "Worcester" [Wooster] (1711–1777) in New Haven, Connecticut, on 18 October 1773, to tell him about her trip. Members of English high society welcomed her "with such kindness[,] Complaisance, and so many marks of esteem and real Friendship as astonishes me on the reflection." Wheatley told Wooster that she had toured much of greater eighteenth-century London—from Westminster in the west to the City of London in the east, Greenwich in the south, and Sadler's Wells in the north. She saw the Observatory, Park, and Royal Hospital for Seamen in Greenwich, as well as the Tower of London and Westminster Abbey. Although her visit to Westminster brought her within blocks of where Ignatius Sancho was living, they never met. She could not have met Olaudah Equiano during the "no more than 6 weeks" she was in England because he was on a voyage seeking a northeast passage over the North Pole to Asia.

Phillis Wheatley's new friends took her to an impressive number of tourist attractions. Almost all the places she visited were (and still are) included in standard tourist guides to London, such as the contemporaneous *Companion to Every Place of Curiosity and Entertainment in and about London and Westminster.*[11] She arrived in London just after the fashionable season, which ended on 4 June, George III's birthday. Consequently, the Drury Lane and Covent Garden theaters were closed. But less reputable venues were available, and they understandably dazzled the young woman from the colonies who had never before seen a performance on stage. Wheatley attended the light entertainment at Sadler's Wells, where "various pleasing and surprising Performances in LADDER DANCING," as well as the "new Entertainment of Music and Dancing, call'd VINEYARD REVELS; Or, HARLEQUIN BACCHANAL" were staged during her stay in London.[12] Among the "too many things & Places to trouble" Wooster with "in a Letter" may have been a performance of the musical comedy *The Padlock* by Charles Dibdin (1745–1814), which was playing at the Hay-Market theater while she was in town. Dibdin performed in blackface the role of Mungo, the wily servant-hero of the play, the most famous comic black figure in eighteenth-century drama.

Phillis went to the British Museum, which allowed very few members of the public to view its collections of natural history, antiquities, manuscripts, and books. She also visited Cox's Museum, "the most elegant of eighteenth-century London exhibitions in respect to both contents and clientele."[13] Located next to present-day Admiralty Arch, the museum opened by the jeweler James Cox (ca. 1723–1800) at the beginning of 1772 was the talk of the town for the next three years because of its precious jewels, metals, and curios designed by such artists as Joseph Nollekens (1737–1823) and Johann Zoffany (1733–1810). Its contents were valued at the astounding sum of £197,000, equivalent to approximately £16 million or $26.4 million in today's money. Someone other than Phillis presumably paid the 10 shillings, 6 pence (equivalent today to about £40 or $66) for her admission ticket to Cox's Museum, as well as the smaller fees to see the paintings displayed in the great hall of the Royal Hospital in Greenwich, and the charge to visit the Tower of London, with its collections of armor, jewels, and animals from all over the world. What may she have thought of "Phillis," one of "two ravenous wolves from Saxony" in the Tower?[14] For many of the people Phillis Wheatley met while she was in London, a pious, enslaved, teenaged, female poet of African descent from the colonies must have seemed as much a curiosity as anything they would have paid to see in Cox's Museum or the Tower.

Phillis found liberation from her accustomed status, duties, and regimen exhilarating. She spent her time in London very differently from the early-to-bed, early-to-rise schedule followed in the home of a successful Boston merchant. The social circle she travelled in while she was in London normally ate breakfast at 10:00 a.m., dinner (lunch) between 2:00 and 4:30 p.m., and supper between 10:00 and 11:00 p.m. Social calls were made between breakfast and dinner. Treated like an exotic visiting celebrity, Wheatley "Was introduced to Lord Dartmouth and had near half an hour's conversation with his Lordship, with whom was Alderman Kirkman.—Then to Lord Lincoln, who visited me at my own Lodgings with the Famous Dr. Solander, who accompany'd Mr. Banks in his late expedition round the World." John Kirkman (1741–80), a silk merchant, was an alderman of the City of London from 1768 to 1780. Lord Lincoln, a courtesy title for Henry Fiennes Pelham Clinton (1750–78), was a Member of Parliament for Aldborough in 1772–74 and a supporter of the North ministry. He was styled Lord Lincoln because he was the eldest son of Henry Fiennes Pelham Clinton (1720–94), whose highest title had been the 9th Earl of Lincoln until he succeeded his uncle Thomas Pelham-Holles (1693–1768) in 1768 as 2nd Duke of Newcastle. Dr. Daniel Solander (1736–82) was a Swedish-born botanist who accompanied Sir Joseph Banks (1743–1820) as a researcher in the South Pacific from 1768 to 1771, aboard the *Endeavor*, commanded by Captain James Cook (1728–79). Solander became keeper of the natural history collections in the British Museum in 1773.[15]

Others Phillis met in London included Israel Mauduit (1708–87), who had represented governor Hutchinson as his private agent in London since 1771.[16] Brook Watson (1735–1807), a future Lord Mayor of London, was a prominent London merchant who had spent much of his youth in Boston and Nova Scotia before returning to London in 1759. His loss of a leg to a shark in Havana in 1749 would become the subject of a famous and controversial painting by John Singleton Copley (1738–1815) in 1778. Lady Cavendish and Lady Carteret Webb, sisters, were followers of the Countess of Huntingdon. Mary (Reynolds) Palmer (1716–94) was the sister of the famous painter Sir Joshua Reynolds (1723–92). Dr. Thomas Gibbons was a dissenting minister who taught rhetoric at the Mile End Academy. He had published *Juvenalia: Poems on Various Subjects of Devotion and Virtue*

(London, 1750) and a Latin poem on the death of Whitefield in 1771. He was a member of Dartmouth's social and religious circles. Gibbons, who had met Occom during his visit to London in 1766, recorded his meeting with Wheatley on Thursday, 15 July 1773: "Was visited this Morning by Phillis Wheatley a Negro young Woman from Boston in New England A Person of fine Genius, and very becoming Behaviour."[17]

Wheatley did not tell Wooster that during her brief London trip she had also visited the ailing statesman and man of letters Baron George Lyttelton (1709–73), who died the month after she left for America. Nor did she mention any plan to have met King George III. According to Margaretta Matilda Odell, great grandniece of Susanna Wheatley, Phillis was to have been presented to the King, but her mistress's illness intervened. Odell's claim is plausible. Occom "Saw the King" and had the "Pleasure of Seeing him put on his Royal Robes and Crown" during his own trip to London in 1766.[18] Phillis Wheatley also failed to mention to Wooster that she had spent part of her stay in London in the home of John Thornton. Thornton later wrote to a friend in York that "Phillis the African Girl . . . was over lately from Boston & staid with me about a Week[.] [S]he has surprising natural parts & they are sanctified by Grace, that she is indeed a prodigy, she was brot [sic] to Boston in 1761 being betwixt 7 & 8[,] & has been a Slave in a Family at that place ever since & with but little aid she has made an uncommon progress in Learning, writes an uncommon good hand, understands Latin[,] is conversant wth Scripture[,] very humble & teachable." Thornton was concerned that the adulation Wheatley received in London would make her sinfully proud. After she returned to Boston he sent her a "friendly hint" regarding her "present situation & the kindness you met with from many good people & the respect that is paid to your uncommon Genius. . . . I have no reason to charge you with any indiscretions of this kind. I mean only to apprize you of the danger I feared for you when here, lest the notice many took of you should prove a Snare."[19]

Of the people Phillis Wheatley met in London, Benjamin Franklin (1706–90) is today the best known. He had been representing the colonial interests of Pennsylvania, Georgia, New Jersey, and Massachusetts in London since July 1757 and would return to America in 1775. He visited Wheatley and offered her his services at the prompting of Jonathan Williams, his nephew-in-law in Boston. Phillis's owners had encouraged Williams to mention Phillis in his letters to his uncle. On 7 July 1773 Franklin described his meeting with Phillis to Williams: "Upon your Recommendation I went to see the black Poetess and offer'd her any Services I could do her. Before I left the House, I understood her Master was there and had sent her to me but did not come into the Room himself, and I thought was not pleased with the Visit. I should perhaps have enquired first for him, but I had heard nothing of him. And I have heard nothing since of her." Nathaniel Wheatley was probably almost as much of an oddity in England as Phillis. New Englanders rarely visited London, and they were generally viewed as much less sophisticated and far more mercenary than other British Americans.[20] Phillis's master may have seemed to Franklin to exemplify Edmund Burke's characterization of New Englanders as "a mean shifting peddling nation."[21] In light of Nathaniel Wheatley's uncivil behavior towards Franklin, Williams responded on 17 October 1773, "The Black Poetess master and mistress prevailed on me to mention her in my Letter but as its turned out I am Sorry I Did."[22]

Like many of his white contemporaries on both sides of the Atlantic, Franklin initially accepted both slavery and the transatlantic slave trade. For years before meeting Phillis Wheatley, Franklin's attitudes toward both the transatlantic slave trade and the institution of slavery were ambivalent, and they continued to be so until just before his death.[23] By 1773 Franklin had been a slave owner for decades, even though he had printed antislavery writings while living in Philadelphia, including one of the earliest antislavery arguments published in America. He also published advertisements for runaway slaves in his *Pennsylvania Gazette*, and in 1731 and 1732 he advertised his own slaves for sale: "To be sold: A likely Negro wench about fifteen years old and talks English. Inquire of the printer hereof. A breeding Negro woman about twenty years of age. Can do any household work." Franklin supported the establishment in America of schools for blacks, and he sent his own slaves to the school in Philadelphia. As the agent in London representing the economic interests of the originally slave-free colony of Georgia, after 1750 Franklin defended the colony's right to have slaves. Franklin's strong objections to slavery in 1751 in "Observations on the Increase of Mankind" were based on economic rather than moral grounds. In his will, written in 1757, Franklin granted his slaves freedom at his death, but he continued to own slaves until 1781. Franklin argued in the "Conversation on Slavery" he published anonymously in 1770 that slavery in North America was uncommon and benign. He likened the English "working poor" to slaves in the way their employers treated them. And he demeaned enslaved blacks in America: "the majority are of a plotting disposition, dark, sullen, malicious, revengeful and cruel in the highest degree."[24] Two years later marked a turning point in Franklin's moral development. In April 1772 the Philadelphia Quaker abolitionist and emancipationist Anthony Benezet (1713–84) began to correspond with Franklin. Franklin, however, did not publicly embrace and privately practice an emancipationist position opposing slavery until very late in his life. When Phillis Wheatley met Franklin, she may also have met his slave, Peter, whom he had brought with him to England. King, the other slave he had brought to England, ran away from Franklin within two years of arriving there. Franklin took Peter with him back to America in 1775, where he remained his slave.

Some of the politically and socially prominent people Wheatley met in London also gave her gifts. She tells Wooster that Dartmouth gave her "5 guineas, and desird me to get the whole of Mr. Pope's Works, as the best he could recommend to my perusal, this I did, also got Hudibrass, Don Quixot, & Gay's Fables—[I] was presented with a Folio Edition of Milton's Paradise Lost, printed on a Silver Type, so call'd from its elegance, (I suppose) By Mr. Brook Watson Mercht.[,] whose Coat of Arms is prefix'd." The books Wheatley mentions include: Alexander Pope's translations of Homer's *Iliad* and *Odyssey* and the nine volumes of Pope's own works; the translation of Cervantes' *Don Quixote* by Tobias Smollett (1721–71); *Paradise Lost* by John Milton (1608–74); *Hudibras* by Samuel Butler (1612–80); and *Fables* by John Gay (1685–1732). Wheatley does not mention to Wooster that Granville Sharp gave her a copy of his *Remarks on Several Very Important Prophecies, in Five Parts* (London, 1768) on 21 July 1773. Although *Remarks* is not one of Sharp's antislavery texts, it may not have been the only book he gave Wheatley.[25] Phillis Wheatley received a far greater gift than books and money from Sharp and others she met in England. She informed Wooster that "Since my return to America my Master, has at the desire of my friends in England given me my freedom."

The risk Nathaniel Wheatley had taken in bringing Phillis to London in 1773 was vastly increased by her primary London tour guide: "Grenville [*sic*] Sharp Esqr.[,] who attended me to the Tower [of London] & Show'd the Lions, Panthers, Tigers, &c. The Horse Armoury, Sma[ll] Armoury, the Crowns, Sceptres, Diadems, the Fount for christen[in]g the Royal Family." Granville Sharp had led the campaign to have the courts refute the unofficial 1729 opinion of Charles Talbot (1685?–1737), the solicitor general, and Philip Yorke (1690–1764), the attorney general, that slavery was legal in England.[26] Sharp sought an official court judgment declaring the *de facto* illegal status of slavery in England *de jure* as well.

Born in Durham on 19 November 1735 as the youngest son of the Archbishop of Northumberland and the grandson of the Archbishop of York, Sharp had received only a grammar-school education and was destined for a trade. While apprenticed to a Quaker linen draper in London, Sharp taught himself Greek and Hebrew to better understand the Bible. His first publications were on biblical scholarship and linguistics. In 1758 he obtained a position in the ordnance department, which he felt compelled to resign in 1776 because of his opposition to the war with the rebellious American colonies.

Sharp's introduction to the question of the legality of slavery came in 1765 in the person of Jonathan Strong, a slave aged sixteen or seventeen. Strong's master, a lawyer and planter named David Lisle, had brought him to London from Barbados. Lisle was a brutal owner. He had thrown Strong out into the street after nearly fatally pistol-whipping him. Sharp met Strong outside the house door of Sharp's brother William, who gave free medical help to the poor. Two years later, Lisle ran into Strong, now fully recovered with the medical and financial aid of the Sharps. Lisle sold Strong to James Kerr, a Jamaica planter, for £30, to be paid when Lisle delivered Strong to a ship bound for Jamaica. Lisle hired two slave catchers, who seized Strong and put him in jail. Strong sent word of his situation to Granville Sharp, who gained his release through the intervention of the Lord Mayor of London. Kerr sued Sharp for loss of property, and Lisle challenged him to a duel. When Sharp's solicitors advised him that Strong was legally a slave and thus a piece of property, he bought a complete law library to prepare himself to challenge the law. The results of Sharp's legal research intimidated the plaintiffs' lawyers so much that they declined to pursue the case.

Sharp won by default, but the experience determined him to gain a definitive legal ruling rejecting the Yorke and Talbot opinion. Sharp published his refutation of Yorke and Talbot while waiting for a suitable case. *A Representation of the Injustice and Dangerous Tendency of Tolerating Slavery; or of Admitting the Least Claim of Private Property of Men, in England* (London, 1769) also includes a denunciation of the hypocrisy of the American colonists who practiced slavery while objecting to political oppression. Sharp's intervention on Strong's behalf quickly became well known in London's African-British community. His aid was sought in the cases of the kidnapped former slaves Mary Hylas in 1766 and Thomas Lewis in 1770. Both were physically and legally rescued through Sharp's efforts. But neither case resulted in the definitive ruling Sharp sought against the institution of slavery. He did not have to wait long for the case he wanted.

In London in 1771 the slave James Somerset (c. 1741–72?) ran away from his master, Charles Stewart, or Steuart, a high-ranking colonial customs official, whose responsibilities covered the Atlantic coast of North America from Quebec to Virginia. Somerset had been enslaved in Africa and brought to Virginia, where Stewart bought him on 1 August 1749. Stewart brought Somerset from Massachusetts to England in November 1769. He was baptized James Summersett at St. Andrew's church, Holborn, on 10 February 1771. Somerset fled from Stewart on 1 October 1771. Stewart recaptured Somerset on 26 November 1771 and intended to send him out of the country on a ship bound for Jamaica under the command of captain John Knowles. Sharp immediately took action when members of London's black community brought word of Somerset's situation to him. Sharp and several others successfully urged Mansfield to issue a writ of habeas corpus ordering the captain to bring Somerset before the court two days after he had been recaptured. Sharp convinced several lawyers to argue Somerset's case free of charge. The inexperienced Francis Hargrave (1741–1821), who wrote an influential account of his defense and went on to a distinguished legal career, also volunteered his legal services on behalf of Somerset.

All interested parties anticipated Mansfield's ruling in favor of Somerset. Samuel Estwick (1736–96) predicted dire consequences in his proslavery *Considerations on the Negroe Cause Commonly So Called*. He warned that were "the decision [to] be in favour of the Negroe . . . the knowledge of their being free might spirit them up to insurrections in America, yet it would put a stop to their importation [into England] by their owners, and they should be more usefully kept and employed in the colonies to which they belonged."[27] Estwick was living in England at the time as the assistant agent for Barbados, representing the interests of the colony's slave-owning planter class. Franklin also anticipated Mansfield's ruling. He nearly endorsed Benezet's argument against slavery itself, as well as against the transatlantic slave trade. Franklin posed as a Quaker to point out anonymously in the *London Chronicle* on 20 June 1772 that Britain's expected self-congratulatory response to a decision in Somerset's favor would not be fully justified. Americans did not have a monopoly on hypocrisy when the subject was slavery: *"Pharisaical Britain!* To pride thyself in setting free *a single Slave* that happens to land on thy coasts, while thy Merchants in all thy ports are encouraged by thy laws to continue a commerce whereby so many *hundreds of thousands* are dragged into a slavery that can scarce be said to end with their lives, since it is entailed on their posterity!"

Mansfield's attempts to get the opposing parties to settle the case out of court failed, forcing him to render his decision on 22 June 1772. He ruled that an owner could not legally force a slave in England back to the colonies.[28] Because the practice of officially recording the oral opinions delivered from the King's Bench did not begin until the nineteenth century, various accounts of Mansfield's words exist. According to the report by Capel Lofft (1751–1824), Mansfield ruled that "The state of slavery is of such a nature, that it is incapable of being introduced on any reasons, moral or political: but only positive law, which preserves its force long after the reasons, occasion, and time itself from whence it was created, is erased from memory: It's so odious, that nothing can be suffered to support it but positive law."[29]

With the *Somerset* ruling, Sharp went from winning battles to apparently winning the war against slavery in England. Mansfield's ruling technically established only that a slave could not be seized by his master and forced against his will to leave England, and that a slave could get a writ of habeas corpus to prevent his master's action. But the judgment was widely considered then and since as the moment slavery was abolished in England. The Mansfield ruling did not abolish slavery in England *de jure*, but it certainly undermined it *de facto* by indisputably denying slave owners the legal coercive power of removal to the colonies. Lacking that power, slave owners could no longer legally enforce their claims of possession because slaves on English soil could legally emancipate themselves by flight. Sharp made sure through his publications that the ruling's implications would not be ignored.

Friend and foe of slavery alike immediately recognized that the Mansfield decision of 1772 clearly allowed colonial slaves to emancipate themselves in England.[30] In contrast, the Declaration of Independence, signed four years later in Philadelphia, offered nothing to the nearly five hundred thousand blacks in North America, or 20 percent of the total population. (The five hundred thousand blacks in the British West Indies, more than 90 percent of the population, were unaffected by either the Mansfield ruling or the Declaration of Independence.) The popular and pamphlet press in Britian and its colonies quickly announced the ruling and discussed its possible significance. Supporters of slavery recognized that they could no longer assume that the British courts and public would continue to passively accept slavery as an institution. The former Jamaica magistrate and legislator Edward Long warned that the decision meant "that the laws of *Great Britain* do not authorize a master to reclaim his fugitive slave, confine or transport him out of the kingdom. In other words; that a Negroe slave, coming from the colonies into *Great Britain*, becomes, *ipso facto*, Free."[31]

London's African-British community greeted the Mansfield decision euphorically. The *Gentleman's Magazine* reported in its June 1772 issue:

> June 22. The Court of the King's Bench gave judgment in the case of Somerset the slave, viz. that Mr. Stuart his master had no power to compel him on board a ship, or to send him back to the plantations. Lord Mansfield stated the matter thus: The only question before us is, Is the cause returned sufficient for remanding the slave? If not, he must be discharged. The cause returned is, the slave absented himself, and departed from his master's service, and refused to return and serve him during his stay in England; whereupon, by his master's orders, he was put on board the ship by force, and there detained in secure custody, to be carried out of the kingdom, and sold. So high an act of dominion was never in use here; no master was ever allowed to take a slave by force to be sold abroad, because he had deserted from his service, or for any other reason whatever. We cannot say the cause set forth by this return is allowed or approved of by the laws of this kingdom: therefore, the man must be discharged.

The *Morning Chronicle* noted on 23 June 1772 that Mansfield's speech was "as guarded, cautious, and concise, as it could possibly be drawn up." The newspaper went on to describe the reaction of the blacks in the audience to the ruling:

> Several Negroes were in court yesterday, to hear the event of a cause so interesting to their tribe, and after the judgment of the court was known, bowed with profound respect to the Judges, and shaking each other by the hand, congratulated themselves upon the recovery of the rights of human nature, and their happy lot that permitted them to

breathe the free air of England.—No sight upon earth could be more pleasingly affecting to the feeling mind, than the joy which shone at that instant in these poor men's sable countenances.

The *Public Advertiser* reported on 25 June that black Britons expressed their gratitude more materially: "A Subscription is now raising among a great Number of Negroes, in and about this Metropolis, for the purpose of presenting Somerset with a handsome Gratuity, for having so nobly stood up in Defence of the natural Rights of the sable Part of the human Creation."

Many contemporaneous observers on both sides of the Atlantic understandably construed the Mansfield ruling as the practical implementation of the constitutional prohibition of slavery that Sir William Blackstone (1723–80) had described in his extremely influential *Commentaries on the Laws of England*.[32] Although Blackstone later qualified his statement in light of the Mansfield decision, he declared in the first edition of his *Commentaries on the Laws of England* "that a slave or negro, the instant he lands in England, becomes a freeman."[33] Blackstone's position was widely known in North America. Edmund Burke (1729–97) reported in 1775 that "I hear that they have sold nearly as many of Blackstone's Commentaries in America as in England."[34] Burke understood the Mansfield judgment to mean in 1777 that "every man putting his foot on English ground, every stranger owing only a local and temporary allegiance, even a negro slave, who had been sold in the colonies and under an act of parliament, became as free as every other man who breathed the same air with him."[35] Building on the precedent Mansfield set, in 1778 the Scottish court declared slavery illegal in Scotland. Thomas Hutchinson had been governor of Massachusetts at the time of the Mansfield ruling but fled to England after hostilities broke out. During dinner at the home of the Lord Chief Justice Mansfield on 29 August 1779, Hutchinson, now an exiled Loyalist, told his host that "all Americans who had brought Blacks [to England after the ruling] had, as far as I knew, relinquished their property in them, and rather agreed to give them wages, or suffered [allowed] them to go free." "His Ldship" responded "that there had been no determination that they were free, the judgment (meaning the case of Somerset) went no further than to determine the Master had no right to compel the slave to go into a foreign country, &c."[36]

Many Britons, especially the thousands of African descent, considered the Mansfield decision an emancipation proclamation. Advertisements for sales of slaves, notices of runaway slaves, and attempts to enforce co-lonial slave laws in Britain—all already rare in England—disappeared in the wake of Mansfield's ruling.[37] Granville Sharp's heroic status within the black community was undisputed. On 3 August 1779 Ignatius Sancho sent a copy of "Mr. Sharpe's [sic] strictures upon slavery" to a friend, telling him, "I think [it] of consequence to every one of humane feelings."[38] In an undated letter of thanks to Sharp, ten blacks described themselves to him as "those who were considered as slaves, even in England itself, till your aid and exertions set us free."[39] Quobna Ottobah Cugoano, the most radical African-British voice in the eighteenth century, celebrated the ruling in a later version of his *Thoughts and Sentiments on the Evil of Slavery* (London, 1791):

> For so it was considered as criminal, by the laws of Englishmen, when the tyrannical paw and the monster of slavery took the man [Som-erset] by the neck, in the centre of the British freedom, and thought henceforth to compel him to his involuntary subjection of slavery and oppression; it was wisely determined by some of the most eminent and learned counsellors in the land. The whole of that affair rested solely upon that humane and indefatigable friend of mankind, GREN-VILLE [sic] SHARP esq. whose name we should always mention with the greatest reverence and honor. The noble decision, thereby, before the Right Hon. Lord Chief Justice MANSFIELD, and the parts taken by the learned Counsellor HARGRAVE, are the surest proofs of the most ami-able disposition of the laws of Englishmen.[40]

Not surprisingly, by the 1770s Equiano was also aware of the role Sharp had played in the Mansfield decision and of his consequent reputation as a "well-known philanthropist" to blacks. Years before Equiano himself turned against the institution of slavery he attempted to save a fellow black from being illegally forced from England back into West Indian slavery. In early 1774, disillusioned by the behavior of "those, who in general termed themselves Christians," Equiano "determined at last to set out for Turkey, and there to end my days." He "sought for a master, and found a Captain John Hughes, commander of a ship called Anglicania, fitting out in the river Thames, and bound to Smyrna in Turkey. I shipped myself with him as a steward; at the same time I recommended to him a very clever black man, John Annis, as a cook." Annis had spent many years on the Caribbean island of St. Kitts as the slave of William Kirkpatrick, "from whom he parted by consent," before Annis went to England.[41] Unfortunately, like many other West Indian whites in Equiano's experience, Kirkpatrick was not a man of his word. On his frequent trips to England, he had paid a number of captains trading to St. Kitts to kidnap Annis and bring him back to the Caribbean. "[W]hen all their attempts and schemes of kidnapping proved abortive, Mr. Kirkpatrick came to our ship at Union-stairs,[42] on Easter Monday, April the 4th, with two wherry-boats and six men, having learned that the man was on board; and tied, and forcibly took him away from the ship, in the presence of the crew and the chief mate, who had detained him after he had information to come away." Equiano reasonably suspected that Captain Hughes and his mate conspired with Kirkpatrick in the kidnapping. They made no attempt to regain Annis's freedom. Nor did the captain agree to give Equiano the nearly five pounds in wages he owed Annis. Equiano "proved the only friend he had, who attempted to regain him his liberty, if possible, having known the want of liberty myself." As soon as he could, Equiano discovered the name of the ship his friend had been taken to downriver. Equiano successfully sought Sharp's advice, but the attorney he hired failed to act before the vessel sailed.

The Annis affair was newsworthy because Kirkpatrick's actions were clearly illegal after the recent Mansfield decision. According to an account in the 27 April 1774 issue of the *London Chronicle*, legal action was underway "to proceed against the Master; and also on the Captain's return to proceed against him for violently and by force taking a man out of the kingdom." But such actions could no longer help Annis. From "two very moving letters" by Annis, and from reports Equiano later received "by some very respectable familes, now in London," Equiano learned that "when the poor man arrived at St. Kitt's, he was, according to custom, staked to the ground with four pins through a cord, two on his wrists, and two on his ancles, was cut and flogged most unmercifully, and afterwards loaded cruelly with irons about his neck." Annis remained a slave "till kind death released him out of the hands of his tyrants."[43] Despite the Mansfield decision, blacks remained in jeopardy as long as slavery was legal in any of the British colonies, and as long as an owner was willing to risk arrest for illegally taking a black from England to the Americas.

Some colonists anticipated the application of the Mansfield judgment to America. For example, on 8 January 1774, the Loyalist Richard Wells wrote anonymously in the *Pennsylvania Packet*, "I contend, that by the laws of the English constitution, and by our *own declarations*, the instant a Negro sets his foot in America, he is as free as if he had landed in England."[44] The question of whether the Mansfield decision applied to the American colonies arose because it was rendered in the court of common law, based on the unwritten English constitution and historical precedent. It was not a ruling on a positive law that had been passed by both houses of Parliament and signed by the monarch. Unlike the colonies, England had no positive laws regarding the institution of slavery on its soil, though of course the English constitution allowed for the making of such positive laws and applying them at home and in the colonies. Blackstone explained that in the absence of any positive metropolitan law regarding slavery the distinction between "two species of colonies" authorized each colony to write its own positive law on the subject. The British-American colonies were considered "conquered or ceded countries, that have already laws of their own."[45]

The Mansfield judgment brought to public attention the legal status of people of African descent who were British yet not English. Their political status and humanity became subjects of public argument in light of the ideological conflict during the American Revolution.[46] The Mansfield ruling also called attention to the plight of people of African descent living in England. It probably helped create a transatlantic audience for Gronniosaw's spiritual autobiography, *A Narrative of the Most Remarkable Particulars in the Life of James Albert Ukawsaw Gronniosaw, an African Prince, as Related by Himself*, dedicated to the Countess of Huntingdon and first published in Bath, England, at the end of 1772. The *Narrative* was reprinted at least twelve times before 1800 on both sides of the Atlantic, including twice in Rhode Island (1774, 1781). Phillis Wheatley very likely read it during her stay in England, and its popularity probably influenced Huntingdon's decision to support the publication of Wheatley's *Poems*.

After the Mansfield ruling, Phillis Wheatley, like many of her contemporaries of African descent during the 1760s and 1770s, was understandably ambivalent about which side to identify with in the growing conflict between Britain and its North American colonies. The hypocrisy of the white North Americans who demanded liberty for themselves while they enslaved others underscored the difference between the legal statuses of African-Britons in the Mother Country and the colonies. Their hypocrisy prompted criticism by Granville Sharp and others on both sides of the

Atlantic. Benjamin Rush published the second edition of his *Address to the Inhabitants of the British Settlements* in Philadelphia by the beginning of October 1773, a few days after Phillis Wheatley's return from London. He urged his readers to press "our assemblies [to] unite in petitioning the king and parliament to dissolve the African committee of merchants," since "the Clamors of the whole nation are raised against them" in response to the Mansfield decision.[47] Wheatley sarcastically commented to Occom in 1774, "How well the Cry for Liberty, and the reverse Disposition for the Exercise of oppressive Power over others agree,—I humbly think it does not require the Penetration of a Philosopher to determine."[48]

The position of many white Americans gave their English opponents an easy opportunity to assert moral and political superiority. Samuel Johnson famously asked in 1775, "How is it we hear the loudest yelps for liberty among the drivers of Negroes?"[49] In a letter written to an American correspondent the following year Thomas Day (1748–89), the author of best-selling antislavery poetry and fiction, observes that

> Slavery . . . is a crime so monstrous against the human species that all those who practise it deserve to be extirpated from the earth. . . .
>
> If men would be consistent, they must admit all the consequences of their own principles; and you and your countrymen are reduced to the dilemma of either acknowledging the rights of your Negroes, or of surrendering your own.—If there be certain natural and universal rights, as the declarations of your Congress [including the Declaration of Independence] so repeatedly affirm, I wonder how the unfortunate Africans have incurred their forfeiture.—Is it the antiquity, or the virtues, or the great qualities of the English Americans, which constitutes the difference, and entitles them to rights from which they totally exclude more than a fourth part of the species?—Or do you choose to make use of that argument, which the great Montesquieu has thrown out as the severest ridicule, that they are black, and you white; that you have lank, long hair, while theirs is short and woolly?[50]

Paradoxically, although Britain was well on its way to becoming the most significant participant in the transatlantic slave trade, for years it had also been the promised land of freedom to slaves in British colonies, particularly those in North America. As Equiano's experiences on ships of the Royal Navy and in England demonstrated, the legal status of slavery in Britain was contested long before the American Revolution. His owner would not have felt the need to sneak Equiano out of England in 1762 had he believed he had an unquestioned right to sell him. And Equiano would not have threatened to take his owner to court in London had he not believed he had legal standing there that he knew he lacked in the British-American colonies.

It is unimaginable that while Wheatley and Sharp were looking at caged African animals, as well as the emblems of British regal glory, Sharp would not have brought up the subject of his judicial triumph the preceding year in extending British liberty to enslaved people of African descent. Sharp considered himself ethically and morally bound to help people in Wheatley's condition: "the glorious system of the gospel destroys all *narrow, national partiality*; and makes us *citizens of the world*, by obliging us to profess *universal benevolence*: but more especially are we bound, as Christians, to commiserate and assist to the utmost of our power all persons in *distress*, or *captivity*."[51] Nothing would demonstrate the significance of the Mansfield ruling more than the emancipation of the most celebrated enslaved person of African descent in the British empire. A slave owner could not have thought of a more dangerous tour guide than Granville Sharp for an enslaved celebrity newly arrived from the colonies.

But was Wheatley aware of the status of slavery in England before she reached London on 17 June 1773? Was she willing to take advantage of the opportunity that that knowledge might have offered her? The circumstantial evidence that she knew about the Mansfield ruling before she left Boston is compelling. Colonial newspapers, including ones that had advertised and published Wheatley's poems since 1767, were reporting and discussing the possible significance of the Mansfield decision by the end of the summer of 1772. In reporting news from June in London, the *Massachusetts Spy* noted on 27 August that "the Court of King's Bench gave judgment in the case of Somerset the Negro, finding that Mr. Stewart, his master, had no power to compel him on board a ship, or to send him back to the plantations." Four days later the *Boston Evening Post* reproduced, without acknowledgment, the account that the *Gentleman's Magazine* had published in London in its June issue.

On the same Thursday in June 1773 that Phillis arrived in London, the *General Evening Post* and the *London Evening Post* advertised the forthcoming publication on the following Monday of "THE DYING NEGRO, a Poetical

Epistle. Supposed to be Written by a BLACK (who lately shot himself on board a vessel in the river Thames) to his intended wife." The poem has been aptly called "a suicide note in verse" that "arguably opened the poetic campaign against slavery."[52] An actual event inspired the twenty-one-page sentimental poem coauthored by the philanthropist and best-selling author Thomas Day and John Bicknell, a lawyer. On 28 May 1773 the *Morning Chronicle and London Advertiser* reported that on "Tuesday a Black, Servant to Capt. Ordington, who a few days before ran away from his Master and got himself christened, with the intent to marry his fellow-servant, a White woman, being taken and sent on board the Captain's ship in the Thames, took an opportunity of shooting himself through the head."[53]

Day and Bicknell elaborated this terse account of the illegal attempt to kidnap an enslaved person in England and force him into colonial slavery into the fictional autobiography of an African who was rendered "a thing without a name" (p. 9) by the treachery of a European who had kidnapped him from "Ye streams of Gambia" (p. 8). The poem reminded readers of how vulnerable people of African descent were in England even after the Somerset ruling. Like Wheatley, Day and Bicknell appealed to the emotions of their readers to demonstrate the humanity people of African and European descent shared, coupled with an argument for the moral superiority of enslaved Africans to hypocritical Christians. *The Dying Negro* was so popular that a revised and expanded version was published in 1774, accompanied by an antislavery essay. The poem was further expanded in a third edition published in 1775, and it prompted several sympathetic poetic responses.

If Wheatley went to England aware of the opportunity for self-emancipation that the Mansfield decision offered her, she was not the only clever and trusted African-British slave who made travel plans with the recent *Somerset* case in mind. The *Boston Gazette* was one of the first colonial newspapers to point out, on 21 September 1772, the implications of the Mansfield decision for any slave owner who considered taking a slave to England: *"June 22. A* Correspondent observes, that as Blacks are free now in this country [England], Gentlemen will not be so fond of bringing them here as they used to be, it being computed that there are about 14000 blacks in this country." The *Virginia Gazette* (Williamsburg, Virginia) published on 27 August 1772 a full account of the Mansfield decision taken, without acknowledgment, from the June 1772 issue of the *Scots Magazine* (Edinburgh). It also reported several cases of slaves seeking the promised land of England. By 1773 even illiterate rural American slaves were aware of England as a sanctuary. John Austin Finnie advertised in the *Virginia Gazette* on 30 September 1773 for two runaway slaves, "a Wench, named AMY, of a very black Complexion, about 27 Years old," and "a Fellow, *African* born, named BACCHUS, about 19 Years of Age, [who] speaks somewhat broken [English]." Finnie noted that he had "some Reason to believe they will endeavour to get out of the Colony, particularly to *Britain*, where they imagine they will be free (a Notion now too prevalent among the Negroes, greatly to the Vexation and Prejudice of their Masters)." On 30 June 1774, Gabriel Jones of Augusta, Georgia, advertised in the same newspaper for a runaway slave named Bacchus. He predicted that Bacchus would "probably endeavour to pass for a Freeman by the Name of *John Christian*, and attempt to get on Board some Vessel bound for *Great Britain*, from the Knowledge he has of the late Determination of *Somerset*'s Case." Like Wheatley, Bacchus was a domestic servant with an active imagination. His assumed alias of "*John Christian*" suggests that, like Cugoano, he hoped to use religion to doubly ensure his claim to freedom if he reached England. Given the press coverage of the significance of the Mansfield ruling, as well as the local connection to Boston of Somerset and his master, Mansfield's judgment was very likely the talk of the town and almost certainly known to Phillis Wheatley and her owners in print as well as by word of mouth.

At least two of Wheatley's poems circulated in North America and Britain after news of the Mansfield decision became available in North America in August 1772, but before her trip to England. Read with the Mansfield ruling in mind, Wheatley's "To the Right Honourable WILLIAM, Earl of Dartmouth" and "A Farewel to America" are more nuanced and more directly about chattel slavery than commonly recognized. She wrote "To the Right Honourable WILLIAM, Earl of Dartmouth, His Majesty's Principal Secretary of State for North America, &c." in October 1772 at the suggestion of Thomas Wooldridge, an Englishman who had gone to America to assess the state of the colonies for Dartmouth. Dartmouth had been appointed secretary of state for the colonies and president of the Board of Trade and Foreign Plantations in August 1772, during the ministry of Lord North (1732–92), a position he held until November 1775.

When Wooldridge forwarded Wheatley's poem, with its accompanying letter from her, to Dartmouth in November 1772 he included his own account of the poem's genesis:

> While in Boston, I heard of a very Extraordinary female Slave, who had made some verses on our mutually dear deceased Friend [Whitefield]; I visited her mistress, and found by conversing with the African, that she was no Imposter; I asked if she could write on any Subject; she said Yes; we had heard of your Lordships appointment; I gave her your name, which she was well acquainted with. She, immediately, wrote a rough Copy of the inclosed Address & Letter, which I promised to convey or deliver. I was astonishd, and could hardly believe my own Eyes. I was present while she wrote, and can attest that it is her own production; she shewd me her Letter to Lady Huntington [*sic*], which, I dare say, Your Lordship has seen; I send you an Account signed by her master of her Importation, Education &c. they are all wrote in her own hand.[54]

The "Account" Wooldridge mentions was actually dictated by Nathaniel, not John, Wheatley to Phillis. It became the basis of the first two paragraphs of the statement attributed to John Wheatley that prefaces Phillis's *Poems* published in 1773.

The letter Phillis Wheatley gave Wooldridge to send with her poem to Dartmouth expresses the hopes she and many other colonists invested in Dartmouth, hopes that would soon be disappointed:

> The Joyful occasion which has given me this Confidence in addressing your Lordship in the enclos'd Peice will, I hope, Sufficiently apologize for this freedom from an African, who with the (now) happy America, exults with equal transport, in the view of one of its greatest advocates Presiding, with the Special tenderness of a Fatherly heart, over the American department.
>
> Nor can they, my Lord, be insensible of the Friendship so much exemplified in your endeavours in their behalf, during the late unhappy disturbances. I sincerely wish your Lordship all Possible Success, in your undertakings for the Interest of North America.

The revised version of "To the Right Honourable William, Earl of Dartmouth, His Majesty's Principal Secretary of State for North America, &c."

is one of the most carefully crafted poems in the 1773 volume. Wheatley re-appropriates the concept of *slavery* from its common metaphorical use in the colonial discourse of discontent, which described any perceived limitation on colonial rights and liberty as an attempt by England to "enslave" (white) Americans.[55] Wheatley appears to use *slavery* in this conventional sense in the poem:

> No more, *America*, in mournful strain
> Of wrongs, and grievance unredress'd complain,
> No longer shall thou dread the iron chain,
> Which wanton *Tyranny* with lawless hand
> Had made, and with it meant t'enslave the land. (ll. 15–19)

But Wheatley's reference to her authority to speak against this conventionally metaphorical slavery reminds her readers of the reality of chattel slavery trivialized by the political metaphor:

> Should you, my lord, while you peruse my song,
> Wonder from whence my love of *Freedom* sprung,
> Whence flow these wishes for the common good,
> By feeling hearts alone best understood,
> I, young in life, by seeming cruel fate
> Was snatch'd from *Afric's* fancy'd happy seat[.]
> . . . .
> Such, such my case. And can I then but pray
> Others may never feel tyrannic sway? (ll. 20–25, 30–31)

Revolutionary rhetoric made many colonists question for the first time the hypocrisy of owners of chattel slaves protesting metaphorical slavery. Accusations against the British authorities of the illegality and immorality of their alleged attempts to "enslave" the (white) colonists may have contributed to the decline in the number of "Servants for Life" in Boston from just over eight hundred in 1761 to 261 ten years later. Wheatley subtly reminds her readers that physical enslavement has already led to "*Freedom*" in America on the spiritual level. In retrospect, her kidnapping in Africa was an act of only "seeming cruel fate" because she has since discovered that it was a fortunate fall into religious liberation. Thus, "*Afric's* fancy'd happy seat" is "fancy'd" (alive in her imagination) in two senses: *now* (at the time of writing the poem) because "*Afric*" can only be recalled; but also *then* (at the time when she was kidnapped) because she mistook her pagan condition for a state of happiness. Complete *"Freedom"*—political, social, and religious—may be realized and restored by the new political order that the poet hopes Dartmouth represents, and by the new judicial order represented by the *Somerset* ruling.

Doubts Wheatley probably had about the applicability of the *Somerset* decision outside of England may account for the Janus-like ambivalence found in the various versions of "A Farewel to America. To Mrs. S.W.," dated *"May 7, 1773."* Boston newspapers published the poem on 10 May 1773, as Wheatley sailed with her master's son to London. Less than two weeks after Phillis reached London, the poem appeared in the *London Chronicle* (1–3 July), with a prefatory note intended to stimulate interest in her soon-to-be-published volume. The advertisement assumed that English readers already knew of Phillis:

> Sir,
>
> You have no doubt heard of Phillis the extraordinary negro girl here [i.e., in Boston], who has by her own application, unassisted by others, cultivated her natural talents for poetry in such a manner as to write several pieces which (all circumstances considered) have great merit. This girl, who is a servant to Mr. John Wheatley of this place, sailed last Saturday for London, under the protection of Mr. Nathaniel Wheatley; since which the following little piece of her's [*sic*] has been published.

"A Farewel" has been called "both a parting tribute to America and an expression of regret for the coming separation from Susannah Wheatley."[56] But "A Farewel" looks forward as well as back. The poem's second half looks ahead, anticipating the speaker's arrival in England, the restoration of her health, and, I believe, the possibility of the restoration of her freedom:

VII.
While for *Britannia's* distant shore
      We sweep the liquid plain,
And with astonish'd eyes explore
      The wide-extended main.

VIII.
Lo! *Health* appears! celestial dame!
      Complacent and serene,

With *Hebe's* mantle o'er her Frame,
      With soul-delighting mein.

IX.
To mark the vale where *London* lies
      With misty vapours crown'd,
Which cloud *Aurora's* thousand dyes,
      And veil her charms around,

X.
Why, *Phoebus*, moves thy car so slow?
      So slow thy rising ray?
Give us the famous town to view,
      Thou glorious king of day!

XI.
For thee, *Britannia*, I resign
      New-England's smiling fields;
To view again her charms divine,
      What joy the prospect yields!

XII.
But thou! Temptation hence away,
      With all thy fatal train
Nor once seduce my soul away,
      By thine enchanting strain.

XIII.
Thrice happy they, whose heav'nly shield
      Secures their souls from harms,
And fell *Temptation* on the field
      Of all its pow'r disarms! (ll. 25–52)

Stanzas VIII–XI express the speaker's increasingly impatient desire to reach London and "Give us the famous town to view." In the course of the poem, "*Health*," "Celestial maid of rosy hue" (stanza III), transforms into the image of "*Aurora*"—a figure of resurrection and restoration: her "thousand dyes" are both her colors and her repeated nocturnal deaths and subsequent rebirths—associated in stanza IX with "*London*" and "*Health*."

Wheatley's association of England with the recovery and restoration of physical health appears elsewhere in *Poems*: in "To a Gentleman on His Voyage to Great-Britain for the Recovery of His Health," as well as in "Ode to Neptune. On Mrs. W—'s Voyage to England." We do not, however, find in Wheatley's poems a simple dichotomy in which America equals illness and England health. As her poem "To a Lady on her coming to North-America with her Son, for the Recovery of her Health" demonstrates, Philadelphia and Boston are healthier than the West Indies, the diseased heart of the empire and of course the area most dependent upon and associated with slavery—the part of the empire that Equiano calls "this land of bondage."[57] In "To a Lady," Wheatley's "ideal [imagined] view" (l. 13) of *"Jamaica's* fervid shore" (l. 3), where "Each branch, wide-spreading to the ambient sky, / Forgets its verdure, and submits to die" (ll. 17–18), is the negative equivalent to the image of *"Afric's* fancy'd happy seat" (l. 25) in her poem to Dartmouth.

The health that Wheatley locates in England in "A Farewel to America" is not only physical. It is also social and political because in England she will face the opportunity to resurrect herself from the social death of slavery.[58] Legally as well as geographically, England is even further than New England from *"Jamaica's* fervid shore." The speaker in "A Farewel" sees herself as choosing in stanza XI between *"Britannia"* and *"New-England,"* and in the version of "A Farewel" published in *Poems* she expresses a seemingly clear desire to return to America: "To View again her charms divine, / What joy the prospect yields!" But the stanzas that follow indicate possible ambivalence about the attractiveness of America. At the end of the first stanza of the poem Wheatley slyly plays on the contemporaneous meanings of the word *tempt* as both *to attempt* and *to lure or solicit to ill* to introduce a tone of ambiguity into the poem:

> ADIEU, *New-England's* smiling meads,
> Adieu, the flow'ry plain:
> I leave thine op'ning charms, O spring,
> And tempt the roaring main. (ll. 1–4)

What is the *"Temptation"* that threatens her later in the poem? Is it something far more significant than the enticements any urban "Sink of Sin" offers to an innocent girl from the provinces? Is *"New-England"* the "thou" addressed in stanza XII? Does the speaker consider returning to America the equivalent of returning to slavery rather than choosing the self-emancipation available to her in England, and thus a temptation to be resisted? As she says in stanza XIII, the choice before her requires a different kind of heroism than that displayed in battle.

Or might the *"Temptation"* be *"Britannia"* and freedom? Was the version of "A Farewel" published "by request" in *The Massachusetts Gazette and Boston Post-Boy and Advertiser* intended to warn Wheatley's owners that she was aware of the possibility for freedom that would, from her owners' point of view, tempt her in England not to return to America? The speaker's desire to see America again—"To view again her Charms divine, / One short reluctant Space"—is certainly less enthusiastic in the newspaper version than in the one that appears in *Poems*. Is she regretting the separation itself or its shortness? Wheatley demonstrates her ability to exploit the rhetorical possibilities that ambivalence and ambiguity offered her. To a colonial audience of slave owners, post-*Somerset* England represented temptation to a slave, and "Virtue" (line 52 in the newspaper version) was returning to one's condition as a slave. To an enslaved audience, and Wheatley herself, the temptation to be resisted was returning to America without having seized the opportunity for freedom that England offered.

A decade before Wheatley gained her freedom, Equiano recognized that "[h]itherto I had thought only slavery dreadful; but the state of a free negro appeared to me now equally so at least, and in some respects even worse, for they live in constant alarm for their liberty, which is but nominal."[59] Because he was aware of how vulnerable a former slave was in a slave society, Equiano chose to redeem himself from slavery by legal means that would enable him to document his new status, rather than to free himself by escaping and trying to make his way to England. Even in post-*Somerset* England, documentation of manumission was considered a wise insurance policy. In his April 1782 will, Lord Mansfield "[r]eaffirm[ed] to Dido Elizabeth Bell[e], her freedom and after the death of my dear wife, £100 a year during her life."[60] Mansfield had raised Dido (1761?–1804), the natural mulatto daughter of his nephew, Sir John Lindsay (1737–1788), from her birth.

Like Equiano before her, who chose to purchase his freedom rather than take advantage of an opportunity to escape West Indian slavery by flight, Wheatley apparently chose the method of emancipation that appeared to grant her the most freedom of movement. As Equiano had done several years earlier, Phillis Wheatley had the foresight to have her manumission put in writing. Had she taken advantage of the Mansfield decision to emancipate herself in London, she could not return to Boston without risking being legally re-enslaved. Given recent events in England and Massachusetts, emancipation in New England probably seemed easily within reach in 1773. Ambivalence and caution, however, would explain why Wheatley did not share her hopes with the Countess of Huntingdon in the farewell letter of 17 July 1773 that Wheatley wrote to her on the eve of her departure for America.

We have increasingly come to appreciate Wheatley as a manipulator of words; perhaps we should have more respect for her as a manipulator of people as well. Rather than being a gift passively received from her master "at the desire of my friends in England," the promise of freedom was probably a concession Phillis Wheatley coerced from Nathaniel Wheatley in exchange for her promise to return to Boston: one promise for another. As a businessman engaged in transatlantic commerce, Wheatley's word was his bond. In this negotiation, Phillis Wheatley had the stronger hand. Phillis Wheatley could neither legally nor practically be forced back to the colonies from England following the *Somerset* ruling. She could insist that her master's son give his word in the presence of Sharp and other "friends in England" that she would be freed if she agreed to return to Boston. The choice of freedom, the terms, and the place were hers to make.

Wheatley tells Wooster that she also shrewdly took out an extra insurance policy by sending a copy of her manumission papers to Israel Mauduit in London. She is clear about her motives for having done so: "The Instrument is drawn, so as to secure me and my property from the hands of the Exectutrs [executors], administrators, &c. of my master, & secure whatsoever should be given me as my Own. A Copy is sent to Isra. Mauduit Esq. F.R.S. [Fellow of the Royal Society]." Phillis apparently already had property, besides her own person, to protect, and she clearly expected to gain more, all of which she sought to keep out of the hands of John Wheatley and his heirs. She knew the truth that Equiano had learned a decade earlier about how vulnerable any free person of African descent remained in a society where slavery was legal.

Phillis Wheatley departed London for Boston on 26 July 1773. She left England without ever having met her patron, the Countess of Huntingdon, and nearly two months before her *Poems* was published. She arrived back in Boston on 13 September, a day whose weather was as "fair" as her future seemed to be.[61] Three days later the *Boston News-Letter* and the *Massachu-*

setts Spy were the first of many colonial newspapers to proclaim the return of "the extraordinary Poetical Genius" and "celebrated young negro poetess, Phillis."[62] The few weeks Phillis Wheatley spent in England rendered 1773 her *annus mirabilis*, a wondrous year. It brought her freedom, fame, and the hope of fortune yet to come. But she would soon be disappointed. Had she chosen the road not taken and remained as a self-emancipated woman in England, she might have found the publisher for her second volume of poetry that she failed to find in America.[63]

Chapter 6

"Now upon my own Footing"

Phillis Wheatley's likely ambivalence about choosing between Boston and London as the site of her anticipated emancipation is understandable. So, too, is her decision to return to America as a slave. She certainly knew before she left London that she could have emancipated herself there. To rely on Nathaniel Wheatley's word of honor that she would be freed when she returned to Boston was a calculated risk, but a risk that seemed well worth taking. Besides, in addition to his word she had the insurance policy she left with Mauduit. The familiarity with current events that Wheatley frequently displays in her writings indicates that she was well aware of the rapidly evolving attitude about slavery in Massachusetts. The legal end of slavery in Massachusetts probably appeared imminent to her in 1773, even though it did not actually happen until the next decade.[1] The Mansfield ruling and revolutionary rhetoric together energized the abolitionist movement in New England that had been developing since the 1760s.[2] Phillis Wheatley had good reason to believe that growing opposition to slavery in Boston would increase the pressure on her owner to free her.

Repeated attempts to legislate the end of the importation of slaves into Massachusetts failed until 1771, when "An Act to prevent the Importation of Negro Slaves into this Province" passed. Governor Thomas Hutchinson rejected it on the grounds that it was a law "of a new and unusual nature" that challenged Parliament's authority. Hutchinson had no time to respond to a subsequent "Act to prevent the importation of Negroes or other Persons as Slaves into this Province," which the legislature sent to him in 1774 as he was about to flee from Massachusetts to England in the face of growing colonial opposition.

The abolitionist movement was increasingly conflated in the northern colonies with opposition to imperial rule. In *The Rights of the British Colonies Asserted and Proved* (Boston, 1764), James Otis (1725–83), who grew up in a slave-owning family, declared that "The Colonists are by the law of nature free born, as indeed all men are, white or black."[3] Boston merchant Nathaniel Appleton (1693–1784) referred to the *de facto* status of slavery in England before the Mansfield ruling when he commented in 1767 in *Considerations on Slavery. In a Letter to a Friend*, "Great-Britain, the envy of the world, does not permit a slave on her happy island; but gives to every one freedom, which stamps him image of his God. . . . Oh! Ye sons of liberty, pause a minute, give me your ear, Is your conduct consistent? Can you review our late struggles for liberty, and think of the slave-trade at the same time, and not blush?"[4]

People of African descent in Boston invoked natural rights and Christian morality to petition the government of Massachusetts for their freedom, the right to own property, and the right to be paid for their labor. They delivered their petition while Phillis Wheatley was on her way to London. James Swan (1754–1830), a Scottish merchant living in Boston, revised his *A Dissuasion to Great-Britain and the Colonies from the Slave Trade to Africa* in 1773 at the request of several people of African descent so that they could submit it with a copy of their petition to the governor and legislature of Massachusetts.[5] On 21 July 1773, five days before Wheatley sailed from London to return to Boston, the abolition of slavery was the subject debated at Harvard's commencement, an annual event that in 1767 had occasioned one of her earliest poems. And several months after her return, other people of African descent alluded to the Mansfield ruling in their 25 May 1774 petition to the governor for freedom.[6]

Attempts to have the government of Massachusetts outlaw slavery were paralleled by attempts to have the courts outlaw it. Lawsuits for freedom for enslaved people of African descent in Massachusetts during the 1760s and 1770s liberated individuals but did not outlaw the institution of slavery. The first came in November 1766, when Jenny Slew brought a freedom suit against John Whipple. Although Slew initially lost her case, she eventually won on appeal on the technical grounds that her mother was white. Several other slaves in Massachusetts successfully sued for their freedom in the course of the next fifteen years. But a court did not rule slavery unconstitutional in Massachusetts until Chief Justice William Cushing (1732–1810) charged the jury to do so in the case of Quok Walker (b. 1753) vs. Nathaniel Jennison in 1783.

Phillis Wheatley fortunately did not have to rely on the slow-moving legal system in Massachusetts to achieve her freedom. The practical effects of her liberty gained "at the desire of my friends in England" were immediate. In her 18 October 1773 letter to Wooster she signifies her transition from slavery to freedom with a new paragraph and a grammatical shift from the passive to the active voice. Rather than emphasize what her "friends" had done for her in England, in her last paragraph she stresses what she is doing for herself now that she is back in Boston and "upon [her] own footing":

> I expect my Books which are publishd in London in [the vessel commanded by] Capt. Hall, who will be here I believe in 8 or 10 days. I beg the favour that you would honour the enclos'd Proposals, & use your interest with Gentlemen & Ladies of your acquaintance to subscribe also, for the more subscribers there are, the more it will be for my advantage as I am to have half the Sale of the Books. This I am the more Solicitous for, as I am now upon my own footing and whatever I get by this is entirely mine, & it is the Chief I have to depend upon. I must also request you would desire the Printers in New Haven, not to reprint that Book, as it will be a great hurt to me, preventing any further Benefit that I might receive from the Sale of my Copies from England. The price is 2/6d [two shillings, six pence] Bound or 2 [shillings]/Sterling Sewed.—If any should be so ungenerous as to reprint them the Genuine Copy may be known, for it is sign'd in my own handwriting.

Phillis Wheatley recognized that emancipation gave her not only freedom and agency, the ability to act on her own behalf, but also new responsibilities. She was now in the vulnerable position of being a freed woman of African descent in a world with very limited economic opportunities for her. It was a very precarious life for anyone trying to live by his or her pen in the eighteenth century. Phillis overestimated by a few months how soon copies of her book would arrive from London. Her concern for protecting the profits from her book reveals a young woman of extraordinary business acumen. Her decision to autograph copies shows that she anticipated that pirated editions would cost her income. She displays in her letter to Wooster a familiarity with the business of bookselling and the need for authentication that increases the likelihood that she had played quite an active role in the marketing of her earlier works.

Although Phillis Wheatley could now keep what she earned, she had to earn her own keep. John and Susanna Wheatley apparently allowed her to continue to live with them after they had freed her, but her former owners were no longer legally obligated to support her. She no longer enjoyed the daily companionship of Mary or Nathaniel Wheatley, however. Mary had married Rev. John Lathrop, pastor of the Old North, the Second Congregationalist Church, in Boston in 1771. Nathaniel Wheatley remained in London, where in November 1773 he married Mary Enderby, the daughter of one of his London business associates.

Wheatley was immediately reminded of just how tenuous her network of support in Boston had become. In a postscript to her letter to Wooster she informed him, "I found my mistress very sick on my return But she is somewhat better. We wish we could depend on it." Susanna had been ill for some time. Elizabeth Wallcut had written to her "Dear Tomy" on 9 September 1773, "Mʳˢ Wheetly Lies near her End Mʳ nat and phillis is gon to England and not Returned yet."[7] Over the next several months Phillis acted as her former mistress's secretary. She wrote to John Thornton on 1 December 1773:

> When I first arrived at home my mistress was so bad as not to be expected to live above two or three days, but through the goodness of God She is still alive but remains in a very weak & languishing Condition. She begs a continued interest in your most earnest prayers, that she may be surly prepar'd for that great Change which [she] is likely Soon to undergo; She intreats you, as her Son is Still in England, that you would take all opportun[i]ties to advise & counsel him; She says she is going to leave him & desires you'd be a Spiritual Fath[er] to h[im]. *She will take it very kind. She thanks you heartily for the kind notice you took of me while in England.*

Susanna Wheatley's "languishing Condition" may have been the final stage of a recurrent illness that had afflicted her for years. She had written Rev. Occom on 29 March 1773, "I am very weak and low, my old indispositions returning upon me, and to Such a degree, as makes me doubtful whether I shall live to See you once more in this World. I must beg your earnest prayers to God for Mr. Wheatley and Me, that when Death comes he may not be a terror, but as the Outward Man decays the inward may be strong in Faith."[8]

Nearly three weeks passed after Susanna's death on 3 March 1774 before Phillis was able to describe her personal loss to Obour Tanner, her most intimate correspondent. Phillis frequently addressed her as "Sister." Her 21 March 1774 letter is the most reliable evidence we have of the familial relationship Phillis felt she had with the Wheatleys:

> I have lately met with a great trial in the death of my mistress; let us imagine the loss of a Parent, Sister or Brother the tenderness of all these were united in her.—I was a poor little outcast & a stranger when she took me in: not only into her house but I presently became a sharer in her most tender affections. I was treated by her more like her child than her Servant; no opportunity was left unimprov'd, of giving me the best of advice, but in terms how tender! how engaging! This I hope ever to keep in remembrance. Her exemplary life was a greater monitor than all her precepts and Instruction, thus we may observe of how much greater force example is than instruction. To alleviate our sorrows we had the satisfaction to se[e] her depart in inexpresible raptures, earnest longings & impatient thirstings for the *upper* Courts of the Lord. Do, my dear friend, remember me & this family in your Closet, that this afflicting dispensation may be sanctify'd to us.

Phillis offered the fullest account of Susanna's exemplary Christian death and further evidence of Phillis's place in the Wheatley family in a letter to John Thornton on 29 March 1774:

> She has been labouring under a languishing illness for many months past and has at length took her flight from hence to those blissful regions, which need not the light of any, but the Sun of Righteousness. O could you have been present, to See how She long'd to drop the tabernacle of Clay, and to be freed from the cumbrous Shackles of a mortal Body, which had so many Times retarded her desires when Soaring upward. She has often told me how your Letters hav[e] quicken'd her in her Spiritual Course: when She has been in darkness of mind they have rais'd and enliven'd her insomuch, that She went on, with chearfuln[ess] and alacrity in the path of her duty. She did truely, *run with patience the race that was Set before her*, and hath, at length obtained the celestial Goal. She is now Sure, that the afflictions of this present time, were not worthy to be compared to the Glory, which is now, revealed in her, Seeing they have wrought out for her, *a far more exceeding and eternal weight of Glory*. This, Sure, is sufficient encouragement

under the bitterest Sufferings, which we can endure.—About half an hour before her Death, She Spoke with a more audible voice, than She had for 3 months before. She calld her friends & relations around her, and charg'd them not to leave their great work undone till *that* hour, but to fear God, and keep his Commandments, being ask'd if her faith faild her She answer'd, No. Then Spr[ead] out her arms crying come! come quickly! come, come! O pray for an eas[y] and quick Passage! She eagerly longed to depart to be with Christ. She retaind her Senses till the very last moment when "fare well, fare well" with a very low voice, were the last words She utter'd. I sat the whole time by her bed Side, and Saw with Grief and Wonder, the Effects of Sin on the human race. Had not Christ taken away the envenom'd Sting, where had been our hopes? what might we not have fear'd, what might we not have expectd from the dreadful King of Terrors? But *this* is matter of endless praise, to the King eternal immortal, invisible, that, *it is finished*. I hope her Son will be interested in Your Closet duties, & that the prayers which she was continually putting up, & wch are recorded before God, in the Book of his remembrance for her Son & for me may be answer'd. I can Scarcely think that an Object of so many prayers, will fail of the Blessings implor'd for him ever Since he was born. I intreat the same Interest in your best thoughts for my Self, that her prayers, in my be-half, may be favour'd with an Answer of *Peace*.

Phillis had of course much besides Susanna's declining health and eventual death to occupy her mind once she had returned to Boston. On 30 October 1773 she wrote to Obour Tanner that the trip to London had more than achieved its purpose of improving at least her psychological health: "I can't say but my voyage to England has conduced to the recovery (in a great measure) of my Health. The Friends I found there among the Nobility and Gentry, Their Benevolent conduct towards me, the unexpected, and unmerited civility and Complaisance with which I was treated by all, fills me with astonishment. I can scarcely Realize it." But as a pious Christian Phillis immediately adds her hope that her reception in London will not go to her head: "This I humbly hope has the happy Effect of lessning me in my own Esteem."

Her return to Boston, however, brought the recurrence of the physical illness she had sought to escape. Once back home, she told Tanner, she had been "visited by the asthma." Phillis was unable to keep up with her correspondence, "being much indispos'd by the return of [her] Asthmatic complaint, besides, the sickness of [her] mistress who has been long confin'd to her bed, & is not expected to live a great while."[9] Wheatley wrote Tanner on 21 March 1774, "I have been unwell the great Part of the winter, but am much better as the Spring approache[s]." Her "Asthmatic complaint" would continue to afflict her for the remaining ten years of her life, particularly during the winters, and may have caused her death. Wheatley never says how she was treated for her "complaint." If she followed the advice of Benjamin Rush, with whom we know she corresponded at some point, the treatment was certainly not what would be recommended today. Rush advises in *A Dissertation on the Spasmodic Asthma of Children* (London, 1770), which first appeared in the *Pennsylvania Gazette*, "1. *Bleeding*. . . . A physician should always be directed by the age, sex, habit of body, and state of the pulse of his patient. The season of the year likewise, as well as the nature of the weather, should influence him considerably with regard to the use of his lancet. . . . 2. *Vomits*. Our chief dependence should be placed on these. They may be given at all times of the disorder."[10]

But despite her own and Susanna's illnesses, Phillis Wheatley had to attend to her own economic interests. She wrote to Thornton on 30 October 1774 that Susanna's death made her appreciate how important her mistress's friendship and support had been: "The world is a severe Schoolmaster, for its frowns are less dang'rous than its Smiles and flatteries, and it is a difficult task to keep in the path of Wisdom. I attended, and find exactly true your thoughts on the behaviour of those who seem'd to respect me while under my mistresses patronage: you said right, for Some of those have already put on a reserve."

She ended her 30 October 1773 letter to Tanner with a request: "I enclose Proposals for my Book, and beg youd use your interest to get Subscriptions as it is for my Benefit." Copies of her *Poems* arrived in Boston from London by the beginning of December 1773 and were soon distributed to her American subscribers.[11] Cox and Berry first advertised the book by "Phillis Wheatley, a Negro Girl" in the *Boston Gazette* on 24 January.[12] Subscribers could pick up their copies at the booksellers' shop, and new buyers could purchase a bound copy for 3 shillings and 4 pence.

By the end of the year Wheatley's book was also on sale in New York, Pennsylvania, Connecticut, Rhode Island, and Nova Scotia, Canada.[13]

Phillis Wheatley wrote to Rev. Hopkins in Newport on 9 February 1774, "I take with pleasure the opportunity by the Post, to acquaint you of the arr[iva]l of my books from London. I have Seal'd up a package, containing 17 for you 2 for Mr. Tanner and one for Mrs. Mason, and only wait for you to appoint some proper person by whom I may convey them to you. I rec[eive]d some time ago 20/sterling upon them by the hands of your Son, in a Letter from Obour Tanner." Significantly, now that Phillis Wheatley was "on [her] own footing" the advertisements no longer identified her as "A Negro Servant to John Wheatley," though he presumably allowed her to continue to live with him after Susanna's death. Friends and relatives of the Wheatleys considered her still part of the family. Thomas Wallcut, at the time living in Montreal, wrote her a playful letter on 17 November 1774 in response to some admonitions she had sent him. He closed by asking her to remember him "to all Your Dear Family."

Although Wheatley's *Poems* was apparently not reviewed in America, news of the book soon spread informally throughout the colonies as well as through the transatlantic distribution of the published British reviews. The tutor Philip Vickers Fithian (1747–76) recorded on 5 March 1774 the reactions he and his pupil, Robert Bladen Carter (1759–93), had to two of the early reviews and the copy of "Recollection" that accompanied one of them:

> I was reading in the Evening to *Bob* in the Monthly Review the remarks on the Poetry and writings of *Phillis Wheatley* of Boston; at which he seem'd in astonishment; sometimes wanting to see her, then to know if she knew grammer [*sic*], Latin, &c. at last he expressed himself in a manner very unusual for a boy of his turn. & suddenly exclaimed, Good God! I wish I was in Heaven! Like *Bob* I am at once fill'd with pleasure & surprise, when I see the remarks of the Reviewers confirmed as to the Writings of that ingenious *African Phillis Wheatley* of Boston; her verses seem to discover that she is tolerably well acquainted with *Poetry, Learning, & Religion*. In the Universal Magazine for September 1773 are the following Lines on her being brought from *Africa* to *America* by herself.[14]

At least one of Wheatley's subscribers anticipated that she was already planning a career as an author. John Andrews told William Barrell on 28 January 1774, "After so long a time, [I] have at last got Phillis's poems in print, which will be also [brought to] you . . . these don't seem to be near all her productions. She's an *artful* jade, I believe, & intends to have ye benefit of another volume." Events would soon prove Andrews right. In 1779 the *"artful* jade" began to try to find a publisher for a proposed but ultimately never published second volume, this time to include correspondence as well as poems.

Phillis Wheatley continued to produce poetry on demand for people, as she had done before she had published her book and gained her freedom. Deborah Fletcher Cushing (ca. 1727–90) wrote from Boston on 19 September 1774 to her husband, Thomas Cushing, Esq. (1725–88), in Philadelphia, to tell him of Wheatley's success as a saleswoman: "I rote you by M^r [Richard] Cary and sent you one of phillis whetlys books which you will wonder att but Mrs Dickerson and Mrs Clymer Mrs Bull with some other Ladys ware so pleasd with phillis and her performances that they bought her Books and got her to compose some peices for them which put me in mind of Mrs Vanhorn to hume I thought it would be very agreabel."[15] Mrs. Cushing's spelling and syntactical errors remind us of just how extraordinary Phillis Wheatley's education was. Thomas Cushing was a prominent Boston merchant and politician who had graduated from Harvard in 1744. He was the Speaker of the Massachusetts House of Representatives and in Philadelphia headed the province's delegation to the first Continental Congress. It had been convened on 5 September 1774 because Britain's passage of the Boston Port Act in March 1774, in response to the Boston Tea Party in December 1773, had galvanized colonial opposition to imperial rule. Like Phillis Wheatley, Deborah and Thomas Cushing were members of the Old South Congregational Church in Boston. Cushing's son-in-law was John Avery, son of the slave dealer John Avery, who may have sold Phillis to the Wheatleys in 1761.

Wheatley also continued to publish poems in response to current events after her return to Boston. Her elegy on the death of the Presbyterian minister John Moorhead, which she published as a broadside on 15 December 1773, differs notably from her earlier elegies. It stresses the effect of "the afflicting Providence" (l. 76) felt by those he left behind, rather than the theme of Christian consolation that pervades the previous poems. Moorhead had died on 6 December. His obituary in the 13 December issue of the *Boston Post Boy* attributes to him many of the qualities Wheatley mentions in her poem and describes his death: "Nature had blessed him with a hale constitution, which he assiduously cultivated and preserved until two or three years since, when a disorder cruel in its nature seized him, and although it did not confine him for any great space of time, yet its repeated attacks wasted and destroyed his health, and finally put a period to his usefulness and life." Several reasons may account for the somber treatment of death in Wheatley's "An ELEGY To Miss. Mary Moorhead, on the DEATH of her Father, The Rev. Mr. JOHN MOORHEAD." Phillis Wheatley probably knew the Moorhead family far better than she did most of the other subjects of her elegies. She frequently saw Rev. Moorhead. When Susanna Wheatley told Rev. Occom on 29 March 1773, "I wrote you before of the Sad accident which befell Mr. Wheatley from a fall, who remains in such a Situation, that he has never been able to get out of his Bed without the assistance of 5 or 6 men: and it is now near 5 weeks Since it happen'd," she also told him that "the revd. Mr Moorhead . . . is very kind to Mr. Wheatley & visits him almost every Day." Furthermore, Susanna's declining health and Phillis's own languishing illness during the winter of 1773–74 may have made the progress of Moorhead's death feel all too familiar.

Phillis Wheatley recovered her health and spirits by the end of 1774. She took part in a light-hearted exchange of poems with a member of the royal navy in the first two issues of the *Royal Magazine*, published in Boston in December 1774 and January 1775 during a period of rapidly deteriorating relations between Britain and its North American colonies. George III reacted to the increasing protests and actions against the economic regime Britain sought to impose on its colonies by sending a fleet of twenty-six ships under the command of Vice Admiral Samuel Graves (1713–87) in the summer of 1774 to patrol the North American coast from Nova Scotia to Florida and to enforce the Boston Port Act. Part of Graves's charge was to blockade Boston until restitution was made for the destroyed tea.

But none of the historical context finds its way into the poems exchanged between Wheatley and John Prime Iron Rochfort (b. 1751). Born in Dublin, Ireland, the twenty-four-year-old Rochfort was rated, or ranked, an able seaman on the *Preston*. He would be discharged from the *Preston* on 30 December 1775 to be promoted to lieutenant on the *Nautilus*. Serving with Rochfort on the *Preston* was Third Lieutenant John Graves, a nephew of Vice Admiral Samuel Graves. Also in the British fleet was Lieutenant Thomas Graves (1747?–1814), one of John's brothers, who was serving on the *Lively*, and whom his uncle would promote in 1775 to command of the *Diana*. The "Greaves" (a phonetically accurate alternative spelling of

"Graves") Wheatley mentions in her poem was probably either Thomas Graves, who had served as a lieutenant on the *Shannon* off the coast of Gambia in 1765, or his younger brother John.[16]

The editorial comment that prefaces the exchange indicates that publication of the poems, which could not have been done without Wheatley's cooperation, demonstrates the intellectual equality of Europeans and Africans, proves the validity of the stadial theory of cultural development, and reveals the moral superiority of the enslaved to their enslavers:

> *By particular request we insert the following Poem addressed, by Philis [sic], (a young* Affrican *[sic], of surprising genius) to a gentleman of the navy, with his reply.*
>
> *By this single instance may be seen, the importance of education.— Uncultivated nature is much the same in every part of the globe. It is probable* Europe *and* Affrica *would be alike savage or polite in the same circumstances; though, it may be questioned, whether men who have no artificial wants, are capable of becoming so ferocious as those, who by faring sumptuously every day, are reduced to a habit of thinking it necessary to their happiness, to plunder the whole human race.*

Wheatley closes her poem of praise for the friendship between Rochfort and "Greaves" and her celebration of Britain's naval might with an address to the young men:

> Cerulean youths! your joint assent declare,
> Virtue to rev'rence, more than mortal fair,
> A crown of glory, which the muse will twine,
> Immortal trophy! Rochfort shall be thine!
> Thine too O Greaves! for virtue's offspring share,
> Celestial friendship and the muse's care.
> Yours is the song, and your's the honest praise,
> Lo! Rochfort smiles, and Greaves approves my lays. (ll. 33–40)

Rochfort responded in his "Answer" with the greatest public praise Wheatley received during her lifetime. He deemed her poetic powers preferable to Britain's martial might:

> Celestial muse! sublimest of the nine,
> Assist my song, and dictate every line:

Inspire me once, nor with imperfect lays,
To sing this great, this lovely virgins praise:
But yet, alas! what tribute can I bring,
WH———TL———Y but smiles, whilst I thus faintly sing,
Behold with reverence, and with joy adore;
The lovely daughter of the Affric shore,
Where every grace, and every virtue join,
That kindles friendship and makes love divine;
In hue as diff'rent as in souls above;
The rest of mortals who in vain have strove,
Th' immortal wreathe, the muse's gift to share,
Which heav'n reserv'd for this angelic fair.
. . . .
For softer strains we quickly must repair
To Wheatly's song, for Wheatly is the fair;
That has the art, which art could ne'er acquire:
To dress each sentence with seraphic fire.
        Her wondrous virtues I could ne'er express!
To paint her charms, would only make them less. (ll. 1–14, 59–62)

Rochfort's "Answer" includes a very romanticized pastoral image of the Gold Coast of Africa:

    Blest be the guilded shore [the Gold Coast], the happy land,
Where spring and autumn gently hand in hand;
O'er shady forests that scarce know a bound,
In vivid blaze alternately dance round:
Where cancers torid heat the soul inspires;
With strains divine and true poetic fires;
(Far from the reach of Hudson's chilly bay)
Where cheerful phoebus makes all nature gay;
Where sweet refreshing breezes gently fan;
The flow'ry path, the ever verdant lawn,
The artless grottos, and the soft retreats;
"At once the lover and the muse's seats." (ll. 15–26)

In "PHILIS's [*sic*] Reply to the Answer in our last by the Gentleman in the Navy," Wheatley assumes a conventional pose of humility. Her pose is consciously ironic in light of her transatlantic renown:

> The generous plaudit 'tis not mine to claim,
> A muse untutor'd, and unknown to fame.
> . . . .
> My pen, least favour'd by the tuneful nine,
> Can never rival, never equal thine;
> Then fix the humble Afric muse's seat
> At British Homer's and Sir Isaac's feet. (ll. 9–10, 13–16)

The poets' exchange of flattery suggests at least an imaginary flirtatious relationship between Rochfort and Wheatley.

Both Rochfort and Wheatley use poetic diction to depict Africa as "display'd" in a "painting" of a golden age, where winter never comes and sin is nowhere to be found. They are engaged in a traditional classical competition of corresponding pastoral poems, with neither attempting to convey accurate cultural, geographical, or historical information. Certainly the slave trade has no place in either Rochfort's or Wheatley's depiction of Africa. Notwithstanding a recent critic's assertion that Phillis's corresponding image of Africa is "a poetic description . . . which plausibly resembles today's Gambia," her poem is at least as conventionally pastoral and idealized as Rochfort's and gives no evidence whatsoever that she is describing an actual place or time, or that she is speaking from personal experience:[17]

> In fair description are thy powers display'd
> In artless grottos, and the sylvan shade;
> Charm'd with thy painting, how my bosom burns!
> And pleasing Gambia on my soul returns,
> With native grace in spring's luxuriant reign,
> Smiles the gay mead, and Eden blooms again,
> The various bower, the tuneful flowing stream,
> The soft retreats, the lovers golden dream,
> Her soil spontaneous, yields exhaustless stores;
> For phoebus revels on her verdant shores;

Whose flowery births, a fragrant train appear,
And crown the youth throughout the smiling year. (ll. 19–30)

Wheatley may have mentioned "Gambia" because "Greaves" had been there.[18] Senegal and Gambia had been idealized in descriptions of Africa since 1759, when Michel Adanson's *Histoire Naturelle du Sénégal* was translated and published in London as *A Voyage to Senegal*.[19] Anthony Benezet's quotation of Adanson's edenic description of Senegambia in his *Some Historical Account of Guinea*, first published in Philadelphia in 1771, made the account widely available to later opponents of the transatlantic slave trade and slavery. Benezet probably brought Adanson's description to the attention of Thomas Day and John Bicknell. Their note to the lines "Nine days we feasted on the Gambian strand, / And songs of friendship echo'd o'er the land" in *The Dying Negro* reads:

> "Which way soever I turned my eyes on this pleasant spot, I beheld a perfect image of pure nature, an agreeable solitude bounded on every side by charming landscapes; the rural situation of cottages in the midst of tress; the ease and indolence of the Negroes, reclined under the shade of their spreading foliage; the simplicity of their dress and manners; the whole revived in my mind the idea of our first parents, and I seemed to contemplate the world in its primitive state. They are, generally speaking, very good natured, sociable, and obliging. I was not a little pleased with this, my first reception; it convinced me that there ought to be considerable abatement made in the accounts I had read and heard of the savage characters of the Africans." *M. Adanson's* Voyage to Senegal, &c.[20]

The idyllic fictional memory in *The Dying Negro* of "Ye streams of Gambia, and thou sacred shade! / Where, in my youth's first dawn I joyful stray'd" may have suggested "pleasing Gambia" to Wheatley's mind.[21] Pastoral poetry, however, could be only a temporary diversion in 1774 from the march to war between Britain and its rebellious colonists.

When Nathaniel Wheatley returned home from England with his wife, Mary, on 22 September 1774 to settle some of his affairs following his mother's death, the naval blockade forced them to land at Salem and travel overland to Boston. On 27 October 1774 Samuel Quincy (1735–89), the Wheatley family lawyer, signed a deposition regarding the transfer of the vast bulk of John Wheatley's property to Nathaniel in 1771 and 1774 for token sums. Nathaniel and Mary Wheatley remained in New England for several years. Wheatley wrote from Boston to Nicholas Brown & Company in Providence, Rhode Island, on 13 February 1775 to order forty-five tons of strained whale oil.[22] On 27 February 1775 Wheatley advertised "Cheshire Cheese and London Porter" for sale at his store on King Street in Boston. Nathaniel Wheatley moved his business to Providence after the British occupied Boston. He and his wife were among the great majority of Bostonians who fled the town to avoid the British occupation following the battles of Lexington and Concord on 19 April 1775. Boston's population fell from more than fifteen thousand in 1770 to less than three thousand in 1776 during the occupation, which lasted until 17 March 1776. Wheatley advertised a house and various products for sale during the first three weeks of October 1775 in the *Providence Gazette*. He was still there in January 1776, when the tax assessed on the property of "Wheatly Nathanael" was significantly higher than the average.[23] Later that year he and his wife went back to Boston, where their daughter Elizabeth was baptized on 27 May 1776.[24] Nathaniel Wheatley remained in New England through 1777. The *London Gazette* reported on 2 December 1777 that on 31 July the British warship *Flora* had seized "the *Hero*, Alexander Coffin Master, Nathaniel Wheatley Owner," at sea on its voyage from Nantucket to France. The *Flora* sent its prize to Newport, Rhode Island, which had been under British control since 1776. Nathaniel Wheatley and his family were back in England by the summer of 1778. He probably returned to America alone in 1780. He may have subsequently gone back to London and again returned to Boston, where he died. The Episcopal Trinity Church record of his death reads, "6 September 1783 Mr. Nathanael Wheatly Mercht. 40y."[25]

Rev. John and Mary (Wheatley) Lathrop were among the refugees who moved to Providence, Rhode Island, during the 1775–76 British occupation of Boston. Phillis Wheatley probably accompanied them. She shared Rev. Lathrop's social and religious values. Several years later, Lathrop wrote from Boston to Benjamin Rush in Philadelphia: "Hearing what had been done in Europe—what your Society had done in Philadelphia, and what the Quakers were doing for the abolition of Slavery. . . . I long for the time when War & Slavery shall come to an end:—When, not only every Sect of *Christianity*, but when Jews & Gentiles, when all the Nations of Men on the face however differing in colour, and in other circumstances, shall embrace as Brethren Children of one common Father, & members of one great Family.—I long for the time when all flesh shall know the Lord."[26]

Phillis and the Lathrops were in Providence by the beginning of May 1775, when John preached "an animated and excellent Sermon" in the Congregationalist church "on the anniversary Election of the Independent Company of Cadets, and the United Company of the Train of Artillery."[27] On 21 November 1775 John Lathrop wrote to Moses Brown (1738–1836), a wealthy Providence merchant. Brown was raised in a slave-owning Baptist family. He and his three brothers managed the trading and manufacturing firm Nicholas Brown and Company, and they were founders of Rhode Island College (now Brown University). Moses Brown became a Quaker in 1774 after his wife's death the preceding year. He freed his own slaves after he embraced the emancipationist position of the Society of Friends. He expanded the program to aid Quakers suffering during the British occupation of Boston to include needy people of all denominations. Lathrop asked Brown to aid a minister who "called on me this morning for a little assistance in his pilgrimage but as I am a Pilgrim myself, thought it would not be out of character to recommend him to you, as one of the sufferers in the present unhappy Times."[28] Brown apparently granted Lathrop's request. On 30 December 1775 Rev. Lathrop appealed to Brown for aid for other indigent refugees from Boston.[29]

Prior to the British occupation of Boston, Phillis Wheatley had quite carefully balanced her public expressions of revolutionary and loyalist sentiments. Her agreement to return to Boston from London in 1773 had set her on the path to fully embracing an African American identity. As her "To His Excellency General Washington" demonstrates, she pledged her allegiance in 1776 to the revolutionary cause, hoping that even the most eminent slave owner in the colonies would ultimately apply the revolutionary ideology of equality and liberty to people of African as well as European descent. Wheatley was probably unaware of just how ironic her appeal to George Washington (1732–99) was. A number of Washington's slaves took advantage of his absence after 1774 from his Virginia plantation to emancipate themselves by joining the British forces. Washington resisted as long as possible the call to enlist militiamen of African descent among his own troops. When he arrived in Cambridge, Massachusetts, to drive the British out of Boston, he was shocked to see armed black men alongside their white fellow New Englanders. As Wheatley was writing to him in October 1775,

Washington was encouraging his officers to stop recruiting blacks. And while Washington was responding to Wheatley in February 1776, he was telling Congress that although he would begrudgingly allow black soldiers to reenlist because of the troop shortage he was suffering, he discouraged the recruitment of more men of African descent.

Wheatley's poem and the letter that accompanied it established her claim to the status of the unofficial poet laureate of the new nation-in-the-making. Wheatley was aware that she was being rather presumptuous in addressing Washington. He was in his camp at Cambridge besieging Boston when she wrote to him from Providence on 26 October 1775 (coincidentally the same day that George III declared to Parliament in London that the colonies were in rebellion):

> SIR,
>
> I Have taken the freedom to address your Excellency in the enclosed poem, and entreat your acceptance, though I am not insensible of its inaccuracies. Your being appointed by the Grand Continental Congress to be Generalissimo of the armies of North America, together with the fame of your virtues, excite sensations not easy to suppress. Your generosity, therefore, I presume, will pardon the attempt. Wishing your Excellency all possible success in the great cause you are so generously engaged in. I am,
>
> Your Excellency's most obedient humble servant,
> PHILLIS WHEATLEY

The poem itself combines a paean to Washington with Wheatley's conviction that the revolutionary ideology of America ("Columbia") has universal application. In language that anticipates Washington's heavenly reward, Wheatley's concluding couplet envisions him supplanting George III as America's patriot king:

> Fix'd are the eyes of nations on the scales,
> For in their hopes Columbia's arm prevails.
> Anon Britannia droops the pensive head,
> While round increase the rising hills of dead.
> Ah! cruel blindness to Columbia's state!
> Lament thy thirst of boundless power too late.
> Proceed, great chief, with virtue on thy side,

Thy ev'ry action let the goddess guide.
A crown, a mansion, and a throne that shine,
With gold unfading, WASHINGTON! be thine. (ll. 33–42)

As one of Wheatley's most astute critics has remarked, "Wheatley's poem should be read as a plea and challenge from a Boston refugee, rather than primarily as a poem of praise."[30]

Washington responded to Wheatley from Cambridge on 28 February 1776. He addressed her only by her first name, refusing, as was his custom, to acknowledge black surnames:[31]

> [Miss] Phillis, Your favor [i.e., letter] of the 26th of October did not reach my hands, 'till the middle of December. Time enough, you will say, to have given an answer ere this. Granted. But a variety of important occurrences, continually interposing to distract the mind and withdraw the attention, I hope will apologize for the delay, and plead my excuse for the seeming but not real neglect. I thank you most sincerely for your polite notice of me, in the elegant Lines you enclosed; and however undeserving I may be of such encomium and panegyrick, the style and manner exhibit a striking proof of your poetical Talents; in honor of which, and as a tribute justly due to you, I would have published the Poem, had I not been apprehensive, that, while I only meant to give the World this new instance of your genius, I might have incurred the imputation of Vanity. This, and nothing else, determined me not to give it place in the public Prints.
>
> If you should ever come to Cambridge, or near Head Quarters, I shall be happy to see a person so favored by the Muses, and to whom Nature has been so liberal and beneficent in her dispensations. I am, with great Respect, your obedient humble servant.

Washington sent Wheatley's poem and letter to his former secretary, Colonel Joseph Reed (1741–85) on 10 February 1776, telling him:

> I recollect nothing else worth giving you the trouble of, unless you can be amused by reading a letter and poem addressed to me by Miss Phillis Wheatley. In searching over a parcel of papers the other day, in order to destroy such as were useless, I brought it to light again. At first, with a view of doing justice to her poetical genius, I had a great

mind to publish the poem; but not knowing whether it might not be considered rather as a mark of my own vanity, than a compliment to her, I laid it aside, till I came across it again in the manner just mentioned.

Reed apparently took Washington's hint and sent the poem and letter with his own headnote to the editors of the *Virginia Gazette*, who published them on 20 March 1776. Thomas Paine (1737–1809) republished them in the April 1776 issue of his *Pennsylvania Magazine or American Monthly Museum*.

Despite Washington's invitation to Wheatley to visit him in Cambridge, it is very unlikely that she would have tried to cross British lines on land and at sea to do so before the British forces withdrew from Boston on 17 March 1776. Wheatley and the Lathrops probably remained in Providence until the liberation of Boston seemed secure.[32] Ezekiel Price (1727–1802) recorded in his diary on 19 April 1776, "The town [Boston] yet looks melancholy; but few of the inhabitants being removed back into it, occasioned by its not being sufficiently fortified and garrisoned against any further attempt of the enemy, to which it now lies much exposed. This day is the anniversary of the famous battle of Lexington."[33] Smallpox was another reason people hesitated to return to Boston, which had been afflicted by the disease since the summer of 1775. On 31 March 1776 Abigail Adams (1744–1818) explained to her husband, John, who was attending the Continental Congress in Philadelphia, that she had not yet reentered Boston because "I am fearfull of the smallpox, or I should have been in before this time."[34]

If Washington and Wheatley ever met, the likeliest place was Providence, where Washington stopped on 5 April 1776 and stayed two nights during his march to New York to face the British there. Wheatley was still in Providence at least as late as 14 February, when she wrote to Obour Tanner from there. Wheatley may have been among the crowds that welcomed Washington to Providence. Theodore Foster (1752–1828) described Washington's reception in his diary: "there was a great Concourse of People many having come a Number of Miles to have a Sight of his Excellency = the Houses through the Street were full of women the Eminemes [Eminences] without covered with Men."[35]

Although Wheatley represents herself in her letter and poem to Washington as deeply invested in the revolutionary cause, she describes herself to Tanner in February 1776 as "a mere spectator . . . of this unnatural civil

Contest."[36] Wheatley anticipated the way Ignatius Sancho was to exploit his social and ethnic status, enabling him to assume the position of a disinterested outsider commenting on sensitive subjects. In a letter dated 4 May 1778 Sancho asserts, "I say nothing of politics—I hate such subjects"; and on 7 September 1779, immediately after giving a very circumstantial account of recent military events and their likely political consequences, he insists that "[f]or my part, it's nothing to me—as I am only a lodger—and hardly that."[37] The context belies Sancho's comments, as does the fact that he was the only known eighteenth-century person of African descent who exercised his right to vote for members of Parliament. The discrepancies between the public and private statements and actions of Sancho and Wheatley probably reflect what W. E. B. Du Bois (1868–1963) calls the double consciousness of a person of African descent living in a white society. Although the loyalist Sancho and the revolutionary Wheatley could not disagree more about the character of the man Sancho mockingly called "Washingtub," they shared a sense of alienation from the respective societies in which the transatlantic slave trade had placed them.[38]

Wheatley was back in Boston by the end of 1776, probably living again with John Wheatley. Her 1779 "Proposals" includes a poem later titled "On the Capture of General Lee," which she dates from Boston 30 December 1776. She sent the manuscript poem to James Bowdoin with a headnote: "The following thoughts on his Excellency Major General Lee being betray'd into the hands of the Enemy by the treachery of a pretended Friend; To the Honourable James Bowdoin Esqr. are most respectfully Inscrib'd." General Charles Lee (1731–82) was a headstrong officer who was frequently reprimanded, and who aggressively sought to replace Washington as commander-in-chief of the Continental army. British troops who had served under him during the Seven Years' War took him prisoner in a New Jersey tavern on 13 December 1776. Although Wheatley probably knew that Lee had been with Washington in Cambridge during the siege of Boston, she apparently was unaware of his reputation. Her poem is an imagined dialogue between a patriotic Lee and his oppressive captors. It concludes with the fictionalized Lee challenging his captors to "'Find in your train of boasted heroes, one / To match the praise of Godlike Washington. / Thrice happy Chief! in whom the virtues join, / And heaven-taught prudence speaks the man divine!'" (ll. 65–68). Lee's behavior during the Battle on Monmouth, New Jersey, on 28 June 1778, caused him to be charged with insubordination and court-martialed. He was convicted and suspended from duty for a year. Some evidence indicates he may have been disloyal to the revolutionary cause. Wheatley's poem was not published until the late nineteenth century, probably because Bowdoin knew how greatly it misrepresents the relationship between Lee and Washington.[39]

National politics was not the only public subject on which the now-free Wheatley commented during the 1770s. In the same period she joined the developing transatlantic conversation about slavery. She wrote a letter to Samson Occom on the subject in February 1774. He had recently helped her sell copies of her *Poems*.[40] Part of the letter was soon widely distributed in print. The *Connecticut Gazette; and the Universal Intelligencer* was the first of many colonial newspapers to reprint Phillis Wheatley's most direct condemnation of slavery and the hypocrisy of self-styled freedom fighters.[41] Readers would have seen Wheatley as a powerful voice in the chorus of calls for rebellious Americans to be consistent in their demands for personal and political freedom. For example, the *Massachusetts Spy*, which reprinted Wheatley's letter to Occom in its 24 March 1774 issue, had the month before published a letter purportedly by an "African." The "African" argues that on the grounds of natural rights, legal precedent, and Christianity, "the Americans can't make a law to enslave the Africans without contradicting the law of God and the law of Great-Britain."

Wheatley's own emancipation allowed her to adapt Revolutionary rhetoric to openly equate contemporaneous slave owners—"Modern Egyptians" —with Old Testament villains, and by implication people of African descent with the Israelites, God's chosen people.[42] Wheatley's equation of slave owners with Egyptians may have inspired David Margate to adopt the same equation the following year. Like Moses Bon Sáam before her, Wheatley anticipated one of the most common metaphors found in nineteenth-century African American resistance to slavery. She was an African American pioneer in the development of what would come to be called liberation theology, the belief that God favored the oppressed. Her own liberation allowed her to use an ironic tone bordering on sarcasm to close her indictment of slave owners:

> *The following is an extract of a Letter from Phillis, a Negro Girl of Mr. Wheatley's, in Boston, to the Rev. Samson Occom, which we are desired to insert as a Specimen of her Ingenuity.—It is dated 11th Feb., 1774.*

Rev'd and honor'd Sir,

I have this Day received your obliging kind Epistle, and am greatly satisfied with your Reasons respecting the Negroes, and think highly reasonable what you offer in Vindication of their natural Rights: Those that invade them cannot be insensible that the divine Light is chasing away the thick Darkness which broods over the Land of Africa; and the Chaos which has reign'd so long, is converting into beautiful Order, and [r]eveals more and more clearly, the glorious Dispensation of civil and religious Liberty, which are so inseparably united, that there is little or no Enjoyment of one without the other: Otherwise, perhaps, the Israelites had been less solicitous for their Freedom from Egyptian Slavery; I do not say they would have been contented without it, by no means, for in every human Breast, God has implanted a Principle, which we call Love of Freedom; it is impatient of Oppression, and pants for Deliverance; and by the Leave of our Modern Egyptians I will assert, that the same Principle lives in us. God grant Deliverance in his own Way and Time, and get him honor upon all those whose Avarice impels them to countenance and help forward the Calamities of their Fellow Creatures. This I desire not for their Hurt, but to convince them of the strange Absurdity of their Conduct whose Words and Actions are so diametrically opposite. How well the Cry for Liberty, and the reverse Disposition for the Exercise of oppressive Power over others agree,—I humbly think it does not require the Penetration of a Philosopher to determine.

By 1774 political ideology as much as religious belief motivated Wheatley's argument for equality. Her position is consistent with Enlightenment philosophy: "the glorious Dispensation of civil and religious Liberty" is "reasonable." Liberty does require exposure to Christianity because "in every human Breast, God has implanted a Principle, which we call Love of Freedom; it is impatient of Oppression, and pants for Deliverance."

Occom was not alone in seeking Wheatley's advice and support on public issues. Rev. Hopkins, Obour Tanner's pastor in Newport, Rhode Island, called on Wheatley to participate in "chasing away the thick Darkness which broods over the Land of Africa." Hopkins had been minister of the First Congregational Church in Newport since 11 April 1770. His familiarity with the transatlantic slave trade, one of the foundations of Newport's prosperity, prompted him to become one of New England's most outspoken abolitionists. Hopkins and Rev. Ezra Stiles (1727–95), pastor of the Second Congregational Church in Newport (and a slave owner), circulated a petition during the summer and fall of 1773, first in manuscript and later in print, soliciting funds to be used to train Bristol Yamma and John Quamine (or Quamino) at what is now Princeton University to become Christian missionaries to Africa. Both men had been enslaved in the 1750s on the Gold Coast of Africa (present-day Ghana) and brought to Newport, where they had recently bought their freedom with money from a winning lottery ticket. They were keen to be sent back to their homeland. As Wheatley's 9 February 1774 letter to Hopkins indicates, he had sent her a copy of the solicitation:

> I received at the same time a paper by which I understand there are two Negro men who are desirous of returning to their native Country, to preach the Gospel; But being much indispos'd by the return of my Asthmatic complaint, besides, the sickness of my mistress who has been long confin'd to her bed, & is not expected to live a great while; all these things render it impracticable for me to do anything at present with regard to that paper, but what I can do in influencing my Christian friends and acquaintance, to promote this laudable design shall not be wanting. Methinks Rev'd Sir, this is the beginning of that happy period foretold by the Prophets, when all shall know the Lord from the least to the greatest, and that without the assistance of human Art & Eloquence. My heart expands with sympathetic Joy to see at distant time the thick cloud of ignorance dispersing from the face of my benighted Country; Europe and America have long been fed with the heavenly provision, and I fear they loathe it, while Africa is perishing with a Spiritual Famine. O that they could partake of the crumbs, the precious crumbs, Which fall from the table, of these distinguished children of the Kingdome.
>
> Their minds are unprejudiced against the truth therefore tis to be hoped they woud recieve it with their Whole heart. I hope that which the divine royal Psalmist Says by inspiration is now on the point of being Accomplish'd, namely, Ethiopia Shall Soon Stretch forth her hands Unto God.

Right around when Hopkins sent Wheatley the proposal he also sent it to Philip Quaque (1741?–1816) in Cape Coast, in present-day Ghana, seeking to find out whatever he could about Quamine's family. The relative of an African ruler, Quaque had been brought in 1754 from Cape Coast to England to be educated at the expense of the Society for the Propagation of the Gospel (SPG). In 1765 Quaque became the first African to be ordained an Anglican priest. The SPG sent Quaque and his English wife back to his native land the following year. He spent the next fifty years in Africa. He was the SPG's "Missionary, Catechist and Schoolmaster to the Negroes on the Gold Coast in Africa." He was at the same time the chaplain of the Company of Merchants Trading to Africa at Cape Coast Castle. During that period, he wrote some fifty letters back to London and to correspondents in North America reporting on his success (or more often lack thereof) as a missionary, his relationships with European and African authorities, his personal feelings, and his observations on the effects that the American and French revolutions had on Africa. Initially writing when the legitimacy of the transatlantic slave trade went largely unquestioned, Quaque wrote his last letters during the period of abolitionist fervor and after the abolition of the slave trade in 1808. Although the SPG supported slavery, and the Company of Merchants invested heavily in the slave trade, Quaque's letters reveal his evolving opposition to both slavery and the trade. He corresponded during the 1760s and 1770s with several early abolitionists in New England who sought information about his success as a missionary. Except for a brief period in 1784–85, when he returned to England to arrange for his children's education, he spent the rest of his life trying to pursue his mission at Cape Coast Castle, with very limited success. He quickly discovered that Africans were not keen to embrace the religion of those who were enslaving their neighbors.

Hopkins initiated a transatlantic correspondence with Quaque in March 1773 to ask his advice on how best to proceed in the plan to send Yamma and Quamine back as missionaries, and to ask Quaque to discover whatever he could about their families. Quaque shared Wheatley, Equiano, and Cugoano's conviction that Africans should welcome exposure to Christianity: "Thanks to *God* Omnipotent that [there] are still numbers of Africans, the supposed Race of *Cain*, able to embrace Christianity were they in a Country that yields the Light and Knowledge of the hidden Gospel."[43] Disappointed by his own lack of success, Quaque's response to Hopkins in May 1773 was pretty discouraging, but nonetheless he wished Hopkins "Success in your goodly Plan, and may God prosper the intent."[44]

John Thornton wrote to Wheatley from London to encourage her to play an active part in that "goodly Plan." He was probably encouraged to do so by comments Wheatley had made to him at the end of 1773. She suggested then that she might welcome having such a mission in life:

> O pray that I may be one also, who Shall Join with you in Songs of praise at the Throne of him, who is no respecter of Persons: being equally the great Maker of all:—Therefor disdain not to be called the Father of Humble Africans and Indians; though despisd on earth on account of our colour, we have this Consolation, if he enables us to deserve it. "That God dwells in the humble & contrite heart." O that I were more & more possess'd of this inestimable blessing; to be directed by the immediate influence of the divine Spirit in my daily walk & Conversation.[45]

Thornton was not the first to suggest that Wheatley be sent to Africa as a Christian missionary. Rev. Occom had asked Susannah Wheatley on 5 March 1771, "Pray Madam, what harm would it be to Send Phillis to her Native Country as a Female Preacher to her kindred, you know Quaker Women are alow'd to preach, and why not others in an Extraordinary Case."[46] We do not know if Phillis Wheatley was ever told of Occom's idea, but she rejected Thornton's request politely but firmly, and with good reason, on 30 October 1774. She might also have pointed out to the pious Thornton how unlikely it was that anyone who had recently achieved her freedom and international celebrity, with every reason to believe that more fame and fortune lay ahead, would give up so much to go to Africa:

> You propose my returning to Africa with Bristol yamma and John Quamine if either of them upon Strict enquiry is Such, as I dare give my heart and hand to, I believe they are either of them good enough if not too good for me, or they would not be fit for missionaries; but why do you hon'd Sir, wish those poor men so much trouble as to carry me So long a voyage? Upon my arrival, how like a Barbarian Should I look to the Natives; I can promise that my tongue shall be quiet for a strong reason indeed being an utter stranger to the Language of Anamaboe. Now to be Serious, This undertaking appears too hazardous, and not sufficiently Eligible, to go—and leave my British & American Friends—I am also unacquainted with those Missionaries

in Person. The reverend gentleman who unde[r] [ta]kes their Education has repeatedly informd me by Letters of their pro[gress] in Learning also an Account of John Quamine's family and Kingdo[m.] But be that as it will I resign it all to God's all wise governance; I thank you heartily for your generous Offer.

Unlike Wheatley (and Quaque), Yamma and Quamine were still able to speak their native language despite having spent many years living outside of Africa. Wheatley later met Quamine. In her 14 February 1776 to Obour Tanner, she mentions that she had "passed the last evening very agreeably" with "Mr. Quamine" in Providence.

Quaque and Wheatley became aware of each other through their separate correspondences with Hopkins, and although they never met, they formed an early link in the network of Black Atlantic writers. Hopkins sent the proposal on behalf of Yamma and Quamine to Quaque on 10 December 1773. He also sent him "the *proposals, &c.* [for Wheatley's *Poems*], supposing it will give you pleasure to see what a remarkable African appears in N. England. She has lately been to Europe, and was taken much notice of there. She will, I hope, be a means of promoting ye best interest of Africans."[47] Hopkins told Wheatley about Quaque's failings as a missionary. She wrote to Hopkins on 6 May 1774:

> I am very sorry to hear, that Philip Quaque has very little or no *apparent* Success in his mission.—Yet, I wish that what you hear respecting him, may be only a misrepresentation.—Let us not be discouraged, but still hope that God will bring about his great work, tho' Philip may *not* be the Instrument in the Divine Hand to perform this work of wonder, turning the Africans "*from darkness to light.*" Possibly, if Philip would introduce himself properly to them, (I don't know the reverse) he might be more Successful; and in setting a good example which is more powerfully winning than Instruction.

Through Hopkins, Quaque and Wheatley became the first authors of African descent to have their writings published together. Ezra Stiles and Hopkins included parts of two letters from Quaque to Hopkins, as well as an edited version of Wheatley's 9 February 1774 letter to Hopkins, in a circular titled *To the Public* (Newport, Rhode Island), dated 10 April 1776. *To the Public* is a progress report of the success Stiles and Hopkins have had in raising funds in America and Britain, as well as in having trained Yamma and Quamine for their mission to Africa, a mission interrupted by "the state of our public affairs."[48] Stiles and Hopkins quote Wheatley and Quaque to bear witness to the promising prospects and rewards of converting people of African descent on both sides of the Atlantic to Christianity.

The increasing hostilities between Britain and its colonies aborted the missionary project of Stiles and Hopkins. Hopkins fled Newport when the British occupied it in December 1776. So did the Tanner family, taking Obour Tanner with them to Worcester, Massachusetts. Quamine did not survive the war. He died in 1779 while serving on a privateer, a privately owned vessel authorized by the American Congress to seize enemy vessels. He had joined in hopes of gaining the money needed to buy his wife's freedom.[49]

The war probably helps to account for Wheatley's relative public silence during the next several years. Her *Poems* and separately published works, however, made her widely known in the English-speaking world during the 1770s and 1780s. George Washington was not the only Revolutionary War hero who corresponded with her. In an undated note probably written in late 1777, John Paul Jones (1747–92) asked fellow officer Hector MacNeill (1746–1818) to give a now-lost enclosure to Wheatley: "I am on the point of sailing . . . pray be so good as put the Inclosed into the hands of the Celebrated Phillis the African Favorite of the Nine and of Apollo, should she Reply, I hope you will be the bearer."[50] Jones may have been attempting to initiate a poetic exchange like that Rochfort had earlier had with "the Lovely daughter of the Affric shore."

Wheatley's publications also brought her to the attention of prominent continental Europeans. Both sides in contemporaneous arguments about the intellect, educability, and literary achievements of people of African descent quoted and cited her. Voltaire (1694–1778) wrote to a correspondent in 1774 that Wheatley's very fine English verse disproved the contention by Bernard le Bovier de Fontenelle (1657–1757) that no black poets existed.[51] To Bernard Romans (1741–84), however, Wheatley was one of a kind rather than representative of people of African descent: "Do we not see Solomon's words verified in Negroes? *A servant will not answer though he understand.*[52] The very perverse nature of this black race seems to require the harsh treatment they generally receive, but like all things, this is carried into the extreme; far be it from me to approve or recommend the vile usage to which this useful part of the creation is subjected by some of our western nabobs, but against the Phyllis of Boston (who is the *Phoenix* of her race) I could bring at least twenty well known instances of the contrary effect of education on this sable generation."[53] A Frenchman travelling in America in 1779 was more positively impressed by Wheatley's abilities, but he did not consider her representative of people of African descent:

> I shall tell you instead about Phyllis, one of the strangest creatures in the country and perhaps in the whole world.
>
> Phyllis is a negress, born in Africa, brought to Boston at the age of ten, and sold to a citizen of that city. She learned English with unusual ease, eagerly read and re-read the Bible, the only book which had been put in her hands, became steeped in the poetic images of which it is full, and at the age of seventeen published a number of poems in which there is imagination, poetry, and zeal, though no correctness nor order nor interest. I read them with some surprise. They are printed, and in the front of the book there are certificates of authenticity which leave no doubt that she is its author.[54]

Wheatley quickly gained recognition as an author in the growing tradition of women writers. The celebrity that Phillis Wheatley enjoyed in London during her brief six-week visit in 1773 continued in her absence during the 1770s and 1780s. There she earned what we today might call cultural capital. In his 1774 poem "Wrote after reading some Poems composed by PHILLIS WHEATLLY [*sic*]," "Alexis" praises "Afric's muse" as emblematic of what people of African descent could achieve if given access to education.[55] In a poem titled *The Female Advocate* (London: Printed for Joseph Johnson, 1774), Mary Scott [Taylor] (1752–93) praises the literary achievements of her female contemporaries, including the authors Catherine Macaulay (1731–91) and Elizabeth Robinson Montagu (1720–1800). Scott notes in her "Dedication" that "of late, Female Authors have appeared with honour, in almost every walk of literature. Several have started up since the writing of this little piece; the public favour has attested the merit of Mrs. Chapone's 'Letters on the Improvement of the Mind;' and of Miss More's elegant Pastoral Drama, intituled, 'A Search after Happiness,' 'Poems by Phillis Wheateley [*sic*], a Negro Servant to Mr. Wheateley [*sic*] of Boston;' and, 'Poems by a Lady,' printed for G. Robinson in Pater-noster-row, lately published, also possess considerable merit."[56] Scott effectively enrolls Phillis Wheatley in the informal society of literary women known as the Bluestockings.

The lines, diction, and footnotes in *The Female Advocate* devoted to Wheatley place her in the canons of English and philosophical poetry:

> Daughter of SHENSTONE* hail! hail charming maid,
> Well hath thy pen fair nature's charms displaye'd!
> The hill, the grove, the flow'r-enamell'd lawn,
> Shine in thy lays in brightest colours drawn:
> Nor be thy praise confin'd to rural themes,
> Or idly-musing Fancy's pleasing dreams;
> But still may contemplation+ (guest divine!)
> Expand thy breast, and prompt the flowing line. (ll. 305–10)

* See original Poems by Miss *Wheatley*.
\+ This couplet alludes to a fine Poem of that Lady's, intituled,
   "the Pleasures of Contemplation." [Scott's notes][57]

The association of Wheatley with the English poet William Shenstone (1714–63) is particularly interesting. He published *Poems on Various Occasions, Written for the Entertainment of the Author* (London, 1737) and *The Works in Verse and Prose of William Shenstone, Esq.* (London, 1744). The latter includes "Elegy XX," one of the earliest sympathetic accounts of the sufferings of enslaved people of African descent. Wheatley owned a copy of Shenstone's *Works*. Mary Everleigh of Charleston, South Carolina, gave it to her on 24 September 1774. Wheatley had in turn given Everleigh a copy of her *Poems*, which is now at Duke University. Wheatley and Everleigh may have exchanged the books in person when Everleigh was in Boston during the summer of 1774.[58]

Hannah More (1745–1833) was amused to be associated with Wheatley. More wrote on 10 September 1774 to Sir Joshua Reynolds's sisters Frances Reynolds (1729–1807) and Mary Reynolds Palmer. Wheatley had met Mrs. Palmer in London in 1773. More asked,

> Have you seen a little Poem called the *Female advocate*? The Author (a Woman) sent me a copy tho I do not know her. She seems to write with some ease and spirit. Mrs Chapone [1727–1801] and I are under infinite obligations to her, for ranking us with Phillis Wheatley the

black girl. I have a notion the comparison of Phillis and *I* occurred to her from the similarity of our *complexions* as well as *Talents*; the complexion of Mrs Chapone's *person* I have not the honour to know, that of her *mind*, I well know and greatly venerate.[59]

Mary Scott's association of Wheatley with More did not go unchallenged, however. The anonymous critic of *The Female Advocate* in the November 1774 issue of the *Monthly Review* objected that "Surely Miss Scott has impeached her own judgment in thus associating the celebrated Miss More with the poor Negro girl, whose talent for poetical imitation we mentioned some time ago."

A very different image of a threatening Phillis Wheatley appears in a brief series of three essays that appeared in the London newspaper the *Public Advertiser* on 11 June, 14 July, and 23 July 1777. The anonymous satirist includes Wheatley in his attacks on the achievements of contemporaneous literary women, specifically Elizabeth Carter and Elizabeth Montagu in philosophy and criticism, Catherine Macaulay in history, and Wheatley and especially Hannah More in poetry. By association with these women, Wheatley is implicitly categorized as what we today might call Black English, but she is *never* classified as *American* in these satires.

Wheatley plays a minor role in the satirist's initial essay. He alleges that women who pursue intellectual interests, particularly in public, are unnatural and either sexually deviant or lascivious. Thus, in his ironic celebration of "our *Literary Triumph*" over the Classical Greeks and Romans "in the noble Walk of Literature," he asks rhetorically and ironically, "where can Antiquity match my fair Friend Mrs. *Catharine Macaulay*, whose *Diction* and *Sentiments* could not be more *Man-like*, were she to wear as many Pair of Breeches as a *Dutch Skipper*." The satirist assumes that Wheatley is as familiar to his readers as the English members of the so-called Blue Stocking Circle of literary ladies that Mary Scott had praised several years earlier: "in Poetry, *Phillis Wheatley* and Mrs. *Hannah More* have quite eclipsed poor *Sappho*, the only Poetess of Antiquity; unless you will allow that the *Pythoness*, or the *old Hag of Cuma*, was inspired by the *Devil*." He reserves Wheatley for a future attack because at the moment he is concerned primarily with Hannah More: "[a]s for that *Ebon Beauty*, Miss Phillis, I shall say nothing about *her*, for the present; but as Mrs. *Hannah More* takes a *Stroke*, in the poetical Line . . . I think she cannot be much offended, if I give her a *Touch* in her own Way."

The value of "Phillis Wheatley" to the satirist becomes clear in the 14 July issue. The satirist's "Wheatley" is a doubly transgressive figure of the oversexed African woman writer who acts mannishly. The satirist elaborates the sexual subtext he established in the first essay with the *double entendres* aimed at Hannah More. His "Wheatley" assumes the masculine role to defend her fellow writers. She challenges this "*white-faced* (I might have added *white-livered*) Enemy of modern *Poetesses*," threatening, "It will . . . be a *black Affair* for him if (to use a Sea Phrase) he comes under my Lee; for I will have no Mercy on a Man who *stands up* against me on that Score." "Wheatley" boasts that from much experience she knows that "I am a Match for the stiffest Pedant in the Republic of Letters," and she warns the satirist, "He holds up his Crest, no Doubt, with Confidence, as he has hitherto met with no Rub for his Impudence in turning up the frail Part of us Female Poets; but I would have him draw back in Time, and not plunge too deep into a Subject whose Bottom his short Line of Understanding can never fathom." The sexual subtext becomes even more explicit in the satirist's ironic 23 July "Palinode to *Phillis Wheatley*." He addresses Wheatley as the "Poetic Queen of parch'd WHIDAW [an area on the slave coast of Africa]! / With *sable* Beauties, void of Flaw." Although obviously negative in intent, the satiric series in the *Public Advertiser* demonstrates Phillis Wheatley's enduring fame in England. Satire, after all, is a form of recognition.

Praise as well as satire could distort the image of Phillis Wheatley. Mary Deverell (fl. 1774–97) published her somewhat clumsily constructed eighteen-line poem titled "On Reading the Poems of Phillis Wheatley" in London in 1781.[60] Deverell's subscribers included Elizabeth Robinson Montagu, her friend Samuel Johnson, the most eminent literary figure in England, and Granville Sharp. Sharp must have been as surprised as we are to find that Deverell transformed the enslaved African he had met in 1773 into an Indian maid:

To shame the formal circle of the school,
That chain their pupils down by pedant rules,
Curbing the insolence of learned lore,
There lately came from India's swarthy shore,
In nature's sable charms, a lowly maid,
By fortune doom'd to languish in the shade;
Till Britain call'd the seeds of genius forth,
Maturing, like the sun, her native worth" (ll. 1–8)

Curiously, the following lines seem to render Wheatley the passive beneficiary of Britain's active artistry:

> Though no high birth nor titles grace her line,
> Yet humble PHILLIS boasts a race divine;
> Like marble that in quarries lies conceal'd,
> Till all its veins, by *polish*, stand reveal'd;
> From whence such groups of images arise,
> We praise the artist, and the sculpture prize. (ll. 9–14)

Once Wheatley's poetic self has been created, however, it gains agency,
spiritual equality, and figurative freedom:

> Go on, sweet maid, of Providence once more
> Divinely sing, and charm another shore;
> No fetters thus thy genius shall controul,
> Nor iron laws restrain thy towering soul. (ll. 15–18)

Phillis Wheatley soon found a place in the developing transatlantic tradition of authors of African descent. Her piety, especially as expressed in
her "On Being Brought from Africa to America," earned her Jupiter Hammon's public praise in Hartford, Connecticut, in 1778. Hammon celebrates
Wheatley's allegedly fortunate fall into Christianity in his *"AN ADDRESS
to Miss PHILLIS WHEATLY, Ethiopian Poetess, in Boston, who came from
Africa at eight years of age, and soon became acquainted with the Gospel of Jesus
Christ*:

> 1.
> O Come you pious youth! adore
>   The wisdom of thy God,   Eccles[iastes]. xii.
> In bringing thee from distant shore,
>   To learn his holy word.

> 2.
> Thou mightst been left behind,
>   Amidst a dark abode;   Psal[ms]. cxxxv, 2, 3.
> God's tender mercy still combin'd,
>   Thou hast the holy word.

To Ignatius Sancho, however, Wheatley's enslavement exposed the hypocrisy of slave owners who called themselves Christians, and who used Wheatley's talent as an excuse for self-congratulation on the "wanton power" they exercised over "a genius superior" to themselves. Sancho, a free African Briton, had been a slave and servant before becoming a grocer. He became the first Black Atlantic literary critic when he thanked the Quaker Jabez Fisher (1717–1806) of Philadelphia on 27 January 1778 for having sent him one of Anthony Benezet's antislavery books and a copy of Wheatley's *Poems*. Fisher's gifts elicited Sancho's most extensive comments on slavery. Sancho did not know that Wheatley had been manumitted in 1773. He believed that what she had been able to achieve despite her enslaved condition reinforced Benezet's case against slavery. To Sancho, although Wheatley's status may have been privileged in relation to that of other slaves, it was nonetheless disgraceful because powerful whites who were willing to praise her while she was a slave refused to help her gain her freedom. Sancho was the first person of any ethnicity known to have questioned the motives of Wheatley's owners and other whites who helped get her book published:

> Phyllis's poems do credit to nature—and put art—merely as art—to the blush.—It reflects nothing either to the glory or generosity of her master—if she is still his slave—except he glories in the *low vanity* of having in his wanton power a mind animated by Heaven—a genius superior to himself—the list of splendid—titled—learned names, in confirmation of her being the real authoress.—alas! shews how very poor the acquisition of wealth and knowledge are—without generosity—feeling—and humanity.—These good great folks—all know—and perhaps admired—nay, praised Genius in bondage—and then, like the Priests and the Levites in sacred writ, passed by—not one good Samaritan amongst them.[61]

The attention Phillis Wheatley received in London in 1773 and the reception of her writings there after her return to Boston gave her good reason to anticipate freedom and literary success in America as well. She did not foresee how greatly the economic and social disruptions caused by the American Revolution would alter her expectations. She would soon discover how many of the "good great folks" in Boston would come to her aid once she was a free woman of color.

Chapter 7

"An Elegy on Leaving"

Much about Phillis Wheatley's life between 1776 and her death in 1784 remains a mystery. She probably returned with John and Mary Lathrop in 1776 to Boston from their self-imposed exile in Providence. She probably remained a member of Rev. Lathrop's congregation when they accepted Rev. Ebenezer Pemberton's invitation to join with members of the New Brick Church to re-form the Second Church. (The British had destroyed Lathrop's Old North Meeting House during the occupation.) The 1779 "Proposals" for her never-published second book prove that she continued to write during the last eight years of her life, but very few of her poems and letters from that period have yet been discovered. Only four of Wheatley's poems were published between 1776 and her death in 1784. All of them appeared in 1784. She no doubt played a significant role in the production of the three poems published in Boston. We do not know whether the fourth, which appeared in London in John Wesley's Methodist *Arminian Magazine*, was published with either her consent or prior knowledge. Who or what accounts for her relative silence in America during her final years despite her continuing celebrity in Europe? The answer may be John Peters (1746?–1801), the free black man Phillis Wheatley married in 1778.[1]

When, where, or under what circumstances Phillis Wheatley and John Peters met are unknown. One critic, however, suggests that Wheatley mentions Peters in her 30 October 1773 letter to Obour Tanner: "[t]he young man by whom this is handed you seems to me to be a very clever man [who] knows you very well & is very Complaisant and agreable [*sic*]."[2] Although Peters was a free man when he first appears in records in 1776, we do not know whether he had ever been enslaved. He may have been born free. Phillis Wheatley almost certainly met Peters before John Wheatley died on 12 March 1778. John Wheatley's will names Rev. John Lathrop as his executor and Mary Wheatley Lathrop as the heir to "all the Residue of my

Estate both real & personal in Action or possession to hold the same to her & her heirs Forever."[3]

Phillis Wheatley's former owner left her nothing. Now more than ever she was on her "own footing." Wartime Boston was a particularly challenging place and time for a single woman, a *feme sole* in the language of the law, especially a free woman of African descent. On 1 April 1778 Phillis Wheatley and John Peters announced their intention to marry. Her willingness to marry was no doubt prompted at least in part by her desire for some degree of social and economic security. Their announcement came in the midst of unseasonably cold and snowy weather and general economic stress. John Tudor (1709–95) wrote in his diary on 31 March 1778 that it was "Still snowing & cold, Trees & everything cover'd as in the dep's of Winter, wind at N," and on 5 April 1778, "Sabbath, A.m. 8 O'clock, Snowing fast, wind at N. It began Yesterday P.m. at 5 and snow'd all night, for the morning it was near 12 inches deep & tho' the 5th of April looks like the dep's [depths] of Winter. Everything looks dark, as War & good Lord deliver us & ours from Enemies abroad, & extortion among ourselves every Nesacry [necessity] of life is exceeding dear."[4]

Phillis Wheatley and John Peters did not rush into marriage.[5] Rev. Lathrop performed the marriage between John Peters and Phillis Wheatley, "Free Negroes," in Boston's Second Congregational Church on 26 November 1778, a "fair Cold Annual Thanksgiving" day.[6] Lathrop had performed the marriage of "Cato Franklin & Susannah Williams, Free Negroes," in that church two days earlier.[7] Mary Wheatley Lathrop did not live to see Phillis marry. Two months earlier Rev. Lathrop recorded that "My Wife, Mary Lathrop died Sepr 24 1778 of a tedious Bilious & nervous complaint AE [aged] 35."[8]

Although Wheatley and Peters did not marry until the end of November 1778, they started living together soon after John Wheatley's death. When Wheatley wrote on 29 May 1778 to Obour Tanner, still living in Worcester, she mentioned that "The vast variety of Scenes that have pass'd before us these 3 years past will to a reasonable mind serve to convince us of the uncertain duration of all things Temporal." She asked Tanner to "Direct your letters under cover to Mr. John Peters in Queen Street." Phillis continued to write and manage her own business affairs until she married. She sent a letter signed "Phillis Wheatley" from Peters's house in Queen Street on 15 July 1778 to David Wooster's widow, Mary Clap Wooster, whom she had

never met. The enclosed poem, titled "On the Death of General Wooster" in Wheatley's 1779 "Proposals," was occasioned by Wooster's death on
2 May 1777.

Major General Wooster had been mortally wounded in battle a few days
earlier at Danbury, Connecticut. He had commanded six Connecticut
regiments since 1775. Wheatley's poem served multiple purposes. It is an
elegy for "a martyr in the Cause of Freedom" in which Wheatley imagines
Wooster's dying speech. Speaking through Wooster, Wheatley again casti-
gates the hypocrisy of self-styled patriots who are fighting for the freedom
to enslave others:

> ["]But how, presumptuous shall we hope to find
> Divine acceptance with th' Almighty mind—
> While yet (O deed ungenerous!) they disgrace
> And hold in bondage Afric's blameless race?
> Let virtue reign—And thou accord our prayers
> Be victory our's, and generous freedom theirs.["] (ll. 27–32)

Sending the poem to Wooster's widow also gave Wheatley an occasion
for tending to business. As soon as the poem ends Wheatley addresses Mrs.
Wooster: "You will do me a great favour by returning to me by the first oppy
[opportunity] those books that remain unsold and remitting the money for
those that are sold—I can easily dispose of them here for 12 [shillings]/
Lm.o [lawful money] each—I am greatly obliged to you for the care you
show me, and your condescention [generosity] in taking so much pains for
my Interest." Wheatley's book was obviously still in demand five years after
first being published. The higher price of twelve shillings lawful money she
expected to be able to charge for a copy reflects both the continued demand
for her work and the inflationary effects of the war.

We can only speculate as to why John Peters and Phillis Wheatley waited
months to wed. Although she had much to gain in terms of security by marrying, she surely knew that marriage would mean losing the independence
she had enjoyed during the previous five years. By exchanging her status of
feme sole for that of *feme covert* by marrying, Wheatley effectively erased the
legal identity she had gained in 1773: "By marriage, the husband and wife are
one person in law: that is, the very being or legal existence of the woman is
suspended during the marriage, or at least is incorporated and consolidated
into that of the husband: under whose wing, protection, and cover, she per-

forms every thing; and is therefore called in our law-French a feme-covert."[9] Wheatley's marriage compounds the problems her biographer faces in trying to reconstruct her life. Once her identity was submerged beneath that of her husband she becomes even more difficult to trace than before.

Records of eighteenth-century people of African descent are often difficult, if not impossible, to find. Paradoxically, we often know more about them when they were enslaved than when they were free because as slaves they were considered property. Human property was usually recorded in various ways for purposes of taxation, inheritance, and manumission. And human property was normally identified in official records by ethnicity or phenotype (complexion). Free people of color, however, often left few, or no, official records unless they were substantial property owners or were involved in some way with the legal system. And even when free people of color left records, in Massachusetts those records often did not indicate whether the person was of African descent if that information was considered irrelevant. For example, many of the individual surviving records relating to John Peters do not say that he was a black man of African descent. But if we follow the chain of evidence in the records or contextualize them with external information, we can often identify which references to any "John Peters" are to the John Peters who married Phillis Wheatley. Fortunately for Wheatley's biographer, in "a society as culturally litigious as Massachusetts," John Peters had more encounters with the legal system than most of his contemporaries, white or black.[10] Prison, tax, court, and census records enable us to fill in many of the gaps in the narrative of what little was known about John Peters, especially his life after Phillis died.

Few early accounts of John Peters exist. The only contemporaneous description by someone who probably knew Phillis Wheatley personally is the one that Hannah Mather Crocker recorded in the nineteenth century: "She [Phillis Wheatley] married at twenty one a man of noteriety [*sic*] by the name of Peters. he did not treat her will [*sic*] She soon fell a prey, to disapointment [*sic*] and her keen sensibility proved a sudden decline and she died."[11] We have no external evidence that allows us to either verify or reject Crocker's account. The most influential account of John Peters has been the very negative one in Margaret Matilda Odell's 1834 "Memoir." Odell was a collateral descendant of Susanna Wheatley, and she attributes much of her information to unnamed relatives and friends of the Wheatley family. Odell's "Memoir," however, needs to be treated with far more care and skepticism than critics and scholars have given it. Much of the information in Odell's account is either unverifiable, unreliable, demonstrably incorrect, or apparently intended to serve Odell's literary and social agendas. Odell's comparison of Wheatley's life before and after she gained her freedom seems designed to represent the security of enslavement as preferable to the unpredictability of freedom for people of African descent: "Phillis was now, therefore, left utterly desolate. She spent a short time with a friend of her departed mistress, and then took an apartment, and lived by herself. This was a strange change to one who had enjoyed the comforts and even luxuries of life, and the happiness of a fire-side where a well regulated family were accustomed to gather"[12]

Odell represents Peters as the villain in a Dickensian narrative of the decline and death of a sentimental heroine. Odell's John Peters is a vain man and bad husband.[13] He sounds much like Chloe Spear's husband, Caesar, who, "although he possessed none of the refinement, or economy, for which his companion was so remarkable, was, nevertheless, fond of finery and show."[14] Writing in the 1830s, both Odell and the amanuensis of Spear's *Memoir* disapproved of demonstrations of gentility by men of African descent that they probably would have left unremarked had they been describing the behavior of whites. During the eighteenth and nineteenth centuries, free people of African descent were often even more concerned than whites with acting, dressing, and speaking respectably to counteract negative stereotypes. As historians have noted, "[t]he Achilles heel of free black men was their vulnerability to any threat to their reputation."[15] But when people of African descent attempted to enhance their reputations, especially during the nineteenth century, they were frequently mocked and accused of acting "uppity."[16]

Surviving records prove that some of Odell's information is wrong. For example, she says that Phillis Wheatley and John Peters had been married for years before the British occupation of Boston, and that

> After the evacuation of Boston by the British troops, Phillis returned thither. A niece of Mrs. Wheatley's, whose son had been slain in battle, received her beneath her own roof. This lady was a widow, and not wealthy. She kept a small day school to increase her narrow income. Her mansion had been much injured by the enemy, but it afforded a shelter to herself and daughter, and they ministered to Phillis, and her

three suffering children, for six weeks. At the end of that period, Peters came for his wife, and, having provided an apartment, took her thither with her little family.[17]

Elizabeth Wallcut was the "niece of Mrs. Wheatley's" whose son Christopher had been killed in battle with the British on 8 July 1777. He was two years older than his brother Thomas, Phillis Wheatley's correspondent. A comparison of letters written by Phillis with those by Elizabeth Wallcut demonstrates that the former slave would have been the far better educated teacher. Elizabeth Wallcut did eventually open a school, but the first record of it occurs several years after Phillis Wheatley Peters died. The *Boston City Directory for 1789* lists "Walcutt, Widow, school-mistress, Purchase-street" in Ward II. Odell is apparently the source of the often repeated claim that Phillis Wheatley Peters "became the mother of three infants." She may be correct, but no birth, baptismal, or burial records have been found for any children of Phillis and John Peters.

Wheatley may have already met "Shopkeeper" Peters when the Suffolk County Superior Court of Common Pleas in October 1776 awarded him forty pounds lawful money in damages and costs in his suit against Joseph Scott. Scott was a Boston merchant and ironmaster who barely escaped being killed when a mob set fire to his house in September 1774 because he had sold military supplies to General Gage's British troops. Scott was a Loyalist who remained in Boston during the 1775–76 occupation. A writ on Peters's behalf was issued against Scott at the end of March 1776, but he had already fled with the British forces to Nova Scotia when they evacuated Boston two weeks earlier. Scott of course failed to appear in court at the session in April 1776 (the court met quarterly each year, in January, April, July, and October).[18] Scott eventually made his way to England. The Massachusetts legislature officially proscribed and banished him in 1778.[19]

Because of the scarcity of money in the colonies during the eighteenth century, "people relied on promises—the notes, bills, and bonds," which a creditor often could get redeemed only by taking the debtor to court.[20] Consequently, law suits were very common and frequently took years to settle, if they were ever settled at all. Even in relatively prosperous times, such as before the French and Indian War, commercial transactions based so heavily on credit and debt were precarious. As *The Ill Policy and Inhumanity of Imprisoning Insolvent Debtors, Fairly Stated and Discussed* (Newport, R.I.,

1754) warned, "the Man in Trade and Business, who is both a Debtor and Creditor, is therefore liable every Moment to Accidents, unforeseen Casualties, and Contingencies."[21] Peters was one of many tradesmen, shopkeepers, and other creditors who brought another suit against Scott for unpaid debts in 1779. Neither the 1776 nor the 1779 suit identifies Peters as a man of African descent, but in the latter suit he is the only creditor not referred to as "Mr."[22] During Phillis's life and even after her death, John Peters continued to bring successful suits against Scott, never to be paid.

Despite Peters's inability to collect the money Scott owed him, much of the first year of Phillis and John Peters's marriage was prosperous and promising, according to tax and court records. Peters and Josias Byles, a white man, were business partners selling rye, wheat, tea, nails, sugar, and other goods in the counties of western Massachusetts during the spring and summer of 1779.[23] Phillis was apparently also optimistic about the future. While her husband worked in western Massachusetts, she remained in Boston. She wrote from there on 10 May 1779 to Obour Tanner to apologize for having "been Silent" due to "a variety of hindrances."

Those "hindrances" included preparation of a second volume for publication, this time to include correspondence as well as poetry. The description of the proposed book is elaborate and ambitious. It was to be approximately twice as long as her first book. The description of the author in the advertisement does not assume that prospective buyers would be familiar with her. The contents of the proposed book, however, indicate a writer of transatlantic stature. The number of poems on, or addressed to, prominent American military figures is balanced by the number addressed to corresponding British figures. Phillis Wheatley Peters's maturity as an author and her enhanced public profile are reflected in the number of national events that are subjects of the poems, as well as in the status of her correspondents. The titles and addressees reflect her growing interest in secular as well as Christian subjects. Her writings since 1772 also reflect her increasing emphasis on the equality of people of European descent with those of African descent based on natural rights and political theory rather than theological doctrine.

The proposed volume was front-page news in the 30 October 1779 issue of the *Boston Evening Post and General Advertiser*, the newspaper produced by the intended publishers of the book. The lengthy advertisement took up more than the whole first column on the front page. It appeared under the newspaper's motto, "Hail LIBERTY Divine, and PEACE, First-born of Heaven." The same newspaper repeated the advertisement on 6 and 27 November and 4, 11, and 18 December:

Proposals

For Printing By Subscription a Volume of Poems And Letters, on Various Subjects, Dedicated to the Right Honourable Benjamin Franklin Esq; One of the Ambassadors of the United States at the Court of France, By Phillis Peters

Poems
[1] Thoughts on the Times.
[2] On the Capture of General Lee, to I.B. Esq.
[3] To his Excellency General Washington.
[4] On the death of General Wooster.
[5] An Address to Dr—.
[6] To Lieut R— of the Royal Navy.
[7] To the same.
[8] To T.M. Esq. of Granada.
[9] To Sophia of South Carolina.
[10] To Mr. A. M'B— of the Navy.
[11] To Lieut R— D— of the Navy.
[12] Ocean.
[13] The choice and advantages of a Friend to Mr. T— M—
[14] Farewell to England, 1773.
[15] To Mrs. W—ms on Anna Eliza.
[16] To Mr. A McB—d.
[17] Epithalamium to Mrs. H—
[18] To P.N.S. & Lady on the death of their infant son.
[19] To Mr. El—y on the death of his Lady.
[20] On the death of Lt. L—ds.
[21] To Penelope.
[22] To Mr. & Mrs. L— on the death of their daughter.
[23] A Complaint.
[24] To Mr. A.I.M. on Virtue.
[25] To Dr. L—d and Lady on the death of their son aged 5 years

[26] To Mr. L—g on the death of his son.

[27] To Capt. F—r on the death of his granddaughter.

[28] To Philandra an Elegy.

[29] Niagara.

[30] Chloe to Calliope.

[31] To Musidora on Florello.

[32] To Sir E.L— Esq.

[33] To the Hon. John Montague Esq. Rear Admiral of the Blue.

Letters

1. To the Right Hon. Wm E. of Dartmouth, Sec. of State for
   N. America.
2. To the Rev. Mr. T.P. Farmington.
3. To Mr. T.W.—Dartmouth College.
4. To the Hon. T. H. Esq.
5. To Dr. B. Rush, Phila.
6. To the Rev. Dr. Thomas, London.
7. To the Right Hon. Countess of H—.
8. To I.M—Esq. London.
9. To Mrs. W—e in the County of Surrey.
10. To Mr. T.M. Homerton, near London.
11. To Mrs. S. W—
12. To the Rt. Hon. the Countess of H—.
13. To the same.

Messieurs Printers, The above collection of Poems and Letters was put into my hands by the desire of the ingenious author, in order to be introduced to public View.

The subjects are various and curious, and the author a *Female African*, whose lot it was to fall into the hands of a *generous* master and *great* benefactor. The learned and ingenuous as well as those who are pleased with novelty, are invited to incourage the publication by a generous subscription—the former, that they may fan the sacred fire which, is self-enkindled in the breast of this *young* African—The ingenuous that they may by reading this collection, have a large play for their imaginations, and be ex[c]ited to please and benefit mankind, by some brilliant production of their own pens.—Those who are *always* in search of some *new* thing, that they may obtain a sight of this *rara avis in terra* [Latin for "rare bird in the land"]—And every one, that the ingenious author may be encouraged to improve her own mind, benefit and please mankind.

CONDITIONS

They will be printed on good Paper and a neat Type; and will Contain about 300 Pages in Octavo.

The price to Subscribers will be *Twelve Pounds*, neatly Bound and Lettered, and *Nine Pounds* sew'd in blue paper, one Half to be paid on Subscribing, the other Half, on Delivery of the Books.

The Work will be put to the Press as soon as a sufficient Number of Encouragers offer.

Those who subscribe for Six [books], will have a Seventh Gratis.

Subscriptions are taken by [James] White and [Thomas] Adams, the Publishers, in School-Street, *Boston*.

White (1755?–1824) and Adams (1757?–99) may have been approached as potential publishers because they had recently published the sermon Rev. John Lathrop delivered at the funeral of his late wife.[24]

The absence of any reference in the advertisement to Phillis's maiden name probably indicates that her husband played a dominant role in the planning of the proposed book. As a *feme covert* the former Phillis Wheatley was now legally the property of her husband, as was any property or possession she owned. She no longer had the right to sign contracts independently of him. Given his experience with the law, John Peters was undoubtedly well aware of his legal rights and authority. Hence, he was probably responsible for the decision to use only their surname in the advertisement. He may also have been responsible for pricing the book. It was to be significantly more expensive than Phillis's first book, even after accounting for the difference in the size and scope of the proposed larger volume, as well as the depreciation of continental currency. In 1774, 135 Massachusetts pounds equalled one hundred pounds sterling in value. After the onset of hostilities, the value of a Massachusetts pound depreciated rapidly. Between January 1777 and December 1779, when Wheatley sought subscribers for her proposed second volume of works, the value of a Massachusetts pound depreciated at least thirtyfold. One scholar estimates that the sum of 300,000 continental dollars was equivalent in 1780 to "about $7500" in specie.[25]

Phillis Wheatley Peters appeared to be on the verge of an *annus mirabilis* in 1780 equivalent to that of 1773, the year that saw the publication of her book and that brought her freedom. She apparently had a new book ready to be published, and she and her husband were seemingly relatively prosperous. The 1780 "Taking Book" records "John Peters (Negro)" as living in Boston's Ward 2 and assessed "150 Rents," a very respectable sum. Peters heads the list of 172 names in the ward, most of whom are tradesmen. He is the only person in Ward 2 identified as a Negro. The assessed rents range from William White, "Shopkeeper," at 260, to Thomas Volintine, "Cooper," at 7.10. Peters is one of thirty residents with rents of 100 or more. In October 1780 Peters won a suit against his partner Byles, "determining that the Defendant pay to the Plaintif Forty eight shillings Lm. Also that the Deft Relinquish all that part of Goods now at Rutland wch Belonged Jointly to Plaintif and Defendant as companys Stock in Trade, or Pay the Plaintif One hundred pounds in thirty days after Judgment."[26] Peters was now worth in property alone upwards of 250 pounds lawful money. But by October 1780 he and Phillis had already begun their nearly four-year-long absence from public records. Why? And where did they go?

Plausible answers exist in the surviving records. In November 1779, the month after Peters initiated the suit against Byles that was judged in his favor the following October, Susannah Child Sheaffe (d. 1811) brought a suit against Peters himself. She was the widow of William Sheaffe (1706–71), who had been deputy-collector of his Majesty's Customs for the Port of Boston for many years before his death in 1771. Friends helped his widow establish a store at the north corner of Queen-Street, where she sold "All kinds of Grocery, by Wholesale and Retail for cash only, upon as good Terms as can be bought in Town."[27] She also ran a boarding house, which British Major General Hugh Percy (1742–1817) used as his headquarters during the occupation. In 1780 she was living in Boston's Ward 1 and assessed "70 Rents." If Sheaffe was the wholesaler who supplied the goods Peters sold in western Massachusetts, that might explain why the court awarded her the impressive amount of nearly four hundred pounds in July 1780 in her suit against him.[28] Not even liquidating all of his known assets would have covered that judgment against Peters.

Eighteenth-century debtors had several choices: pay the debt; go to jail until either the debt is paid or the creditor gives up trying to collect it; hide in one's house; skip town. Peters apparently chose the latter option. Since Peters's suit against Byles awarded him costs, we have a record of the quarterly expenses he reported to the court. He requested no travel allowance in October 1779 and January 1780, which meant that he was living in Boston during those quarters, but for each of the April, July, and October 1780 quarters he reported traveling thirty miles roundtrip to court.[29] He may have been planning his escape if he anticipated the judgment against him in Sheaffe's suit. But where did he and Phillis go? Odell says that during the occupation of Boston "Phillis accompanied her husband to Wilmington," Massachusetts, which was indeed "an obscure country village" in Essex County north of Boston.[30] Wilmington had fewer than 750 residents at the time.[31] Although Odell is obviously wrong about when Phillis and John Peters might have gone to Wilmington, a move to Wilmington, which is approximately thirty miles roundtrip from Boston, would be consistent with Peters's claim for travel reimbursements. Peters may have considered Wilmington a village especially sympathetic to people of African descent. Wilmington had freed its slaves on 3 March 1779, well before slavery was abolished in Massachusetts. No records of Phillis and John have been found in Wilmington, but that is to be expected if they went there to escape a creditor.[32]

Phillis was not completely out of the public eye in Boston during her years of silence. A woodcut portrait based on the frontispiece of her 1773 *Poems* appeared in *Bickerstaff's Boston Almanack . . . 1782* (Boston, 1781). John and Phillis Peters may have returned to Boston by the beginning of 1784, when she published the pamphlet *An Elegy, Sacred to the Memory of that Great Divine, the Reverend and Learned Dr. Samuel Cooper* (Boston: Printed and Sold by E[zekiel]. Russell, in Essex-Street).[33] Or she may have sent the poem on the death of the minister who had baptized her to the Boston publisher from out of town. The beginning of 1784 was probably also when she published *LIBERTY AND PEACE, A POEM. By PHILLIS PETERS* (Boston: Printed by [William] Warden [1761–86] and [Ezekiel] Russell, At Their Office in Marlborough-Street, 1784). The pamphlet is a celebration of the Peace of Paris that Congress ratified in January 1784. Not surprisingly given its subject, the poem exudes joy and optimism. The tone is even somewhat self-congratulatory.[34] In her description of "Freedom" Phillis Wheatley Peters quotes in italics a couplet from her earlier poem to Washington: "*She moves divinely fair, / Olive and Laurel bind her golden Hair.*" As someone who had endured the Middle Passage, Phillis may also be referring less directly to herself in lines lamenting the fate of British troops "Sent [to America] from th' Enjoyment of their native Shore / Ill-fated—never to behold her more!" Unfortunately, Phillis's vision that "So Freedom comes array'd with Charms divine, / And in her Train Commerce and Plenty shine" would not include her, her husband, and most other people of African descent.[35]

Phillis and John were definitely back in Boston by June 1784, when John Peters, "Labourer," had another writ issued against Joseph Scott. Peters again won his suit by default when Scott, of course, did not appear at the July quarterly session.[36] Winning, however, gained him nothing, since Scott remained in England. The identification of Peters as a "Labourer" should not surprise us. In the eighteenth century, especially during the depression following the Revolutionary War, many men had multiple occupational identities, simultaneously as well as successively.[37] John Wheatley, for example, even before the War is normally listed in records as a tailor, but he was also a shopkeeper who engaged in transatlantic commerce. Peters seems to have been scrambling to try to get back on his feet in 1784. "Shopkeeper" Peters successfully petitioned town officials on 28 July 1784 to allow him to sell liquor at the shop he had recently opened in north Boston "for the purpose of supporting himself & Family."[38]

Peters's mention in his petition of his "Family" is one of only two contemporaneous references to children in the marriage between John Peters and Phillis Wheatley. The other appears in the sympathetic account of Peters recorded by the Venezuelan revolutionary Sebastián Francisco de Miranda y Rodríguez (1750–1816) in his journal. He was visiting Boston between 16 September and 15 October 1784:

> Phillis Wheatley, a Negro slave who, as a child, came from the coast of Guinea to this city [Boston]. Her owner gave her the small beginnings of an education, and see you here that the compositions of Phillis, in prose and poetry, went to press. She went to England and was admired. Afterwards she returned here and suffered the same neglect the talents experience everywhere. She finally married a sagacious Negro named Peters, by whom she had several children, and today is dying in indigence. Here one sees that the rational being is the same in whatever form or aspect. The most cruel laws of forbearance and the enjoyment of the most exalted pleasures are preserved in this Negro being.[39]

The closest we come to having a reference by Phillis herself to any of her own children is a manuscript draft of a poem whose speaker is a pregnant woman. Attribution of the poem to Wheatley, however, is not universally accepted:

Prayer
Sabbath—June 13, 1779
Oh my Gracious Preserver!
hitehero thou hast brot [me,]
be pleased when thou bringest
to the birth to give [me] strength
to bring forth living & perfect a   5
being who shall be greatly in-
strumental in promoting thy [glory]
Tho conceived in Sin & brot forth
in iniquity yet thy infinite wisdom
can bring a clean thing out of an   10
unclean, a vess[el] of Honor filled
for thy glory—grant me
to live a life of gratitude to thee
for the innumerable benefits—
O Lord my God! instruct my ignorance   15
& enlighten my Darkness
Thou art my King, take [thou]
the entire possession of [all] my
powers & faculties & let me be
no longer under the dominion   20
of sin—Give me a sincere &
hearty repentance for all my
[grievous?] offences & strengthen
by thy grace my resolutions
on amendment & circumspection   25
for the time to come—Grant me
[also] the spirit of Prayer & Suppli[cation]
according to thy own
most gracious Promises.[40]

John Peters was unfortunately unable to exploit his temporary success in having his petition to sell liquor approved. Indeed, his petition may have alerted his creditors that he had returned to Boston. The "Taking Book" for 1784, "taken on the 1st Sepr 1784," includes "Jno Peters Negro" in Ward 7. Ward 7 was a far more economically and ethnically diverse ward than the one John and Phillis Peters had lived in in 1780. Of the 297 names in the 1784 list, 78 own real estate of over 100 value, 40 are identified as poor &/or infirm, and 32 Negroes are identified. At the other end of the economic scale, Dr. Joseph Gowen is assessed at 175, and "Physician" Dr. Thomas Bulfinch, at 600, owns 2 houses. Although Peters owns one "Dwellg House," he is described as "In Prison for Debt." His debt to Mrs. Sheaffe may have been what sent him there. She was still living in Boston when he returned: the same "Taking Book" places "Widow Sheaff" in Ward 8, where she "Keeps Boarders" and owns "125 Value Real Estate."[41]

Phillis and John Peters were victims of the severe depression throughout the former colonies that followed the end of the Revolutionary War, when "the decline of prices, the scarcity of cash, depreciation, competition from British manufactures, the obstacles to establishing export markets when no longer part of the British empire, and efforts by British commercial creditors to collect pre-war debts all contributed to a wave of business failures after the Revolution."[42] Peters had no chance of collecting the money Scott owed him. He had almost as little chance of collecting the money Byles owed him because most businessmen in western Massachusetts were in even more dire financial situations than those in Boston: "When the postwar depression arrived . . . [t]he demand of coastal merchants for specie to satisfy their foreign creditors echoed across the state, as debt collection suits flooded the courts and imprisoned debtors crammed the jails. Particularly hard hit were the farmers of Worcester and Hampshire counties, where lawsuits for debt more than tripled over war levels and where debt actions embroiled nearly a third of the adult males of each county. These debtors were at the end of the chain of credit that ran from British merchants to Boston wholesalers to inland retailers and other commercial intermediaries."[43] No doubt complicating the financial situation of Phillis and John Peters was the fact that Massachusetts was the only state that required all debts and taxes be paid in very scarce specie rather than in much depreciated currency.[44]

Boston did not have a separate prison for debtors, and prison records were kept quarterly. They tell us whether a particular person was in the prison on the day the record was made, but not necessarily whether or for how long that person was there before or after the quarterly recording. John Peters is not included on the 6 January, 20 April, 6 July, 5 October 1784 or 4 January and 5 July 1785 prisoner lists, but he is on the 19 April and October 1785 lists. He may have been in and out of prison for debt during much of that period. Peters meanwhile continued to pursue his hopeless suit against Joseph Scott in October 1784 and January 1785.[45] The available evidence does not appear to support either the accusation that Peters "had become so shiftless and improvident, that he was forced to relieve himself of debt by an imprisonment in the county jail," or the insinuation that Phillis Wheatley Peters died alone and in desperate circumstances because her husband had abandoned her.[46] He almost certainly had no choice but to be absent.

Phillis did not vanish from public notice while her husband was in jail. On 20 May 1784 Boston's *Independent Chronicle and Universal Advertiser* published "The Choice," by "the late Mr. Heman Harris" of Wrentham, Massachusetts, which contains the lines:

> And to delight the studious mind,
> I'd in the next gradation find
> The Poets in a pleasing throng,
> From the great source of Grecian Song
> That shines in the page
> Down to the PHILLIS of our age. (ll. 48–53)

Next to "The Choice" the *Independent Chronicle and Universal Advertiser* reprinted an emancipationist attack on slavery that had been published in a London newspaper two months earlier.

Phillis tried again to reassert her own agency during her husband's absence by advertising another proposal for a second volume of her writings in the September 1784 issue of the *Boston Magazine*. The advertisement in the magazine published by Greenleaf and Freeman included a hitherto unpublished poem that Phillis had written before her marriage: "The Poem ['To Mr. and Mrs.—, On the Death of Their Infant Son, By Phillis Wheatly (*sic*)'], in page 488, of this Number, was selected from a manuscript Volume of Poems, written by PHILLIS PETERS, formerly Phillis Wheatly—and is inserted as a Specimen of her Work; should this gain the approbation of the Publick and sufficient encouragement be given, a Volume will be shortly Published, by the Printers hereof, who received subscriptions for said Work."[47] The difference between her elaborate and very confident 1779 "Proposals" and her rather desperate-sounding final one is striking. During her marriage to Peters, Phillis most actively publicly pursued her calling as a poet when he was probably either out of town in 1779 or incarcerated in 1784.

What role, if any, Phillis played in John Wesley's publication and re-publication of some of her poems in 1781 and 1784 is not known.[48] Like Whitefield, Wesley published his own sermons, but he also published the religiously oriented works of others, both indirectly through plagiarism, and openly in abridged versions of classic religious texts. Wesley began publishing the *Arminian Magazine* in London in 1778. It was renamed the *Methodist Magazine* after his death in 1791. During Phillis's lifetime Wesley published variant versions of eight of her previously published poems: "On the Death of a Child, Five Years of Age," "On the Death of a Young Gentleman," "Thoughts on the Works of Providence," "To T. H[ubbard] Esq. on the Death of His Daughter," "To S.M. a Young African Painter, on Seeing His Works," "To the Right Honourable William, Earl of D———t———th, when Secretary of State for North America," "On the Death of J.C. an Infant," and "On Imagination." Abolitionist as well as religious concerns probably motivated Wesley's interest in Wheatley and her writings. Unlike Whitefield and the Countess of Huntingdon, John Wesley opposed the institution of slavery. In *Thoughts upon Slavery* (London, 1774), Wesley drew on accounts of Africa by Adanson, Hans Sloane (1660–1753), and others he had read in Benezet's works to derive a very favorable image of Africans: "Our Forefathers! Where shall we find at this day, among the fair-faced natives of *Europe*, a nation generally practising the Justice, Mercy, and Truth, which are found among these poor black *Africans*? Suppose the preceding accounts are true . . . , and we may leave *England* and *France*, to seek genuine Honesty in *Benin*, *Congo*, or *Angola*."[49] Europeans "first taught Africans drunkenness and avarice, and then hired them to sell one another. . . . When did a Turk or Heathen find it necessary to use a fellow-creature thus?"[50] Slavery, Wesley argues, is inconsistent with "even natural justice."[51] The immorality of slavery made economic arguments for it irrelevant to Wesley. Wesley proclaims that "It were better that all those [West India] Islands should remain uncultivated for ever, yea, it were more desirable that they were all together sunk in the depth of the sea, than that they should be cultivated at so high a price, as the violation of Justice, Mercy and Truth."[52]

Wesley published Phillis's "An ELEGY on leaving—" in the July 1784 issue of the *Arminian Magazine* five months before her death. The next-to-the-last of Phillis Wheatley Peters's writings published during her lifetime is a twenty-eight-line pastoral poem about the fictional speaker's regret at having to leave the peaceful countryside "For crowds and noise" (l. 8). We do not know when Phillis wrote the poem, whether she played any role in having it published, or even if she knew that it was published. The absence of "An Elegy" from Phillis's 1779 "Proposals," however, suggests that it was written sometime after she published the "Proposals" in December 1779. As the opening and closing stanzas show in retrospect, the poem is a fittingly poignant farewell to more than just a life of seclusion:

> FAREWEL! ye friendly bow'rs, ye streams adieu,
>> I leave with sorrow each sequester'd seat:
> The lawns, where oft I swept the morning dew,
>> The groves, from noon-tide rays a kind retreat.
> . . . .
> But, ah! those pleasing hours are ever flown;
>> Ye scenes of transport from my thoughts retire;
> Those rural joys no more the day shall crown,
>> No more my hand shall wake the warbling lyre.
> But come, sweet Hope, from thy divine retreat,
>> Come to my breast, and chase my cares away,
> Bring calm Content to gild my gloomy seat,
>> And cheer my bosom with her heav'nly ray. (ll. 1–4, 21–28)

We can only speculate as to why Phillis Wheatley Peters's proposed second volume was never published. Her first book had to be published in England because she was unable to find an American publisher in 1772. Unfortunately, the war effectively closed the British market to colonial authors in 1779. Her would-be publishers had failed to exploit her continuing celebrity by not referring to her premarital identity as Phillis Wheatley in advertising her proposed book. Her husband may have been responsible for that imprudent choice. Phillis did not have much time to promote her proposed book in 1779 before she and her husband left Boston and disappeared from public view for several years. There is no evidence that anyone had approached Benjamin Franklin about having the book dedicated to him. Her apparent conviction that he would have been agreeable to such a gesture reflects an impressive amount of confidence on her part. If John Peters was as arrogant as Odell claims, he may have been the source of such confidence, as well as the one who made the mistake of overpricing the proposed book in a period of economic depression and wartime turmoil. John Peters was almost certainly in jail when Phillis Peters included a reference to her former identity, Phillis Wheatley, when she readvertised the proposed volume in 1784. When she was on her own she showed some of the same business acumen she had displayed in the production and distribution of her *Poems* before she married Peters.

Phillis Wheatley Peters died a few months after the publication of "An ELEGY on leaving—." John Peters was probably still in prison for debt when his wife died on that "fair" 5 December 1784.[53] The asthmatic condition that had afflicted Phillis in previous winters may have caused or at least contributed to her death. She was about thirty-three years old when she died. That was the average life expectancy of a person of African descent, men as well as women, free as well as enslaved, during the period.[54] Phillis Wheatley Peters may have spent the last months, perhaps even years, of her life in relative obscurity, but like many authors before and since, she was restored to celebrity by death.

The *Independent Chronicle and Universal Advertiser* announced to its readers on 9 December 1784, "Phillis Peters formerly Phillis Wheatley aged 31, known to the literary world by her celebrated miscellaneous poems. Her funeral is to be this afternoon, at 4 o'clock, from the house lately repaired by Mr. Todd, nearly opposite Dr. Bulfinch's at West Boston, where her friends and acquaintances are desired to attend." "Mr. Todd" probably refers to the housewright William Todd. Wealthy Dr. Thomas Bulfinch (1728–1802) lived in the family mansion he inherited in 1757 in quasi-rural Bowdoin Square. He was the brother-in-law of Rev. Samuel Cooper, the subject in 1784 of one of the last poems Phillis Wheatley Peters published. The proximity of Bulfinch's house to the Granary Burial Ground suggests that Phillis may have been buried close to her former owners and their daughter Sarah. Nearby are the remains of Christopher Snider, Crispus Attucks, John Hancock, James Bowdoin, Paul Revere, and many of Phillis's other famous eighteenth-century Bostonians. But Phillis's gravesite, like that of most of her contemporaries of African descent, was unmarked and remains unknown.

John Peters may have still been in jail when he advertised in the *Independent Chronicle and Universal Advertiser* on 10 February 1785: "The person who borrowed a volume of manuscript poems && of Phillis Peters, formerly

Phillis Wheatley, deceased, would very much oblige her husband, John Peters, by returning it immediately, as the whole of her works are intended to be published." According to Odell, the person from whom John Peters was trying to recover Phillis's manuscript was Elizabeth Wallcut's daughter. Given Peters's financial problems and the renewed interest in Phillis and her writings following her death, he surely would have published it had he acquired it. The proposed book so confidently advertised in 1779 unfortunately never appeared. Of the poems included in the 1779 "Proposals" that had not previously been published or distributed in manuscript, only a draft version of "Ocean," which turned up at the end of the twentieth century, has been found.

In many ways Peters's life demonstrates the truth of the observation that "While slavery existed in New England, an exceptional man of color could prosper; after emancipation, the barriers became almost insurmountable."[55] From September 1784 until early 1788 Peters was frequently imprisoned in the Suffolk County, Massachusetts, jail for debt, at least occasionally for weeks at a time. Debtors were usually sentenced to jail terms of two to three months, but sometimes to as little as a week at a time. Shurtleff's comment that Peters was employed as a "journeyman baker" is plausible. Through Phillis he could have known Benjamin Wallcut, Elizabeth Wallcut's oldest son. According to the 1784 "Taking Book," or tax assessment, Benjamin Wallcut was a baker in Ward 11. But the only person recorded as working for Wallcut then was "Jon Decosta wth Mr Walcut Baker." If Peters also worked for Wallcut in 1784 he could only have done so for very brief intervals between his incarcerations. Phillis's widower was probably not the John Peters listed on 6 January 1789 as imprisoned for "Burglary."[56] That John Peters was probably the same John Peters listed on 7 July 1789 as imprisoned for "Theft not tried."[57] Phillis's widower was more likely the John Peters, identified as a trader, who took Diamond Morton, Gentleman, to court on 6 January 1789 over the return of 2 horses.[58]

Necessity was often the mother of simultaneous occupations during the eighteenth century. Peters seems to have regained his economic footing by early 1788, when the "Assessors' Taking Book," recorded in April, lists "John Peters Black Man," living in Ward 1. In the "Taking Book" for Ward 1 in April 1789 John Peters is listed as 1 Poll, blank "Rl Estate," "Bl[ac]k Man." By 1790 Phillis's John Peters was clearly financially and socially upwardly mobile. That year's "Taking Book" identifies him as a "Blck M docter pintle" worth $25. A list of "Names of the Inhabitants of the Town of Boston in 1790" includes John Peters as head of a family that includes no "Free white Males of 16 Years and upwards, including Heads of Families," no free white males or females under 16, no slaves, and one other free person.[59] The 1791 "Taking Book" describes John Peters as a "Lawyer Physician Gentn pintlesmith." Peters himself would have been the source of the occupational information recorded in the "Taking Books." Odd though it may be to see someone described as both a doctor and a maker or mender of pintles, John Peters was not extraordinary in practicing medicine, law, and multiple other careers.[60]

Accusations that John Peters practiced law and medicine without a license are correct, but misleading. The accusations need to be historically contextualized. By the time Odell wrote her very influential account of Phillis Wheatley's life, both law and medicine had become professionalized to a degree largely unknown in the eighteenth century. Laymen like John Peters had easy access to medical information: "William Buchan's *Domestic Medicine* (London, 1769) was so popular that it was published at least fifteen times in the colonies and the new United States between 1771 and 1799, and many times afterward. . . . [A]lso within this self-help tradition was Methodist theologian John Wesley's *Primitive Physic* (London, 1747) which was reprinted many times."[61]

Most eighteenth-century medical practitioners lacked medical degrees, and most had more than one occupation: "Not until the proliferation of medical schools during the nineteenth century granting thousands of diplomas did 'physician' become generally equated with the recipient of the M.D. Nowhere in colonial America did there exist effective restraints on the use of the title of 'Doctor' or uniformly accepted qualifications for who could practice. . . . And in an environment that encouraged multiple careers, virtually all doctors were engaged also in other income-producing activity."[62] The relatively few professionally trained physicians had little success in distinguishing themselves from their lay competitors: "in reality the healing arts were practiced chiefly by self-taught or slightly trained 'empirical' doctors, midwives, clergymen, and self-dosing laymen who, in treating themselves, their families, and their neighbors, practiced the most common of the healing arts. Popular medicine dominated colonial and revolutionary Massachusetts."[63] Medical schools existed in Boston, New York, and Philadelphia during Peters's lifetime, but they were not open to people of African descent. John Peters was not the only person of African descent who was recognized as a doctor: "Several black men were called 'Doctor' because they helped their owner, an apothecary and physician, prepare compounds and visit patients."[64] Peters was extraordinary, however, in being a person of African descent who practiced medicine independently.

The situation was similar in the practice of law during the eighteenth century. There were no law schools in colonial America. And although a few opened after the American Revolution, none admitted people of African descent. The overwhelming majority of (white) men who entered the legal profession before the late nineteenth century did so by studying standard legal texts such as Blackstone's *Commentaries* under the tutelage of an experienced attorney. Most colonial printers published books and guides aimed at the common reader who sought legal advice: "Probably the most popular of the American [legal] manuals was *Conductor Generalis . . .* , first published in New York by William and Andrew Bradford in 1711 and reissued in at least seven editions before Independence—all outside Massachusetts. Although *Conductor Generalis . . .* was never printed in Massachusetts, another comparable guide *was* published there: *An Abridgement of Burn's Justice of the Peace and Parish Officer* (Boston: Joseph Greenleaf, 1773)."[65] (Greenleaf later hoped to become a copublisher of Phillis Wheatley Peters's proposed, but never published, second volume.)

Josiah Quincy (1772–1864) recalled that Peters "at one time, practiced law, or professed to." Quincy reportedly "met him in the courtroom."[66] Peters certainly had plenty of practical experience with the law. For at least the last two decades of his life he was repeatedly involved with the court as either a plaintiff or defendant. For example, in 1790 Peters was awarded thirty shillings in his action against Dilly Adkins, who was committed to jail because she defaulted on her debt to him.[67] On 4 October 1791 John Peters was awarded £8 in his suit against Jonathan Booth, a baker. On 17 April 1792 the Court of Common Pleas ruled against Peters in his suit against Francis Booth, who had posted bail for the appearance of Jonathan Booth. The court charged Peters the cost of the suit because Jonathan Booth was in Castle Island prison. John Peters's frequent lawsuits led to his receiving an official reprimand several years later. The Supreme Judicial Court of the County of Suffolk in Boston indicted Peters on 27 August 1793 on a charge of barratry for having been excessively litigious during the past three years: "on the first day of June in the Year of our Lord one thousand seven hundred and ninety and on divers days and times between that day and this [John Peters] was and yet is a *common Barrator* and divers strifes quarrels and controversies between the good citizens of the said commonwealth unlawfully and litigiously did stir up excite and promote in evil example to others against the peace of the said Commonwealth and the dignity of the same." A warrant was issued in September 1793 for the arrest of Peters, but the charge was dropped the following February.[68] The Court seems to have made its point: Peters's lawsuits apparently ended after his indictment.

John Peters's economic situation did not stabilize until twelve years after Phillis's death. The 1796 "Taking Book" identified him as "100 Rl Estate, Physician Bl[ac]k," and in 1798 he was listed as a "Bl[ac]k M[an]. 200 Rl Estate. *The Statistics of the United States Direct Tax of 1798, as Assessed on Boston; and The Names of the Inhabitants of Boston in 1790, as Collected for the First National Census* describes Peters's property: "John Peters, owner and occupier; wooden dwelling; fronting Northerly on Prince Street; Southerly & Westerly on Thomas Hopkins; Easterly on [Thomas] Whitman. Land, 202 square feet; house, 202 square feet; 1 story, 7 windows; value $200." Peters's house was the least valuable one of sixty-three listed in Book 2 "on lots not exceeding 2 acres." The others were two valued at $300, one at $400, four at $500, seven at $600, one at $700, one at $750, one at $800, one at $900, and the rest from $1,000 to $3,000. Phillis's widower was doing so well by the end of the decade that he may have been the John Peters who had enough social ambition to run for senator from the County of Suffolk in 1798. On the list of the twenty-five candidates dated 2 April 1798, Peters received the fewest votes, two. The highest vote-getter, Oliver Wendell, received 1574.[69]

Odell mistakenly says that after Phillis's death Peters "went to the South."[70] He went instead to Charlestown, just north of Boston. Peters's political defeat may have contributed to his decision to leave Boston. The "Taking Book," Ward 1, compiled in May 1799, includes "John Peters, gone to Cambridge, 200 Rl Estate, Doctr Pintle Mender." Peters's story seems to end in 1800, when the "Taking Book 1800" for Ward 1 records "John Peters Bl[ac]k M[an]. dead, 200 Rl Estate."[71] The report of his death proved premature, however. The 9–12 March 1801 issue of the *Independent Chronicle and Advertiser* (Boston) announced his death: "At Charlestown, Dr. *John Peters*, aged 55." The administration of the estate of "John Peters late of Charlestown negro & physician, deceased, intestate" is dated 2 June 1801.[72] On 2 May 1802 his property was valued at $213.93, including "13 Book &

1 Bibel," together worth $10," and "2 small mahogoney" tables valued at $9. One of the tables may be the writing desk now at the Massachusetts Historical Society, believed to have belonged to Phillis Wheatley before her marriage.[73] His books indicate that he was an unusually educated man and probably a religious one as well. His ownership of a "Sorel hors," a sleigh, feather bed, leather-bottomed chairs, and other luxury goods reflects his aspirations to be recognized as a gentleman. Like many of his white as well as black contemporaries, however, Peters died as he had lived—in debt. His debts far exceeded the value of his assets.[74] His remaining possessions suggest some of the reasons Phillis was attracted to him.

Rather fittingly, London was where Phillis Wheatley effectively said her poetic farewell. She had had her greatest success in revising her literary and social identities there. Had she remained in London in 1773, she very likely would have found a publisher for her second volume, financial success, and access to influential literary, political, and social circles. She probably would have come into contact with the most important eighteenth-century patrons of women writers. Had she remained in England rather than gambling on her future by returning to America, Samuel Johnson and Elizabeth Robinson Montagu's Bluestocking Circle might have welcomed her. Even without their aid, interest in her work and her status as a woman writer of color certainly continued in London after her departure. Revised versions of eight separate previously published Wheatley poems appeared in London in John Wesley's Methodist *Arminian Magazine* during the 1780s, perhaps with her knowledge, approval, or even direction.

While she was in London, Wheatley had established relationships directly and indirectly with leaders of the movement that developed in Britain during the 1780s to abolish the transatlantic slave trade. John Thornton had been one of her correspondents since before she went to England. Through him she met another correspondent, Hannah Wilberforce, his half sister and another admirer of Whitefield. Her nephew was the leading abolitionist William Wilberforce (1759–1833). Wheatley may also have met the abolitionist Rev. John Newton (1725–1807), an evangelical Anglican priest who was a former slave trader. Newton, perhaps now best known as the author of the hymn "Amazing Grace," also enjoyed the patronage of the Earl of Dartmouth and Thornton. On 31 March 1774 and 13 October 1774 Thornton showed Newton correspondence between himself and Wheatley. Thornton's references to her simply as "Phillis" suggest that Newton knew her as well. Newton no doubt shared Thornton's opinion that "she is a blessed Girl & has been marvelously preserved" in having survived her voyage back to Boston. Had Wheatley chosen the path not taken and remained with these "friends in England," she might have enjoyed the fame and success she deserved but failed to find in America.

Back in the new United States, however, Wheatley's continuous attempts to control her own destiny failed. She eventually fell into obscurity and desperate poverty, unable to find a patron or a publisher. Ignatius Sancho's indictment of Phillis's white supporters proved to be prescient: "These good great folks—all know—and perhaps admired—nay, praised Genius in bondage—and then, like the Priests and the Levites in sacred writ, passed by—not one good Samaritan amongst them."[75]

"Shielded from the Severe Trials of unpitying Criticism"

Phillis Wheatley Peters received the recognition in America after her death that she had struggled unsuccessfully to regain during the last years of her life. The pseudonymous "Horatio" published his "Elegy on the Death of a late celebrated Poetess" in the December 1784 issue of the *Boston Magazine*. It reads in part:

As Orpheus play'd the list'ning herds among,
They own'd the magic of his powerful song;
Mankind no more their savage nature kept,
And foes to music, wonder'd how they wept.
So PHILLIS tun'd her sweet mellifluous lyre;
(Harmonious numbers bid the soul aspire)
While AFRIC's untaught race with transport heard,
They lov'd the poet, and the muse rever'd.

. . . .

As if by heaven inspir'd, did she relate,
The souls grand entrance at the sacred gate!
And shall the honour, which she oft apply'd,
To other's reliques, be to hers deny'd?
   O that the muse, dear spirit! own'd thy art,
To soften grief and captivate the heart,
Then should these lines in numbers soft array'd
Preserve thy mem'ry from oblivion's shade;
But O! how vain the wish that friendship pays,
Since her own volumes are her greatest praise.

Phillis's *Poems* was not reprinted in the United States while she was alive. Joseph Crukshank (1746?–1836) reprinted her book in Philadelphia in 1786. Joseph James (1754?–1830) reprinted it again in Philadelphia the following year.

Joseph Brown Ladd may not have known that Phillis was dead when he published "The Prospect of America. Inscribed to His Excellency General Washington" in *The Poems of Arouet* (Charleston, South Carolina, 1786). Ladd was a native New Englander practicing medicine in South Carolina when he celebrated in verse the triumph and future of America. His examples of America's literary talents include Philip Freneau (1752–1832) and Joel Barlow (1754–1812), as well as "Phillis Wheatley, a negro, and the authoress of some ingenious poems, which seem to be entitled to a remembrance here, although not written by a native of America."[1] He quotes lines 7–14 from Wheatley's "To Maecenas" to support his claims for her status as a canonical American poet:

> Here the fair volume shews the far spread name
> Of wondrous WHEATLY, *Afric's* heir to fame.
> Well is it known what glowing genius shines,
> What force of numbers, in her polish'd lines:
> With magic power the grand descriptions roll
> Thick on the mind, and agitate the soul. (ll. 390–395)

Wheatley and Ignatius Sancho rarely directly addressed the issues of the abolition of either the slave trade or slavery. Francis Williams never did. But each to some extent was invoked in the arguments of the 1780s and later about the literary and intellectual capacities of Africans because they displayed obvious pretensions to literary achievement. Both sides in the late-eighteenth-century debate over the innate intelligence and even humanity of the African cited the three authors. Such citations contributed to the development of the canon of authors of African descent writing in the English language. Charles Crawford (b. 1752) quotes Anthony Benezet and Phillis Wheatley in *Observations upon Negro-Slavery* in 1784 to demonstrate that "The opinion that is entertained by some, among whom is David Hume, that the capacities of Negroes are not equal to those of white people, is contradicted by those who have a peculiar opportunity of being acquainted with the dispositions and talents of the Negroes." Crawford alludes to David Hume's notorious reference to Francis Williams as evidence of the alleged intellectual inferiority of people of African descent. "The celebrated PHILLIS WHEATLEY," Crawford remarks, "may be produced as an instance of extraordinary genius. It would be difficult perhaps to name any living person as being endowed with superiour talents for Poetry." To prove his point, Crawford quotes John Wheatley's introductory letter and "To the Publick" from the 1773 *Poems*. He also quotes "the following lines [which] appear to be faultless" from "To a Clergyman on the Death of his Lady."[2] When Charles Crawford expanded his original 21-page *Observations upon Negro-Slavery* to 125 pages in 1790, he added Wheatley's "To the University of Cambridge, in New-England" to further demonstrate her "great talents for poetry." He also added Ignatius Sancho and Olaudah Equiano as more examples "Of the natural genius of the Negroes."[3]

Abolitionists opposed to the transatlantic slave trade and emancipationists opposed to the institution of slavery frequently cited the literary quality of Wheatley's poetry, often in combination with that of Sancho's *Letters*, to demonstrate the humanity she and her white readers shared. For example, in his *Essays Historical and Moral* (London, 1785), George Gregory (1754–1808) sees Wheatley's poems and Sancho's letters as "striking instances of genius contending against every disadvantage, resulting from want of encouragement, and of early cultivation."[4] The Reverend Robert Boucher Nikolls considered the poetry of Wheatley and Francis Williams sufficient evidence to refute the racist arguments of people like Edward Long:

> The stupidity of negroes is . . . urged by the friends of slavery as a plea for using them as brutes; for they represent the negroes as little removed above the monkey, or the oran-outang, with regard to intellects. But I am very certain, nothing has been written by the late defenders of slavery, that discovers [displays] half the literary merit or ability of two negroe writers. Phillis Wheatley wrote correct English poetry within a few years after her arrival in Boston from Africa; and there is a Latin ode of considerable length written in classic language by Francis Williams. . . . I never heard of poems by a monkey, or of Latin odes by an oran-outang.[5]

Thomas Clarkson (1760–1846) says of Wheatley, "if the authoress *was designed for slavery*, . . . the greater part of the inhabitants of Britain must lose their claim to freedom."[6] In support of his position, Clarkson quotes liberally from her *Poems*. Clarkson brought Wheatley and her poetry to the attention of Cugoano and Equiano, both of whom were very familiar with his *Essay*.

Not only emancipationists acknowledged the merit of at least some authors of African descent. John Gabriel Stedman (1744–97) admits in his *Narrative of a Five Years Expedition against the Revolted Negroes of Surinam* (London, 1796):

> That these people are neither divested of a good ear, nor poetical genius, has been frequently proved, when they had the advantages of a good education. Amongst others, *Phillis Wheatley*, who was a slave at *Boston* in New England, learned the Latin language, and wrote thirty-eight elegant pieces of poetry on different subjects, which were published in 1773. . . . [Stedman quotes ll. 9–22 from "On Imagination"]
>
> *Ignatius Sancho*, a negro, many years servant to the Duke of Montagu, whose sentimental letters, so generally known, would not disgrace the pen of an European, may also be mentioned on this occasion.[7]

Even those who denied the achievement of authors of African descent implicitly acknowledged the developing black canon by disputing the quality of the authors' literary productions. Thomas Jefferson most notoriously expressed this sort of negative recognition in his *Notes on the State of Virginia* (London, 1787), Query XIV:

> Among the blacks is misery enough, God knows, but no poetry. Love is the peculiar oestrum [inspiration] of the poet. Their love is ardent, but it kindles the senses only, not the imagination. Religion indeed has produced a Phillis Whately [*sic*]; but it could not produce a poet. The compositions composed under her name are below the dignity of criticism. The heroes of the Dunciad are to her, as Hercules to the author of that poem.[8]

The American Gilbert Imlay (1754–1828) was one of the first to answer Jefferson's attack on Wheatley in *A Topographical Description of the Western Territory of North America* (New York, 1793):

> I will transcribe part of her Poem on Imagination, and leave you to judge whether it is poetical or not. It will afford you an opportunity, if you have never met with it, of estimating her genius and Mr. Jefferson's judgment; and I think, without any disparagement to him, that by comparison, Phillis appears much the superior. Indeed, I should be glad to be informed what white upon this continent has written more beautiful lines.[9]

John Quincy Adams (1767–1848), sixth President of the United States (1825–29), alluded to Jefferson's disparaging comments on Wheatley and Ignatius Sancho in *Notes on the State of Virginia* to mock his political enemy's rumored sexual relationship with his slave Sally Hemings. Writing his imitation of "Horace, Book II, Ode 4. To Xanthia Phoceus" under the pseudonym "Thomas Paine," Adams advised Jefferson to invent a worthy ancestry for his illegitimate offspring:

> Yet, from a princess and a king
> Whatever be their hue,
> Since none but driveling idiots spring,
> And GODS must spring from you,
> We'll make thy Tommy's lineage lend;
> Black and white genius both shall blend
> In him their rays divine.
> From Phillis Wheatley we'll contrive
> Or brighter Sancho to derive
> Thy son's maternal line.[10]

Henry Louis Gates Jr. has aptly remarked that "if Phillis Wheatley was the mother of African-American literature, there is a sense in which Thomas Jefferson can be thought of as its midwife."[11] Wheatley's poetry continued to be used by black as well as white antebellum American abolitionists as evidence for the humanity, equality, and literary talents of people of African descent.

During the period from the late nineteenth century to the 1970s, a number of literary critics expressed neo-Jeffersonian denunciations of Wheatley's literary abilities, as well as of her racial loyalty. Wheatley, Gates notes, became "something of a pariah in black political and critical circles, especially in the militant 1960s, where critics had a field day mocking her life and her works (most of which they had not read)."[12] The nadir of this movement was marked by accusations that Wheatley had "a white mind," and was "not sensitive enough to the needs of her own people to demonstrate a kinship to Blacks in her life or writings."[13]

Thanks to the work since the 1980s by editors, critics, and literary historians such as Henry Louis Gates Jr., Julian D. Mason Jr., and John C. Shields, Phillis Wheatley Peters's place in the developing tradition of early transatlantic literature by people of African descent and her role as the mother of African American literature are now secure. The many ways in which Wheatley subtly and indirectly confronted the issues of racism, sexism, and slavery are increasingly appreciated. The prophecy offered by the pseudonymous "Matilda" in "On Reading the Poems of Phillis Wheatley, the African Poetess" (*New York Magazine*, October 1796) has been realized:

> A PHILLIS rises, and the world no more
> Denies the sacred right to mental pow'r;
> While, Heav'n-inspir'd, she proves *her Country's* claim
> To Freedom, and *her own* to deathless Fame.[14]

Notes

Chapter 1. "On Being Brought from Africa to America"

1. Massachusetts Historical Society, Ms. N-641: Robert Treat Paine (1731–1814), Diary, 11 July 1761.

2. Information about Boston's population when Phillis Wheatley arrived is derived from Benton, *Early Census Making in Massachusetts, 1643–1765*.

3. "Moreover of the children of the strangers that do sojourn among you, of them shall ye buy, and of their families that are with you, which they begat in your land: and they shall be your possession.

"And ye shall take them as an inheritance for your children after you, to inherit them for a possession; they shall be your bondmen forever: but over your brethren the children of Israel, ye shall not rule one over another with rigour."

4. Between the Middle Ages and the end of the twentieth century, Islamic traders enslaved approximately twelve million Africans, sending them across the Sahara desert, Red Sea, and Pacific Ocean to eastern markets. Segal, *Islam's Black Slaves*, 55–57.

5. Richardson, "The British Empire and the Atlantic Slave Trade, 1660–1807," 462.

6. Craton, *Sinews of Empire*, 4.

7. The most reliable estimates are by Eltis, "The U.S. Transatlantic Slave Trade, 1644–1867."

8. Eltis, "The Volume and Structure of the Transatlantic Slave Trade."

9. Berlin, *The Making of African America*, 49. See also Sidbury, *Becoming African in America*; Sweet, *Negotiating Race in the American North, 1730–1830*; Gomez, *Exchanging Our Country Marks*.

10. Medford Historical Society: The Medford Slave Trade Letters—1759–1765, letter references A(5), A(7).

11. Miller, "Mortality in the Atlantic Slave Trade"; Miller, *African Way of Death*, 384–85; Klein, *The Middle Passage*; Klein and Engerman, "Long-Term Trends in African Mortality in the Transatlantic Slave Trade"; Klein, Engerman, Haines, and Shlomowitz, "Transoceanic Mortality"; Kiple and Higgins, "Mortality Caused by Dehydration during the Middle Passage."

12. Edward Long (1734–1813), *The History of Jamaica*, vol. 2: 352–53, 404. Long had been a magistrate and legislator in Jamaica, where he was born, until he moved to England in 1769 to recover his health.

13. On 13 July 1761 the *Boston Evening Post* reported the arrival of "Gwin from Africa" two days earlier.

14. Based on information found in *The Trans-Atlantic Slave Trade Database*, www.slavevoyages.org/tast/database/search.faces.

15. *The Trans-Atlantic Slave Trade Database*, www.slavevoyages.org/tast/database/search.faces, 25481.

16. *The Trans-Atlantic Slave Trade Database*, www.slavevoyages.org/tast/database/search.faces, 25215.

17. Morgan, "Africa and the Atlantic, c.1450 to c.1820," 230.

18. *Boston Gazette*, 13 July 1761.

19. "PHILIS's [*sic*] Reply to the Answer in our last by the Gentleman in the Navy" is discussed in chapter 6.

20. Hughes, *Famous American Negroes*, 2, 3, 5–15.

21. For example, John C. Shields, an editor and perceptive critic of Wheatley's writings, refers without qualification to "her native Gambia" twice before he more carefully considers the evidence "that she may have come to America carrying with her a rudimentary knowledge of Arabic script adapted to the Fulani language" of Gambia. But after asserting that he has "established the land of her origins with some degree of probability," Shields leaps from one conclusion to another. He finds it "probable that Wheatley's family comprised members of the ruling class" and "plausible to posit that, as a student between the ages of one and seven, Wheatley absorbed from her African years images of the land of her birth, especially of its worshipped sun, and retained memories of the intellectual and artistic pursuits which characterized the people of that land." Shields, *Phillis Wheatley's Poetics of Liberation*, 20, 82, 97–100, 102, 100, 101, 104.

22. Equiano, *The Interesting Narrative of the Life of Olaudah Equiano*, 58. There is considerable doubt about whether Equiano himself actually experienced the Middle Passage he famously described. See Carretta, *Equiano, the African*.

23. See Christopher, *Slave Ship Sailors and their Captive Cargoes, 1730–1807*; Rediker, *The Slave Ship*; Handler, "The Middle Passage and the Material Culture of Captive Africans."

24. Robert E. Desrochers, Jr., in "Slave-for-Sale Advertisements and Slavery in Massachusetts, 1704–1781," calculates that "Some 87% of all advertisements for imported slaves first appeared between May and October; 41% (42 of 103) debuted in July and August alone" (656).

25. Robinson, *Phillis Wheatley and Her Writings*, 5, is the primary source of this confusion because he overlooked the 13 July 1761 advertisement for the sale of the enslaved aboard the *Phillis* and assumed that the slaves advertised by John Avery (advertisements that Robinson misdates) must have included the future poet. I, like all other critics, have contributed to this confusion in my earlier publications and talks on Phillis Wheatley by having uncritically accepted Robinson's conclu-

sions. Despite Robinson's occasional errors and frustrating frequent failure to cite his sources, however, all subsequent scholars, critics, and biographers are heavily indebted to his pioneering research.

26. Information on Avery, as well as on many of Phillis Wheatley's contemporaries, is available on the CD-ROM *Colonial Collegians: Biographies of Those Who Attended Colonial Colleges before the War of Independence*, ed. Conrad Edick Wright (Boston: Published for the Massachusetts Historical Society by the New England Historic Genealogical Society, 2005).

27. The second advertisement was republished in the 10, 17, and 24 August issues of the *Boston Evening Post*. It was also published during August in the *Boston Gazette*, the *Boston News Letter*, and the *Boston Post Boy*.

28. *Boston Gazette*, 13 July 1761.

29. Mary was apparently also called Polly, a common nickname for Mary. According to Samuel Forman, the account books of Dr. Joseph Warren (1741–75) record treatment of members of the Wheatley family. He refers to only one of them by a first name, "Polly." Warren was apparently either a boarder or tenant of the Wheatleys in 1763–64. Forman plausibly speculates that Warren probably treated Phillis Wheatley during that period as well. Samuel Forman to Vincent Carretta, personal correspondence, 8 August 2010.

30. Margaret Matilda Odell's "Memoir" prefaces the anonymously published *Memoir and Poems of Phillis Wheatley, A Native African and a Slave. Dedicated to the Friends of the Africans*, 9.

31. Grimsted, "Anglo-American Racism and Phillis Wheatley's 'Sable Veil,' 'Length'ned Chain,' and 'Knitted Heart,'" 341, fn. 6, deems Odell's account "careful, rich, and balanced." Odell's "Memoir," however, should be read with a great deal of skepticism. For a perceptive assessment of Odell's "Memoir" and its unfortunate influence on subsequent biographical and literary criticism of Wheatley, see Elrod, "Phillis Wheatley's Abolitionist Text: The 1834 Edition."

32. Dunkle and Lainhart, *Inscriptions and Records of the Old Cemeteries of Boston*, G 1383.

33. Odell, "Memoir," 12.

34. Philip D. Morgan makes the very useful distinction between a *slave-owning* society and a *slave society* in "British Encounters with Africans and African-Americans, circa 1600–1780."

35. For a useful overview and bibliography of the resistance to the conversion of slaves in slave societies in the American South, see Young, *Proslavery and sectional Thought in the Early South, 1740–1829: An Anthology*, 1–67.

36. Lorenzo Johnston Greene, *The Negro in Colonial New England 1620–1776*, 324; Piersen, *Black Yankees*.

37. Sweet, *Negotiating Race*, 155–56.

38. British money was counted in pounds sterling (£), shillings (s.), pence, or pennies (d.), and farthings. One pound sterling = 20 shillings; 5 shillings = 1 crown; 1 shilling = 12 pennies; 1 farthing = 1/4 pence. One guinea = 21 shillings (the coin was so named because the gold from which it was made came from the Gold Coast of Africa, and because the coin was first struck to celebrate the founding in 1663 of the slave-trading monopoly the Royal Adventurers into Africa.)

39. Massachusetts Historical Society, Ms. N-1683: John Tudor (1709–1795) Papers, 1732–1793.

40. Suffolk (County, Massachusetts) Deeds 126: 201.

41. *Boston Gazette, and Country Journal*, 8 July 1771; *Boston News-Letter*, 30 August 1764.

42. *Boston Evening Post*, 19 March 1770.

43. *Boston News-Letter and New-England Chronicle*.

44. *Boston News-Letter and New-England Chronicle*, 1 September 1768; *Boston Evening Post*, 16 July 1770.

45. *Lloyd's Register*, London 1764.

46. *Lloyd's Register*, 1764; *Boston Chronicle*, 25–28 December 1769.

47. *Boston Chronicle*, 4–6 January 1770.

48. *Boston Chronicle*, 15–19 February 1770.

49. *The Massachusetts Tax Valuation List of 1771*, facsimile reprint, ed. Bettye Hobbs Pruitt (Boston: G. K. Hall & Company, 1978). John Wheatley is entry 0101/4515, and Nathaniel Wheatley is entry 0101/4516.

50 Odell, "Memoir," 13.

51. Reverend Samson Occom to Susanna Wheatley, 5 March 1771, in Brooks, *The Collected Writings of Samson Occom, Mohegan*, 97.

52. *Boston Record Commissioners' Reports* (Boston: Boston Registry Department, 1876–1909, Vol. 19: *Boston Selectmen's Minutes, 1754–1763*, 156, 168.

53. *Boston Record Commissioners' Reports*, Vol. 20: *Boston Selectmen's Minutes, 1764–1768*, 314.

54. *Boston Record Commissioners' Reports*, Vol. 19: *Boston Selectmen's Minutes, 1754–1763*, 240.

55. *Boston Record Commissioners' Reports*, Vol. 25: *Boston Selectmen's Minutes, 1776–1786*, 70.

56. See Rozbicki, "To Save Them from Themselves."

57. The National Archives, United Kingdom, High Court of Admiralty 30/258, quoted in Coldham, *Emigrants in Chains*, 131.

58. For a very welcome study of the lives of women of African descent in New England before 1800, see Adams and Pleck, *Love of Freedom*.

59. Norton, *Liberty's Daughters*, 21. See also Zagarri, *Revolutionary Backlash*.

60. Adams and Pleck, *Love of Freedom*, 42.

61. Bernard Page to the Countess of Huntingdon, 19 March 1773, Cheshunt Foundation, Westminster College, Cambridge, United Kingdom: A3/5/17.

62. Anonymous, "Phillis Wheatley," in *Anti-Slavery Record* 2, no. 5 (May 1836): 7–8. This account of the way Timothy Fitch's daughters reacted to their mother's invitation to Phillis Wheatley to join them at tea must be treated with some skepticism because other information in the account regarding Phillis's 1773 trip to London is demonstrably false.

63. Odell, Memoir," 12.

64. Odell, Memoir," 13.

65. Wheatley, *Complete Writings*, 5. Unless indicated otherwise, all quotations from Phillis Wheatley's post-1765 writings in poetry and prose are cited from the Penguin edition hereafter within the text by page number and/or date.

Chapter 2. "Thoughts on the Works of Providence"

1. Julian D. Mason, Jr., *The Poems of Phillis Wheatley*, 3.

2. Scholars disagree about the extent to which colonial New England slave owners encouraged their slaves to embrace Christianity. For an argument that exposure to Christianity gave people of African descent the means and motive to become leaders of the abolitionist movement in late-eighteenth-century Massachusetts, see Cameron, "Freeing Themselves." Sweet, *Bodies Politic*, 126, on the other hand, believes that "many slaves used evangelical religion not so much to challenge their enslavement as to reconcile themselves to a conservative Christian ethos."

3. Boswell, *Life of Samuel Johnson*, 324–325 (30 July 17630); 409 (10 October 1769).

4. Franklin, "*Autobiography*," 1409.

5. Equiano, *The Interesting Narrative*, 132. Equiano could not have heard George Whitefield in Philadelphia in either 1766 or 1767, as he says he did. Whitefield did not leave Great Britain between 7 July 1765 and 16 September 1768. He must have heard him on Sunday, 10 February 1765, in Savannah, Georgia. The weekly newspaper the *Georgia Gazette* (14 and 21 February) reported that Whitefield was in the town on the 9th. The sloop *Prudence*, on which Equiano served under Thomas Farmer, was in port between the 7th and the 16th.

6. Benjamin Rush, Philadelphia, to Ebenezer Hazard, New York, 21 May 1765, Library Company of Philadelphia: Rush Correspondence, vol. 39:7.

7. Capitein, *The Agony of Asar*.

8. Whitefield, *Three Letters*, 13, 15.

9. Cheshunt Foundation, Westminster College, Cambridge, United Kingdom: A4/2 16, 6–8 May 1775; A4/2 13B, 24 January 1775.

10. Cheshunt Foundation: A4/2 16, 6–8 May 1775.

11. Cheshunt Foundation: A4/2 16, 6–8 May 1775. Piercy reported in the same letter to the countess that Margate also alienated the slaves at Bethesda by insisting that "the Lord had told him that he should take a Negro Woman in y^r house to be his Wife that was already Wife to one of your Slaves, & that I must comply as it was from God."

12. Emphasis in original. The periodical the *Prompter* first published "The Speech" anonymously on 10 January 1735, and it was reprinted in the January 1735 issues of the *Gentleman's Magazine* and the *London Magazine*.

13. Equiano, *The Interesting Narrative*, 110–11. Equiano may have learned of "The Speech of Moses Bon Sáam" from James Tobin's *Cursory Remarks upon Mr. Ramsay's Essay*. Tobin mentions Reverend Robert Robertson's proslavery *The Speech of Mr. John Talbot Campo-Bell, a Free Christian Negro, to his Countrymen in the Mountains of Jamaica* (131), which includes "The Speech of Moses Bon Sáam" in an appendix. Equiano published a hostile review of Tobin's *Cursory Remarks* in the *Public Advertiser* on 28 January 1788.

14. See Elrod, "Moses and the Egyptian"; Boulukos, *The Grateful Slave*, 193–95; Carretta, "Equiano's Paradise Lost."

15. Feiler, *America's Prophet*.

16. Cheshunt Foundation: A4/1 20A, 13 June 1775.

17. Cheshunt Foundation: A1/13 10, 16 June 1775.

18. The works of Briton Hammon, Jupiter Hammon, Gronniosaw, Liele, Marrant, George, and King are reproduced in Carretta, *Unchained Voices*.

19. On Phillis Wheatley's association with the transatlantic evangelical movement, see Rawley, "The World of Phillis Wheatley"; Rogal, "Phillis Wheatley's Methodist Connection"; Isani, "The Methodist Connection."

20. *Boston Evening Post*, 27 February 1764 .

21. *Massachusetts Spy*, 14–16, 25–28 August, 17 September 1770.

22. Anonymous, "A Conversation between a New York Gentleman & Phillis," Dr. Williams's Library: Congregational Library, II. b. 7 (13). I thank David Powell for bringing this manuscript to my attention.

23. Hannah Mather Crocker, "Reminiscences and Traditions of Boston: Being An Account of the Original Proprietors of that Town, & the Manners and Customs of Its People" (ca. 1829), New England Historic Genealogical Society, Mss 219, pp. 102–04. I thank Judy Lucey for bringing this manuscript to my attention. See Botting and Houser, "'Drawing the Line of Equality.'"

24. Andrew Eliot to Thomas Hollis, 29 January 1769, quoted in Bridenbaugh, *Mitre and Sceptre*, 192. See Monaghan, *Learning to Read*.

25. Lambert, *Pedlar in Divinity*, 138. Bassard, *Spiritual Interrogations*; Kidd, *The Great Awakening*.

26. Norton, *Liberty's Daughters*, xv.

27. Crocker, *A Series of Letters on Free Masonry*, 8. Emphasis in original.

28. The full title of the *Memoir* is *Memoir of Mrs. Chloe Spear, A Native of Africa, Who was Enslaved in Childhood, and Died in Boston, January 3, 1815. . . . Aged 65 Years. By a Lady of Boston.* The New York Public Library's copy of the *Memoir* identifies Mary Webb (1768–1831) as the "Lady of Boston" who was the amanuensis of this as-told-to slave narrative. The *Memoir* is hereafter cited parenthetically within the text. In addition to the Memoir, the principal sources of information about Chloe Spear include the unpublished "Notes concerning Blacks with the Name Spear, 1798–1815," compiled by William G. Spear and deposited in the manuscript collection of the New England Historic Genealogical Society (NEHGS), Ms. 246; the NEHGS CD-ROM of Annie Thwing, *Inhabitants and Estates of the Town of Boston 1630–1800 and The Crooked and Narrow Streets of Boston, 1630–1822* (Boston: The Massachusetts Historical Society and the New England Historical and Genealogical Society, 2001), commonly known as "the Thwing Index."

29. *Memoir of Mrs. Chloe Spear*, 16.

30. Ibid., 20–21.

31. Ibid., 22–23.

32. Ibid., 24.

33. Ibid., 26.

34. John Carter Brown Library: Brown Family Business Records: B. 20, folder 13, #8, 15 June 1780; B. 311, folder 8, 20 October 1780.

35. Quoted from the letter signed "John Wheatley. *Boston, Nov.* 14, 1772," which prefaces Wheatley, *Poems on Various Subjects.*

36. Adams and Pleck, *Love of Freedom*, 20–21.

37. Winslow, *Diary.*

38. *Boston Gazette, and Country Journal*, 20 January 1772.

39. Winslow, *Diary*, 32.

40. Ibid., 21.

41. Berthold, *American Colonial Printing.*

42. Winslow, *Diary*, 14.

43. Ibid., 37.

44. Ibid., 23.

45. Grimsted, "Anglo-American Racism," 372. Grimsted also plausibly suggests that Obour Tanner attended Sarah Osborn's religious meetings in Newport (375).

46. I thank Bertram Lipincott III, librarian at the Newport Historical Society, Rhode Island, for his help in finding the records relating to Obour Tanner: First Congregational Church, Newport, Rhode Island, Church record book #832, page 27, #200; Church record book #832, page 17, #59; Church record book #832, page 61; Parish Records book #814, page 71.

47. Elrod, *Piety and Dissent*; May, *Evangelism and Resistance in the Black Atlantic*; Brooks, *American Lazarus*; Zafar, *We Wear the Mask*; O'Neale, *Jupiter Hammon and the Biblical Beginnings of African-American Literature*.

Chapter 3. "I prefer the Verse"

1. Brooks, *The Collected Writings of Samson Occom, Mohegan*, 269.

2. The title of the missing "On the Death of the Rev. Dr. *Sewell* [*sic*], when Sick, 1765," however, may indicate that Wheatley composed the poem anticipating Sewall's death.

3. Massachusetts Historical Society: Jeremy Belknap Papers, Ms. N-1827, Diaries 1770–1775.

4. Blake, *Public Health in the Town of Boston, 1630–1822*; Duffy, *Epidemics in Colonial America*.

5. Winslow, *Diary*, 22.

6. Cavitch, *American Elegy*.

7. Philip Freneau, "On Funeral Elogiums" (1790), in Philip M. Marsh, ed., *The Prose of Philip Freneau* (New Brunswick, N.J.: Scarecrow Press, 1955), 268. Quoted in Cavitch, *American Elegy*, 2.

8. See Gerzina, *Mr. and Mrs. Prince*.

9. Franklin, *Writings*, 1318.

10. On the possible influence of Byles on Wheatley, see Shields, "Phillis Wheatley and Mather Byles."

11. Anonymous, "A Conversation between a New York Gentleman & Phillis."

12. Desrochers, "'Surprizing Deliverance': Slavery and Freedom, Language and Identity in the Narrative of Briton Hammon."

13. See Kelley, "Reading Women/Women Reading"; Kelley, "'A More Glorious Revolution'"; and Kelley, *Learning to Stand and Speak*. Foster, *Written by Herself*; Landry, *The Muses of Resistance*; McBride, *Impossible Witnesses*; Scheick, *Authority and Female Authorship in Colonial America*; Foster, "Narrative of the Interesting Origins and (Somewhat) Surprising Developments of African-American Print Culture"; Brooks, "Our Phillis, Ourselves," emphasizes the role women played in the distribution of Wheatley's poetry.

14. Mss. of Hannah Griffitts: Library Company of Philadelphia 7423. F 1–125, Poems, Essays, Extracts (F. 81–90), on deposit at the Historical Society of Pennsylvania. Griffitts's headnote suggests that she recorded the poem soon after it was written: "The following Lines are said to be Composed by a Native of Africa, about 15 years of age,—& who a few Years ago Could not Speak one word of English, she belong'd to John Wheatley of Boston." Other contemporaneous collectors and transcribers of Phillis Wheatley's manuscript verse included Catherine

Haines (fl.1775–98), Julia Stockton Rush (1759–1848), and Pierre Eugène du Simitière (1736?–84).

15. As John C. Shields points out in "Phillis Wheatley's use of Classicism," Wheatley very frequently employs solar imagery in her writings. Shields, *The Collected Works of Phillis Wheatley*, 242, argues that "[i]n her poetry, then, Wheatley has syncretized the memory of her mother's sun worship with Christianity." The only source for Shields's reference to "her mother's sun worship" is Odell, "Memoir," 10: "[Wheatley] does not seen to have preserved any remembrance of the place of her nativity, or of her parents, excepting the simple circumstance that her mother *poured out water before the sun at his rising*—in reference, no doubt, to an ancient African custom."

16. Fox, *Gospel Family-Order*, 13–14 (emphasis in original).

17. Sewall, *The Selling of Joseph*, 3 (emphasis in original).

18. Gates, *The Trials*, 71.

19. Dunlap, *Poems Upon Several Sermons Preached by the Rev'd and Renowned George Whitefield While in Boston*, 17.

20. Kendrick, "Re-Membering America" 72, notes that in her poems Wheatley frequently crosses the boundary between author and speaker, "making the one who speaks synonymous with the one who writes."

21. Mary McAleer Balkun, "Phillis Wheatley's Construction of Otherness and the Rhetoric of Performed Ideology," 131. Bennett, "Phillis Wheatley's Vocation and the Paradox of the 'Afric Muse'"; Nielsen, "Patterns of Subversion in the Works of Phillis Wheatley and Jupiter Hammon."

22. Tolman, *John Jack, the Slave, and Daniel Bliss, the Tory*, 4.

23. Cugoano, *Thoughts and Sentiments on the Evil of Slavery and Other Writings*, 59.

24. *"The Prince of the Kings of the Earth"*: Revelation 1:5.

25. "I may say with Joseph . . . intended for my good": see Genesis 45:4–8. Cugoano probably mentions Joseph here because, as William Bollan (d. 1776) says in *Britannia Libera, or a Defence of the Free State of Man in England, against the Claim of any Man there as a Slave. Inscribed and Submitted to the Jurisconsulti, and the Free People of England* (London, 1772), "[t]he first man certainly known by name, or otherwise, to have been sold for a *slave*, was *Joseph*" (2). Cugoano quotes *Britannia Libera*, 2, later in his *Thoughts and Sentiments*, 68.

26. Cugoano, *Thoughts and Sentiments*, 17 (emphasis in original).

27. Hall, *Things of Darkness*, Introduction.

28. Williams, "To That most upright and valiant Man," in Long, *The History of Jamaica* 2: 483. See Carretta, "Francis Williams: An Eighteenth-Century Black Jamaican Man of Letters."

29. God's elect: the doctrine that God has chosen, or elected, some relatively

few people—the "elect"—who are predestined to be saved while the great majority are doomed to eternal damnation was most often associated with the teachings of John Calvin. See Romans 8:27–9:21.

30. Cugoano, *Thoughts and Sentiments*, 40.

31. Winslow, *Diary*, 2–3.

32. Nearly eight years later, Bacon opposed an attempt to deny people of color the right to vote on the grounds that all people were inherently equal: "Are they not Americans? Were they not (most of them at least) born in this country? Is it not a fact, that those who are not natives of America, were forced here by us, contrary, not only to their own wills, but to every principle of justice and humanity? I wish, Sir, these gentlemen would tell us what they mean by *foreigners*: Do they mean by it, such persons, whose ancestors came from some other country! If so, who of us is not a foreigner." (*Independent Chronicle* [Boston], 23 September 1779; emphasis in original).

33. For the reception history of Phillis Wheatley's publications before 1775, see Isani, "The Contemporaneous Reception of Phillis Wheatley."

34. Sapho was baptized in Trinity Church, Boston, on 28 March 1770 (*Thwing Collection*, Refcode 9907). In November 1768 Coffin was appointed deputy to Charles Stewart, the principal customs collector in North America (see chapter five of this book). Coffin remained a Loyalist after the outbreak of hostilities and fled with the British forces when they evacuated Boston in March 1776.

35. *Boston News-Letter and New-England Chronicle*, 1 October 1767.

36. Wheatley's relationship to Revolutionary events has been frequently noted, for example in Rawley, "The World of Phillis Wheatley," 657–77; Shields, *Phillis Wheatley's Poetics of Liberation*; Erkkila, "Phillis Wheatley and the Black American Revolution"; Erkkila, *Mixed Bloods and Other Crosses*, 77–88; Ennis, "Poetry and American Revolutionary Identity"; Coviello, "Agonizing Affection"; Slauter, "Neoclassical Culture in a Society with Slaves: Race and Rights in the Age of Wheatley," *Early American Studies* (Spring 2004), 81–122; Slauter, *The State as a Work of Art*, 169–214; Richards, "Phillis Wheatley and Literary Americanization"; Richards, "Phillis Wheatley, Americanization, the Sublime, and the Romance of America"; Bruce, *The Origins of African American Literature, 1680–1865*, 39–91; Akers, "'Our Modern Egyptians'"; Burke, "Problematizing American Dissent," 193–209; Willard, "Wheatley's Turns of Praise"; Sidney Kaplan and Emma Nogrady Kaplan, *The Black Presence in the Era of the American Revolution, 1777–1800*; T. H. Breen, "Making History."

37. [Great Britain], Anno Regni Georgii III, 10.

38. Stephen Hopkins, *The Rights of Colonies Examined*, 21.

39. Johnson, *Taxation no Tyranny* (London, 1775), 454.

40. Proper names were commonly spelled in various ways during the eighteenth century.

41. Robinson, *Phillis Wheatley and her Writings*, 455, reprints twelve lines of verse published in the *Boston Evening Post* on 12 March 1770 "because the style, sentiment, and vocabulary are very much like Phillis's, and may be part of" the lost poem. Bly, "Wheatley's 'On the Affray in King Street,'" 177, asserts that "[t]he author of the anonymous lines is unquestionably Phillis Wheatley." The attribution of the lines remains to be proven.

Another early political poem has been tentatively attributed to Wheatley by Dr. Randall K. Burkett, African-American Studies Bibliographer for the Robert W. Woodruff Library of Emory University. One of two copybooks in the Library contains thirty-three complete or partial poems by various hands, including "Hymn to Humanity," identified in the copybook as Wheatley's, as well as the anonymous "The Voice of Freedom," both in the same hand. Dated 12 December 1773, the "Hymn" is a later version of the poem "An Hymn to Humanity. To S.P.G. Esq" published in Wheatley's *Poems on Various Subjects, Religious and Moral* in September 1773. The newly discovered version includes many significant substantive changes and identifies "S.P.G." as "S.P. Gallowy: who corrected some Poetic Essays of the Authoress," about whom nothing more is yet known. Either the newly discovered version is a very unusual instance of Wheatley's revising an already published poem, or it is a revision of Wheatley's poem by another poet. Dr. Burkett acknowledges in an unpublished paper dated August 1998 that "[i]t is yet to be determined whether any portion of the copybook, including 'Hymn to Humanity,' is in Phillis Wheatley's own hand" (2). Julian D. Mason, Jr., a scrupulous editor of Wheatley's writings, says in private correspondence dated 12 May 2000 that the Emory variant "is not her handwriting." He is probably correct. If "Hymn to Humanity" and "The Voice of Freedom" in the Emory copybook are written in Wheatley's hand, the latter would be a significant new political poem by her. Its epigraph is from "A Song for American Freedom" (the Liberty Song), published in Philadelphia in 1768 by John Dickinson (1732–1808). The twenty-line poem refers to him as the "Immortal Farmer" because he was best known for his *Letters from a Farmer in Pennsylvania* (Philadelphia, 1768). The poet's assumption of the voice of the female allegorical figure of "Freedom" and the very domestic simile in line 12 suggest a female author: "'As from the wall, your brooms the cobwebs sweep.'"

I thank Professor Mason for bringing the Emory holdings to my attention, and I am very grateful to him and Dr. Burkett for sharing their thoughts about the documents with me.

42. Gillies, *The Works of the Rev. George Whitefield*, 1:105.

43. Whitefield, "The Good Shepherd," in *Eighteen Sermons Preached by the Late Rev. George Whitefield*, 434.

44. Gordon, *The History of the Rise, Progress, and Establishment, of the Independence of the United States of America*, 1:143–144 (emphasis in original).

45. Samuel Adams, *Writings of Samuel Adams*, 1:26.

46. Gillies, "Memoirs of the Life of the Reverend George Whitefield," in *Works*, 7:248.

47. Whitefield, *Sermons*, 388.

48. Whitefield, *Works*, 3:426 (emphasis in original).

49. E.g., Anonymous, *An Elegiac Poem Sacred to the Memory of the Rev. George Whitefield* (Boston: Isaiah Thomas, 1770); *The Massachusetts Gazette and the Boston Weekly News-Letter*, 4 October 1770. See also Cray, "Memorialization and Enshrinement."

50. Leonard, *Fettered Genius*, 34, observes that Wheatley's elegy on Whitefield "posits [her] as a bard not just for Africans who were slaves; she could also speak to and for whites and for God. In addition to associating her imagination with the democratic spirit and her accomplishment with social inclusion, in other words, Wheatley quite literally joins a mourning community as an equal or even as an advisor, as she had also done in speaking to the graduating students at Cambridge."

51. The ultimate source of Whitefield's prophecy in the poem to "ye Africans" that "You shall be sons, and kings, and priests to GOD" (line 44) is Christ's promise to Christians in Revelations 1:6: "And [Jesus Christ] hath made us kings and priests unto God and his Father." The way Wheatley phrases the prophecy suggests that she was familiar with Samuel Bourn, *Lectures to Children and Young People*. According to Bourn, human happiness is found by establishing "*New Relations* to God, as Sons, as Kings and Priests" (101).

52. Whitefield, *Works*, 4:475.

53. Because the copy of the poem Wheatley sent to the Countess with her cover letter is missing, we do not know whether it was a copy of the printed broadside or a manuscript copy.

54. Thomas Jefferson (1743–1826), for example, ended a letter in 1791 to Benjamin Banneker, a free man of African descent, "I am with great esteem, Sir, Your most obedient Humble Servant."

Chapter 4. "A WONDER of the Age indeed!"

1. Pemberton, *Heaven the Residence of the Saints*.

2. Although Dunlap dates her "Introduction" 1 January 1771 (iii), she later says in "To the Reader," dated 18 March 1771, that she has withheld publication until the later date because she wanted to add some poems in response to the death of her husband.

3. Mason, *Poems*, 35.

4. James Green, in "The Publishing History of Olaudah Equiano's *Interesting Narrative*," notes the relative rarity of asking for advance payment from subscribers.

5. Letter to William Boutcher, December 30, 1775, quoted in Zachs, *The First John Murray and the Late Eighteenth-Century Book Trade*, 69. Zachs notes that Murray reiterates his opinion of publication by subscription in a letter to John Imison, 27 August 1784.

6. The second was Gronniosaw's *Narrative* a few months later, which includes a preface addressed "To the Reader" by the Countess of Huntingdon's cousin Walter Shirley (1725–86). Shirley, a clergyman, writer, collector and publisher of hymns, assures the reader that "This account of the Life and spiritual Experience of JAMES ALBERT was taken from his own Mouth" (Carretta, *Unchained Voices*, 32).

7. Robinson, *Writings*, 377; Mason, *Poems*, 142.

8. Massachusetts Historical Society: Andrews-Eliot Ms N-1774, #7.

9. Massachusetts Historical Society: Andrews-Eliot Ms N-1774, #12.

10. Massachusetts Historical Society: T. Wallcut Microfilm P-391, Thomas Wallcut Papers, 1671–1866, Reel 2 of 3.

11. Thomas Wallcut later became an author, copier of documents, and an antiquarian. Ignatius Sancho (1729?–1780) was the only contemporaneous person of African descent besides Wheatley known to have mentored whites. Several aspiring artists and authors sought his advice.

12. R. F. W. [Robert F. Wallcut, Thomas Wallcut's nephew], "Memoir of Thomas Wallcut," *Proceedings of the Massachusetts Historical Society* 2 (1841): 193–208; 193–94.

13. Rush, *An Address*, 2.

14. Kuncio, "Some Unpublished Poems of Phillis Wheatley."

15. Rush, *An Address*, 2fn.

16. Nisbet, *Slavery not Forbidden by Scripture*, 23.

17. Ibid. Though not named, Williams appears in a footnote in Hume's essay "Of National Characters," in his *Essays and Treatises on Several Subjects*, 234n. Anonymous, *Personal Slavery Established, By the Suffrages of Common and Right Reason. Being a Full Answer to the Gloomy and Visionary Reveries, of all the Fanatical and Enthusiastical Writers on that Subject* (Philadelphia: Printed by John Dunlap, in Market-Street, 1773) is an ironic response to Woolman, Benezet, and especially Rush, which explicitly relies heavily on Nisbet. The anonymous author also refers to Francis Williams: "I will be candid enough to allow there have been surprising instances of *docility* [educability] in Negroes. Such for instance was that of a negro fellow in Jamaica, who seemed to have some parts and learning, and could talk in a manner, that had his colour been concealed, and he had stuck a piece of wax on his nose to make it a little more prominent, might have been mistaken for a rational creature possessing a tolerable knowledge in the law" (21–22; emphasis in original).

18. Several years later, Nisbet greatly qualified his assessment of people of Afri-

can descent in general and Phillis Wheatley in particular, renouncing "the force of evil custom" that had hitherto blinded him to the fact "that every prejudice against this unfortunate people is mere illusion, proceeding from the natural but pernicious abuses which follow an unlimited power of tyrannizing over our fellow creatures." He described Wheatley as "cramped by her condition," and he acknowledged that her ingenious productions demonstrated "ample testimony of, at least, as considerable a portion of mental activity, as falls to the lot of mankind in general." *The Capacity of Negroes for Religious and Moral Improvement*, iii–v, 31.

19. On 11 February 1773 the *Massachusetts Spy or, Thomas's Boston Journal* reported the death of Mrs. Spooner, widow of the late John Spooner. On 18 March the same newspaper reported the death of Mrs. Andrew Oliver.

20. Cheshunt Foundation, Westminster College, Cambridge, United Kingdom: A3/5/6.

21. Cheshunt Foundation: A3/5/17.

22. *Boston Post Boy*, 16 November 1772; *London Chronicle*, 17 December 1772.

23. Connecticut Historical Society: Samson Occom Papers.

24. Massachusetts Historical Society: Andrews-Eliot Ms N-1774, #16.

25. Cox and Berry moved their business to British-controlled New York after the beginning of the American Revolution and were banished from Massachusetts and declared Loyalist outlaws in 1778.

26. Cheshunt Foundation: A3/5/3.

27. Cheshunt Foundation: A3/5/8.

28. Massachusetts Historical Society, Ms. N-641: Robert Treat Paine, "Diary."

29. *Boston News-Letter* (6 May), *Connecticut Journal and New-Haven Post-Boy* (7 May), *Providence Gazette* (8 May), *Boston Evening Post* (10 May), *Boston Gazette* (10 May), *Boston Post-Boy* (10 May), *Connecticut Courant* (11 May), *Boston News-Letters* (13 May), *Pennsylvania Chronicle* (17 May), *Pennsylvania Packet* (24 May), and *New York Gazete and Weekly Post-Boy* (27 May).

30. Wallace Brown, ed., "An Englishman's Views of the American Revolution," 140. Hulton apparently got his information from the 6 May *Boston News-Letter*, which reported that the "extraordinary Negro Poet" was going to London "at the invitation of the Countess of Huntington [*sic*]." On 13 May the newspaper retracted its claim that the Countess of Huntingdon had invited her.

31. *Boston Evening Post* (10 May), *Boston News-Letter* (13 May), *Essex Gazette* (18 May), *Pennsylvania Packet* (24 May), *Connecticut Courant* (25 May), *Massachusetts Spy* (27 May), and *New Hampshire Gazette* (18 June). The *London Chronicle* (3 June) also published Wheatley's "Farewel," with a letter from Boston telling readers that the poem was addressed to Susanna Wheatley.

32. The Countess had been Gronniosaw's patron since at least 3 January 1772,

when he acknowledged her generosity to him and his family: "James allbate [James Albert Ukawsaw Gronniosaw] the Black" to Selina Hastings, Countess of Huntingdon Cheshunt Foundation: F/1: 1574. I thank Ryan Hanley for bringing this letter to my attention.

33. Mason, *The Poems of Phillis Wheatley*, 8.

34. Additional London advertisements for Wheatley's book appeared in the *London Chronicle or Universal Evening Post* (11, 16 September), *Lloyd's Evening Post* (13 September), the *Public Advertiser* (13 September), the *Morning Post and Daily Advertiser* (13, 18 September), and the *General Evening Post* (18 September).

35. Saunders and Miles, *American Colonial Portraits 1700–1776*, 44.

36. Cavendish's frontispiece-portrait appears in her *Philosophical and Physical Opinions*. Rowe's frontispiece appears in her *Poems on Several Occasions*. Haywood's frontispiece-portrait appears in her *Works* and her *Secret Histories, Novels, and Poems*. I thank Isobel Grundy and Paula Backscheider for bringing these frontispiece-portraits to my attention.

37. Saunders and Miles, *American Colonial Portraits 1700–1776*, 44.

38. On Job Ben Solomon, see Grant, *The Fortunate Slave*. The image of Solomon is based on a 1734 etching by William Hoare (c.1707–92). The image of Sessarakoo is based on a 1749 mezzotint by John Faber, Jr. (c.1695–1756) after a 1749 oil painting by Gabriel Mathias (d. 1803).

39. Shaw, "'On Deathless Glories Fix Thine Ardent View,'" 27.

40. I thank Eric Slauter for sharing "Looking for Scipio Moorhead: An 'African Painter' in Revolutionary America," 27 pp. ms., his consideration of the uncertain identification of Scipio Moorhead as the addressee of Wheatley's poem and the designer of her frontispiece.

41. Shaw, "'On Deathless Glories Fix Thine Ardent View,'" assesses the frontispiece-portrait more positively: "It is a portrait not of an objectified and subordinated woman, but of an empowered wielder of agency. It is a portrait of a subject. In the confines of the engraved oval frame, Wheatley sits alone. She is a slim, dark-skinned young woman with a long face. Shown in profile, her head is well-shaped, with a pronounced forehead. Her elbows rest on a small oval writing table on which a pewter inkwell, a book, and a sheet of paper attend her poetic impressions. She wears an elaborately beribboned lace bonnet, full of pleats and accented with a colored ribbon at its top. A black band encircles her neck, ending in a bow at the back, while a white shawl covers her shoulders. The extended index finger of her left hand rests against her cheek, and the other fingers curl inward in support of her chin. She directs her gaze upward, toward heaven, as if searching for inspiration to direct the long quill pen she holds in her right hand. In turn, the top of the feather points back up at her head" (29).

42. *Athenian Mercury*, 24 October 1693.

43. Dabydeen, *Hogarth's Blacks*, 21–26; Aravamudan, *Tropicopolitans*, 33–38; Beth Tobin, *Picturing Imperial Power*, chap. 1.

44. Chapone, *Letters on the Improvement of the Mind*, iii.

45. Darwall, *Original Poems on Several Occasions*, 3–4.

46. Famous as well as obscure poets before and after Wheatley used similar titles for their initial books: Rowe, *Poems on Several Occasions*; Pope, *Poems on Several Occasions*; Shenstone, *Poems on Various Occasions*; Whyte, *Original Poems on Various Subjects*; Wheatley's friend Mather Byles's *Poems on Several Occasions*; Wheatley's London acquaintance Thomas Gibbons's *Juvenalia: Poems on Various Subjects of Devotion and Virtue*; Carter, *Poems on Several Occasions*; George Roberts, *Juvenile Poems on Various Subjects*; Darwall, *Original Poems on Several Occasions*; *Poems on Several Occasions. By John Bennet, a Journeyman Shoemaker* (London, 1774); and Coleridge, *Poems on Various Subjects*.

47. Ladd, *The Poems of Arouet*, vii.

48. Henry Louis Gates Jr. describes the imagined interrogation in *The Trials of Phillis Wheatley*. Gates had earlier imagined the scene in "Writing 'Race' and the Difference It Makes." For a strong argument against the likelihood that such an inquisition ever took place, see Brooks, "Our Phillis, Ourselves."

49 See Levernier, "Phillis Wheatley and the New England Clergy."

50. Wilcox, "The Body into Print," 18.

51. O'Neale, "A Slave's Subtle War." Scheick, "Subjection and Prophecy in Phillis Wheatley's Verse Paraphrases of Scripture."

52. On Wheatley and Classicism, Shields, "Phillis Wheatley's Use of Classicism." Cynthia J. Smith, "'To Maecenas'"; Watson, "A Classic Case." Shields, *The American Aeneas*; Winterer, *The Mirror of Antiquity*; Walters, *African American Literature and the Classicist Tradition*; Mason, "Examples of Classical Myth in the Poems of Phillis Wheatley"; Cook and Tatum, *African American Writers and Classical Tradition*.

53. Shaw, "'On Deathless Glories Fix Thine Ardent View,'" notes that "There remains the possibility, although there is no recorded evidence, that while Wheatley was in London she may have viewed one of Wilson's Niobe paintings in the collection of the Earl of Dartmouth. . . . In fact, she may not have composed the poem until after her arrival in London, which would push the date of the poem's composition to that summer. This possibility is supported by the poem's absence from the listing of the original 1772 proposal for the volume, and by its placement toward the rear of the volume." (42, fn. 30).

54. For a different reading of "Niobe," see Thorn, "'All beautiful in woe.'" Grimsted, "Anglo-American Racism," 369, says that [t]he extraordinary bloodiness of

Wheatley's poems drawn from classical-biblical sources suggests . . . subterranean anger which the gentle young woman expressed only when it was sublimated in distant settings and in religious truisms about God's terrible wrath."

55. Shuffleton, "Phillis Wheatley, the Aesthetic, and the Form of Life." Levernier, "Style as Protest in the Poetry of Phillis Wheatley."

56. Shields, *Phillis Wheatley's Poetics of Liberation*, argues "that Wheatley developed what we may term a relaxed Christianity . . . [that] begins to appear in the middle of 1771" (146). Shields, *Phillis Wheatley and the Romantic Age*, 49, argues that the theme of the freedom of the imagination appealed to Wheatley in part because of her own physical enslavement: "While the exterior world of Boston . . . would confine her in the shackles of slavery, Wheatley claims ownership of her own interior, limitless mind." I thank Professor Shields for showing me a prepublication copy of his *Phillis Wheatley and the Romantic Age*.

57. On the reviews and Wheatley's visit to London, see Robinson, "Phillis Wheatley in London"; Isani, "Wheatley's Departure for London," 123–29; Isani, "The Contemporaneous Reception of Phillis Wheatley."

58. Jefferson, *Notes on the Sate of Virginia*, 149.

59. *Critical Review* 36 (September 1773), 232–33.

60. *London Magazine* 42 (September 1773), 456.

61. *Gentleman's Magazine* 43 (September 1773), 456.

62. *Monthly Review* 49 (December 1773), 457–59. The nine reviews are reproduced in Isani, "The British Reception of Wheatley's *Poems on Various Subjects.*"

Chapter 5. "A Farewell to America"

1. Wrigley, "A Simple Model of London's Importance in Changing English Society and Economy, 1650–1750."

2. Boswell, *Life of Johnson*, 859 (20 September 1777).

3. Occom, *Collected Writings*, 266–67.

4. Library Company of Philadelphia: Benjamin Rush Papers, Vol. 39: 25.

5. The most reliable statistical study of people of African descent in England during the period is Chater, *Untold Histories*. Other studies of Britain's eighteenth-century black population include Gerzina, *Black London*; Walvin, *Black Ivory*; Dabydeen, *Hogarth's Blacks*; Fryer, *Staying Power*; Shyllon, *Black People in Britain, 1555–1832*.

6. After carefully reviewing the contemporaneous and contemporary estimates of the eighteenth-century black population in England, Norma Meyers, *Reconstructing the Black Past*, says that "a figure persistently of at least 5,000 seems highly likely" (31).

7. Drescher, *Capitalism and Antislavery*, 25–49.

8. Lorimer, "Black Slaves and English Liberty."

9. Long, *Candid Reflections upon the Judgement Lately Awarded by the Court of King's Bench*, 48.

10. Fielding, *Extracts from Such of the Laws*,143–45. John was the half-brother of the novelists Henry (1707–54) and Sarah (1710–68) Fielding. Sarah collaborated with Jane Collier on the satiric novel *The Cry: A New Dramatic Fable* (1754). John, although totally or almost totally blind, was the leading magistrate in Middlesex and well known for his efforts to enforce the laws vigorously and to organize a local London police force. The mob burned down his house in the Gordon Riots of 1780. The mob also burned down Mansfield's house, destroying his library and many of his papers.

11. Anonymous, *A Companion to Every Place of Curiosity and Entertainment in and about London and Westminster* (London, 1767; 3rd ed. 1772). The *Companion* reached its ninth edition in 1800.

12. *Public Advertiser*, 1 July 1773.

13. Altick, *The Shows of London*, 69.

14. Anonymous, *A Companion*, 13.

15. A search by Carole Holden, Head of American Collections at the British Library, of the archives of the British Museum and the papers of Daniel Solander in the British Library found no references to Phillis Wheatley (private correspondence 16 and 17 August 2010).

16. Israel Mauduit, a dissenter, was a very familiar figure in Massachusetts. He had assisted his brother Jasper Mauduit (1697–1772) when Jasper was the agent representing Massachusetts (1762–65). Israel published both *A Short View of the History of the Colony of Massachusetts* and *A Short View of the History of the New England Colonies* in London in 1769. In 1773 Ezekiel Russell reprinted a Boston edition of Israel Mauduit's *The Case of the Dissenting Ministers*, an argument supporting greater religious tolerance that was first published in London in 1772. In 1774 Mauduit joined Alexander Wedderburn (1733–1805), the British solicitor-general, in defending governor Hutchinson against Benjamin Franklin's attempt to have him removed from office. Mauduit defended British interests in *Considerations on the American War. Addressed to the People of England.*

17. "The Diary of Rev. Dr. Thomas Gibbons, 1749–1785," Dr. Williams' Library.

18. Occom, *Collected Writings*, 267–68.

19. John Thornton to Rev. William Richardson, 2 June 1774; John Thornton to Phillis Wheatley, 22 April 1774 (MS.Add.7826/1/B. Letters, 1772, from John Thornton to John Newton, Thornton Family Papers, GB 012 MS.Add.7826, Cambridge University Library, Department of Manuscripts and University Archives). I am very grateful to Jeffrey Bilbro for bringing the Thornton correspondence to my attention and for sharing his copies of it with me.

20. Flavell, *When London Was Capital of America*, 127–29.

21. *The Writings and Speeches of Edmund Burke*, vol. 3: *Party, Parliament, and the American War, 1774–1780*, 219. Quoted in Flavell, *When London Was Capital of America*, 127.

22. Labaree, *The Papers of Benjamin Franklin* 20: 291–92, 445.

23. See Waldstreicher, *Runaway America*.

24. Franklin, *Writings*, 648, 649.

25. The copy of Pope's translation of Homer's *Iliad* is at Dartmouth College; Pope's four-volume translation of Homer's *Odyssey* and the nine volumes of his own works are at University of North Carolina at Charlotte; volume two of the translation of Cervantes' *Don Quixote* by Tobias Smollett (1721–71) is in the Schomburg Center for Research in Black Culture of the New York Public Library; John Milton (1608–74), *Paradise Lost* is at the Houghton Library, Harvard University; Sharp's *Remarks* is at the Essex Institute in Massachusetts.

26. See Glasson, "'Baptism doth not bestow Freedom.'"

27. Estwick, *Considerations on the Negroe Cause Commonly So Called*, 41.

28. On the significance of the Mansfield decision and the arguments over its interpretation since its rendering, see Wise, *Though the Heavens May Fall*; Wiecek, "*Somerset*: Lord Mansfield and the Legitimacy of Slavery in the Anglo-American World"; Cotter, "The Somerset Case and the Abolition of Slavery in England." Wiecek argues that *Somerset* abolished slavery in England *de facto*, if not *de jure*; Cotter's argument that *Somerset* abolished it *de jure* as well as *de facto* has been challenged by Ruth Paley, "After Somerset: Mansfield, Slavery and the Law in England"; Carretta, "Phillis Wheatley, the Mansfield Decision of 1772, and the Choice of Identity"; Van Cleve, "The Somerset Case and its Antecedents in Imperial Perspective"; Sword, "Remembering Dinah Nevil: Strategic Deceptions in Eighteenth-Century Antislavery." Chater, *Untold Stories*, denies that Mansfield could have emancipated slaves in England because by law there were none; "There was no need to emancipate them: they were already free in this country, whatever their status in the colonies" (92).

29. Quoted in Wiecek, "*Somerset*," 86.

30. See Swaminathan, "Developing the West Indian Proslavery Position after the *Somerset* Decision."

31. Long, *Candid Reflections*, 56. Long incorrectly conflates the English and Scottish legal systems when he uses the term *Great Britain*.

32. Blackstone, *Commentaries on the Laws of England*.

33. Ibid., book 1, chapter 1. Blackstone had delivered the substance of the *Commentaries* as lectures several years earlier as the first Vinerian Professor of Law at Oxford University. Blackstone revised this passage in the 2nd and subsequent editions at the behest of Lord Mansfield, his mentor and patron. The 2nd (1766) and 3rd (1768) editions read: "A slave or a Negro, the moment he lands in England, falls

under the protection of the laws, and so far becomes a freeman; though the master's right to his service may probably still continue." In the 4th (1770) and later editions, "probably" reads "possibly." Blackstone's *Commentaries* remains the standard legal reference source on English Common Law, and the United States legal system that has developed from it.

34. *The Speech of Edmund Burke Esq; on Moving His Resolutions for Conciliation with the Colonies, March 22, 1775* (London: James Dodsley, 1775), in *The Writings and Speeches of Edmund Burke* 3: 123. Blackstone's *Commentaries* was reprinted in Philadelphia in 1771–72. Maitland, *Historical Essays*, 147, estimates that "Nearly 2500 copies of Blackstone's *Commentaries* were absorbed by the colonies on the Atlantic seaboard before they declared their independence."

35. Burke, *Letter to the Sheriffs of Bristol* (London: James Dodsley, 1777), in *The Writings and Speeches of Edmund Burke* 3: 297.

36. *The Diary and Letters of His Excellency Thomas Hutchinson, Esq* 2: 276–77.

37. On the effects of Mansfield's ruling, in addition to Wiecek and Cotter, see Drescher, *Capitalism and Antislavery*, 25–49.

38. Sancho to John Ireland, in Sancho, *Letters of the Late Ignatius Sancho, an African*, 164.

39. Hoare, *Memoirs of Granville Sharp*, 333.

40. Cugoano, *Thoughts and Sentiments on the Evil of Slavery*, 115–16.

41. Equiano, *Interesting Narrative*, 179.

42. A landing place on the North bank of the Thames, about 3.5 miles downriver from Westminster Palace.

43. Equiano, *Interesting Narrative*, 181.

44. For an account of North American newspaper reports of the Mansfield ruling, see Bradley, *Slavery, Propaganda, and the American Revolution*, 66–80.

45. Blackstone, *Commentaries on the Laws of England* 1: 104–05: "But there is a difference between these two species of colonies, with respect to the laws by which they are bound. For it is held, that if an uninhabited country be discovered and planted by English subjects, all the English laws are immediately there in force. For as the law is the birthright of every subject, so wherever they go they carry their laws with them. But in conquered or ceded countries, that have already laws of their own, the king may indeed alter and change those laws; but, till he does actually change them, the antient laws of the country remain, unless such as are against the law of God, as in the case of an infidel country.

"Our American plantations are principally of this latter sort, being obtained in the last century either by right of conquest and driving out the natives (with what natural justice I shall not at present enquire) or by treaties. And therefore the common law of England, as such, has no allowance or authority there; they being no part of the mother country, but distinct (though dependent) dominions."

46. Quarles, *The Negro in the American Revolution*; Quarles, "The Revolutionary War as a Black Declaration of Independence"; Christopher L. Brown, "The Empire without Slaves"; Nash, *The Forgotten Fifth*: Minardi, *Making Slavery History*.

47. Rush, *Address*, 19.

48. *Connecticut Gazette; and the Universal Intelligencer*, 11 March 1774.

49. Johnson, *Taxation No Tyranny*, 454.

50. Day, *Fragment of an Original Letter on the Slavery of the Negroes*, 24, 34. Although the letter is dated 1776, Day did not publish it until after the American Revolution ended. Day's poem *The Dying Negro*, coauthored with John Bicknell, appeared in 1773. Day's novel *The History of Sandford and Merton, A Work Intended for the Use of Children* appeared in three installments (1783, 1786, and 1789).

51. Sharp, *An Essay on Slavery*, 22–23 (emphasis in original).

52. Carey, *British Abolitionism and the Rhetoric of Sensibility*, 76, 75.

53. The same report also appeared in the *General Evening Post* (25–27 May 1773) and *Lloyd's Evening Post* (26–28 May 1773).

54. Quoted from Mason, *The Poems of Phillis Wheatley*, 149.

55. On the pervasive use of metaphorical slavery in colonial discourse, see Dorsey, *Common Bondage*.

56. Isani, "Wheatley's Departure for London and Her 'Farewel to America,'" 123–129: 123.

57. Equiano, *Interesting Narrative*, 98.

58. On the concept of slavery as social death, see Patterson, *Slavery and Social Death*. For a challenge to Patterson's thesis, see Vincent Brown, "Social Death and Political life in the Study of Slavery."

59. Equiano, *Interesting Narrative*, 122.

60. Quoted from Cotter, "The Somerset Case," 51.

61. Massachusetts Historical Society, Ms. N-641: Robert Treat Paine, "Diary."

62. *Boston Evening Post* (20 September), *Boston Gazette* (20 September), *Boston Post-Boy* (20 September), *Connecticut Courant* (21 September), *New Hampshire Gazette* 24 September), *New London Gazette* (24 September), *Providence Gazette* (25 September), *New Port Mercury* (27 September).

63. The many positive English reviews of Wheatley's first volume of poetry indicate that her second proposed volume, again refused by American publishers, would very probably have found an English publisher.

Chapter 6. "Now upon my own Footing"

1. Exactly when during a series of court decisions slavery legally ended in Massachusetts is much disputed: O'Brien, "Did the Jennison Case Outlaw Slavery in Massachusetts?"; Cushing, "The Cushing Court and the Abolition of Slavery in Massachusetts"; Zilversmit, "Quock Walker, Mumbet, and the Abolition of Slav-

ery in Massachusetts"; Zilversmit, *The First Emancipation*, chs. 5–8; MacEacheren, "Emancipation of Slavery in Massachusetts: A Reexamination, 1770–1790"; Berlin, *Many Thousands Gone*, 229; Spector, "The Quock Walker Cases (1781–1783)"; Downs, "Unlikely Abolitionist."

2. On the early abolitionist movements in British North America, see Zilversmit, *The First Emancipation*.

3. Otis, *Rights*, 29.

4. Appleton, *Considerations*, 4, 19. *Considerations on Slavery. In a Letter to a Friend* was published anonymously in Boston by Benjamin Edes (1732–1805) and John Gill (1732–85).

5. Swan, *A Dissuasion to Great-Britain and the Colonies from the Slave Trade to Africa*.

6. See "The recent Petition," June 1773, Massachusetts Historical Society: Jeremy Belknap Papers, Ms. N-1827; Thomas J. Davis, "Emancipation Rhetoric, Natural Rights, and Revolutionary New England"; Russell, *The Appendix. Or some Observations of the Expediency of the Petition of the Africans, Living in* Boston"; Melish, *Disowning Slavery*.

7. Massachusetts Historical Society: T. Wallcut Microfilm P-391, Thomas Wallcut Papers, 1671–1866, Reel 2 of 3.

8. Connecticut Historical Society: Samson Occom Papers.

9. Phillis Wheatley to Rev. Samuel Hopkins, 9 February 1774.

10. Rush, *A Dissertation*, 19 (emphasis in original).

11. On 29 November 1773 the *Boston Evening Post* reported that the *Dartmouth*, commanded by Captain Hall, had arrived in Boston harbor the previous day. The vessel's cargo was not immediately unloaded because it included a "pernicious Article": "114 Chests of the much talked-of East India Company's TEA." An assembly at the Old South Church voted to force the importer of the tea to send it back to London (*Essex Gazette*, 30 November–7 December 1773).

12. The *Boston Gazette* repeated the advertisement on 31 January and 7 February. The *Boston Weekly News-Letter* carried the advertisement on 3, 10, 17 February.

13. *Rivington's New York Gazeteer* (14 April 1774); *Pennsylvania Journal and Weekly advertiser* (17 August 1774); *Connecticut Gazette; and the Universal Intelligencer* (17 June); *Nova Scotia Gazette and Weekly Chronicle* (11 May and 1 June 1774). The printer of the *Connecticut Gazette; and the Universal Intelligencer*, Timothy Green (1737–96), advertised that not only was he selling copies of Wheatley's *Poems*, but that "a few of the above are likewise to be sold by Samson Occom." The week before the *Nova Scotia Gazette and Weekly Chronicle* reprinted Wheatley's "Farewel," as well as the full London advertisement for her *Poems*, it reprinted the extract of Wheatley's letter to Rev. Occom (see below). Cox and Berry re-advertised Wheatley's *Poems*

as "This Day is Published . . . for the Benefit of the Author" in the *Boston Post-Boy* on 4, 11, and 18 July 1774.

14. Fithian, *Journal & Letters of Philip Vickers Fithian*. Journal entry for Saturday, 5 March 1774.

15. Massachusetts Historical Society: Ms. N-1072 Cushing Family Papers II.

16. The *Boston News-Letter* reported on 4 July 1765, "New York, June 24 [1765]. Commodore [Thomas] Graves [1725–1802], in his Majesty's Ship the *Edgar* [ADM 36/7353, ADM 33/446] and the *Shannon* Frigate [ADM 36/6695, ADM 32/228] and *Hound* Sloop of War [36/5780, 36/5781] were at Gambia the 1st of May." (*Georgia Gazette*, 28 March 1765, reported that they were sent to destroy the French fort at Albreda. Thomas Graves, commander of *Edgar*, promoted his cousin Thomas Graves [1747?–1814] lieutenant of *Shannon* in 1765 while off the coast of Africa. John Prime Iron Rochfort did not serve on either the *Edgar*, the *Shannon*, or the *Hound*.)

Able seaman Rochfort sailed from England 6 May 1774 under the command of Captain John Robinson aboard the *Preston* (ADM 36/8090, ADM 34/562). The 24-year-old Rochfort was one of three hundred men on the fifty-gun ship. Serving on the *Preston* with him were "Richard Graves, 19, Gravesend, County of Derry, Ab to y[e] 28th Sep[t] then Mid. Discharged 30/12/75" (34/574); "Samuel Graves, Scarbro', 3rd Lieutenant"; "John Graves, Edinburgh, 3rd Lieutenant" (brother of Lt. Thomas Graves [1747?–1814], commander of *Diana* in 1775); and "Samuel Graves [1713–87], supernumerary, VAB to 26 May 1775, then VAW" (uncle of John and Thomas Graves; uncle of Admiral Thomas Graves, 1st Baron Graves, who was a first cousin of Rear-Admiral Sir Thomas Graves).

Rochfort was discharged from the *Preston* on 30 December 1775 to become lieutenant on the *Nautilus*, which had 100 men (125 after 22/5/76), until 14/12/78 (ADM 34/530, 574). According to *The Commissioned Sea Officers of the Royal Navy, 1660–1815* (Aldershot: Scolar Press for the Navy Records Society, 1994), Rochfort was promoted to Lieutenant, 30 December 1775, and Commander, 25 October 1809.

Vice Admiral Samuel Graves (1713–87) promoted his nephew Thomas Graves at the beginning of 1775. Graves to Philip Stephens (1725–1809), Secretary of the British Admiralty, 8 January 1775: "I have appointed Lieut. Thomas Graves of his Majesty's Ship *Lively* [20 guns, 130 men, Capt. Thomas Bishop] to command the *Diana* Schooner. . . . The *Diana* will soon be ready for Sea, and I shall send her to Rhode Island." "The Conduct of Vice-Admiral Graves in North America in 1774, 1775 and January 1776," Gay Transcript, Massachusetts Historical Society, I, 42–48; original in British Library, Ms. 14038: 1: 46v.

17. Shields, *Phillis Wheatley's Poetics*, 97.

18. The equation of Rochfort's "guilded shore" and Wheatley's "Gambia" may be traced back to the reference to "Gambia's golden shore" by John Singleton (fl. 1760s)

in *A General Description of the West-Indian Islands*, Book 2, line 49. An abridged version was published the following year under the title *A Description of the West-Indies, A Poem, in Four Books* (London: Printed for T. Becket, the corner of the Adelphi in the Strand, 1767). Rochfort, Wheatley, and Singleton may have all been confusing Gambia with the Gold Coast of Africa.

19. Michel Adanson (1727–1806), *A Voyage to Senegal.*

20. Day and Bicknell, *The Dying Negro*, 11, fn.

21. Day and Bicknell, *The Dying Negro*, 8.

22. Brown Family Business Records, B363, f.5: 13, John Carter Brown Library.

23. Providence Town Papers, Mss. 214 sg1 (1705–89), vol. 230, Rhode Island Historical Society.

24. Massachusetts Historical Society: Second Church (Boston, Mass.) records, Ms. N-2037 Tall Vol. 6: Record Book, 1741–1816: 27 May 1776, "Baptised} Elizabeth of} Nathaniel & Mary Wheatley." Their first daughter had been baptized in the same church in 1774: "Octr 31 Baptised} Susannah of} Nathaniel & Mary Wheatley N[ota] B[ene]. This child was baptized in private at the particular Desire of its parents."

25. By the time of his death, Nathaniel Wheatley had been living in Boston long enough to have been assessed for taxes. Boston Public Library: "Taking Book, Additional & Abatements 1783," Ward 9.

26. Rush Mss. Vol 24:144, 5 May 1788, Library Company of Philadelphia, on deposit at Historical Society of Pennsylvania.

27. *Providence Gazette, and Country Journal*, 6 May 1775.

28. Rhode Island Historical Society: Moses Brown Papers, Part 1, reel 3, 00473.

29. Rhode Island Historical Society, Moses Brown Papers, Part 1, reel 3, 00473; Part 1, reel 3, 00501.

30. Mason, *The Poems of Phillis Wheatley*, 164, fn. 38.

31. Morgan, "'To Be Quit of Negroes,'" 415.

32. If Phillis Wheatley returned to Boston with the Lathrops, she was back in town by 9 May 1776, when Abigail Adams told her husband, John, that "Mr Lothtrope" was participating in the fortification of Boston harbor: Butterfield, Garrett, and Sprague, *The Adams Papers, Series II, Adams Family Correspondence*, 1: 369.

33. Price, "Diary of Ezekiel Price," 252. Price was a respectable Boston merchant and clerk of the Court of Common Pleas and Sessions before the Revolution and from 1776 to 1800. He was a son-in-law of the John Avery who may have sold Phillis to John and Susanna Wheatley in 1761, and thus he was related by marriage to Anna Green Winslow.

34. Abigail Adams to John Adams, 31 March 1776, Butterfield et al., *The Adams Papers* 1: 405.

35. Foster's diary is interleaved in his copy of *The New-England Almanack, or Lady's and Gentleman's Diary . . . 1776, by Benjamin West* (Providence, 1775) at the Rhode Island Historical Society.

36. Wheatley to Tanner, 14 February 1776, published by National Public Radio, 21 November 2005: http://www.npr.org/templates/story/story.php?storyId=5021077

37. Sancho, *Letters*, 116, 177.

38. Sancho to Mrs. Margaret Cocksedge, 5 November 1777, in Sancho, *Letters*, 106.

39. Mason, *The Poems of Phillis Wheatley*, 168, fn. 42.

40. See endnote 13 above.

41. The *Connecticut Gazette* (11 March 1774), *Boston Evening Post* (21 March), *Essex Gazette* (22 and 29 March), *Boston Post-Boy* (22 March), *Boston News-Letter* (24 March), *Massachusetts Spy* (24 March), *Providence Gazette* (26 March), *Essex Journal and Merrimack Packet* (30 March), *Connecticut Journal* (1 April), *Newport Mercury* (11 April), *Nova Scotia Gazette and Weekly Chronicle* (3 May).

42. Feiler, *America's Prophet.* The best-known comparison of American colonists with Old Testament Israelites is probably by Thomas Paine (1737–1809) in *Common Sense* (1776).

43. Quaque, *The Life and Letters of Philip Quaque*, 118: Quaque to Richard Hind, 19 March 1774.

44. Quaque, *The Life and Letters*, 114.

45. Wheatley to Thornton, 1 December 1773. The sentence in quotation marks paraphrases Isaiah 57:15.

46. Occum, *The Collected Writings of Samson Occom*, 97.

47. Quaque, *The Life and Letters*, 115.

48. Hopkins and Stiles, *To the Public*, 5.

49. Piersen, *Black Yankees*, 42, 58–59.

50. John Paul Jones to Hector MacNeill, undated, Pierpont Morgan Library MA0835: Collection of Letters of John Paul Jones, Chiefly to Hector MacNeill, 1781–1790 and undated. Jones arrived at Boston on 16 December 1776, was given command of the *Ranger* on 14 June 1777, and sailed for France on 1 November 1777. Earlier in his life, Jones spent several years serving as a mate on slave ships in the transatlantic trade.

51. Mason, *The Poems of Phillis Wheatley*, 30, quoting Seeber, *Anti-Slavery Opinion in France*, 57, n.54.

52. Proverbs 29:19: "A servant will not be corrected by words; for though he understand he will not answer."

53. Bernard Romans (1741–84), *A Concise Natural History of East and West Florida*, 1: 105.

54. Chase, *Our Revolutionary Forefathers*, 84–85.

55. *Sentimental Magazine, or, General Assemblage of Science, Taste, and Entertainment* (London), 2 (September 1774): 416.

56. Scott (Taylor), *The Female Advocate*, vii, viii.

57. *Ibid.,*, 26–27.

58. I am indebted to Mason, *The Poems of Phillis Wheatley*, 8–9, for the information about the relationship between Wheatley and Everleigh. Mason points out that this relationship is "a heretofore unanticipated southern connection" (9).

59. Houghton Library, Harvard University, MS Hyde 25, Series: I Correspondence (3), 10 September 1774 letter from Hannah More, Bristol, to Frances Reynolds. I thank Zachary Petrea for bringing this letter to my attention.

60. Deverell, *Miscellanies in Prose and Verse*.

61. Sancho, *Letters*, 112.

Chapter 7. "An Elegy on Leaving"

1. Fortunately for Phillis Wheatley's biographer, there are few men named "John Peters" in relevant Boston records, and Phillis's husband can usually be distinguished from them by comparing contemporaneous records. For example, Phillis's husband was certainly neither the John Peters listed in *The Boston Directory* (Boston: John West, June 1796) as "Peters John, labourer, Short street," nor the John Peters, probably the same person, listed in *The Boston Directory* (Boston: John West, 1800) as "Peters John, labourer, Belknap's lane." Tax assessment records prove that Phillis's widower lived in a different ward.

2. Mason, *The Poems of Phillis Wheatley*, 198, fn. 14.

3. Massachusetts Archives: "John Wheatley 1778 Will" (signed "John Wheatly") 16501 Suffolk Probate Record Books, vol. 77, pp. 307, 358, 359. John Wheatley left to "my Son Nathaniel Wheatley the sum of Twenty Shillings, & I give him no more, because I believe I have already given him full two thirds of my Estate already." Mary Wheatley Lathrop survived her father by only a few months. After learning from Rev. Lathrop of the deaths of his father and sister, Nathaniel wrote from London to Lathrop that he planned to return to Boston, without his wife, in spring 1780 to deal with the estate (Massachusetts Historical Society: Ms. N-1552 John Lathrop Sermons 1758–1816 Misc. papers. Box 11 of 11).

4. Massachusetts Historical Society, Ms. N-1683 John Tudor papers, 1732–1793. Massachusetts Historical Society, Ms. N-641: Robert Treat Paine, "Diary," describes 1 April 1778 as "Cloudy dull raw day—Snow Squall."

5. I (along with every other editor and critic of Wheatley) mistakenly assumed that 1 April was the date of their marriage rather than simply the date they announced their intentions, even though we knew that she continued to use her maiden name after 1 April 1778. Julian D. Mason, Jr., for example, proposes that "[t]hough she had become Phillis Peters in April [1778], to Mrs. Wooster, whom she

had not met, Phillis would have been known still as Wheatley" when she wrote to Mrs. Wooster on 15 July 1778 (170–71).

6. Massachusetts Historical Society, Ms. N-641: Robert Treat Paine, "Diary." Paul Revere had a pew in the same church.

7. Massachusetts Historical Society, Second Church (Boston, Mass.) records, Ms. N-2037 Tall

Vol. 7: Record Book, 1768–1815, Marriages 1778: "108 Cato Franklin & Susannah Williams

Free Negroes———— Novr 24. 1778. 109 John Peters & Phillis Wheatley Free Negroes———— Novr 26 1778."

8. Massachusetts Historical Society, Second Church (Boston, Mass.) records, Ms. N-2037 Tall, Vol. 7: Record Book, 1768–1815, 148.

9. Blackstone, *Commentaries* 1: 430–31.

10. Quoted from Egerton, *Death or Liberty*, 104. Egerton does not discuss either Phillis Wheatley or John Peters.

11. Crocker, "Reminiscences and Traditions of Boston," 103.

12. Odell, "Memoir," 19–20. See Elrod, "Phillis Wheatley's Abolitionist Text," 96–109.

13. Odell, "Memoir," 20, 23 (emphases in original): "At this period of destitution, Phillis received an offer of marriage from a respectable colored man of Boston. The name of this individual was Peters. He kept a grocery in Court-Street, and was a man of very handsome person and manners; wore a wig, carried a cane, and quite acted out *'the gentleman.'* In an evil hour he was accepted; and he proved utterly unworthy of the distinguished woman who honored him by her alliance. He was unsuccessful in business, and failed soon after their marriage; and he is said to have been both too proud and too indolent to apply himself to any occupation below his fancied dignity. Hence his unfortunate wife suffered much from this ill-omened union."

"Poor Phillis was left to the care of her negligent husband.

"We now learn nothing of her for a long interval. At length a relative of her lamented mistress heard of her illness, and sought her out. She was also visited by several other members of that family. They found her in a situation of extreme misery. Two of her children were dead, and the third was sick unto death. She was herself suffering for want of attention, for many comforts, and that greatest of all comforts in sickness—cleanliness. She was reduced to a condition too loathsome to describe. If a charitable individual, moved at the sight of so much distress, sent a load of wood, to render her more comfortable during the cold season, her husband *was too much of a gentleman* to prepare it for her use.—It is painful to dwell upon the closing scene. In a filthy apartment, in an obscure part of the metropolis, lay the dying mother, and the wasting child. The woman who had stood honored and respected in the presence of the wise and good of that country which was hers by adoption, or rather compulsion, who had graced the ancient halls of Old England, and rolled about in the splendid equipages of the proud nobles of Britain, was now numbering the last hours of life in a state of the most abject misery, surrounded by all the emblems of squalid poverty!"

14. Spear, "Memoir," 54–55.

15. Adams and Pleck, *Love of Freedom*, 188.

16. Odell's image of a villainous John Peters reappears in subsequent accounts of him. Nathaniel B. Shurtleff repeats Odell's erroneous assertion that Wheatley and Peters "married in April, 1778." Shurtleff relies on Odell's "report . . . that he kept a shop, wore a wig, carried a cane, and felt himself superior to all kinds of labor." Shurtleff, too, says that following the death of Mary Wheatley Lathrop, Phillis "was left entirely to her miserable husband, who proved to be improvident, failing in business," and who refused "to do any thing that would conduce to her comfort in the days of her sickness and sorrow." Shurtleff also reports that "about this time [1783] she lost two of the three children born to her and her husband in their days of extreme poverty and distress." Shurtleff's claim that "poor Phillis! was obliged to earn her own subsistence in a common negro boarding-house, at the west part of the town" while her husband was in prison has not been verified. But some of Shurtleff's information is verifiable: "Soon after his liberation from jail, Peters worked as a journeyman baker. Subsequently he attempted to practice law, and finally imposed upon the credulous by pretending to be a physician." Shurtleff, *Proceedings of the Massachusetts Historical Society* 7 (1863–1864): 270–72.

17. Odell, "Memoir," 22.

18. Massachusetts Archives: Suffolk County Court of Common Pleas, Record Books 1776–1779, Vol. 1776, page 11. "Shopkeeper" Peters was awarded "the Sum of Thirty eight Pounds and four pence lawful money Damage, and Costs of suit, taxed at £1. 18. 8."

19. Jones, *The Loyalists of Massachusetts*, 256. Sabine, *Biographical Sketches of the American Revolution*, 268–69.

20. Mann, *Republic of Debtors*, 18.

21. Anonymous, *The Ill Policy*, 9.

22. Massachusetts Archives: Suffolk County Probate File for Joseph Scott, docket #16956 Absentee 1779.

23. Massachusetts Archives: Suffolk (Massachusetts) Files, Vol. 653, 105248 (series) (cf. 105606, 105612): John Peters vs. Fowler (1788–89), tracing back to Spring-Summer 1779, when Peters was in partnership with Josias Byles (variously spelled) trading nails, tea, sugar, etc. for rye and wheat in Hampshire and Worcester counties. Peters successfully claimed that he and Byles were partners in Worcester County but not Hampshire.

24. Lathrop, *Consolation for Mourners.*

25. Norton, *Liberty's Daughters*, 181. Isani, "'On the Death of General Wooster,'" 308n., suggests that the compositor for the *Boston Evening Post and General Advertiser* may have mistakenly printed twelve pounds rather than 12 Lm° (i.e., 12 shillings, legal money). Robinson, *Phillis Wheatley and Her Writings*, 349n., notes that "Just fifteen months earlier, Phillis had declared that she could easily dispose of remainder copies of her 1773 volume "for 12/Lm°." He also remarks that the prices in the 1779 "Proposals" "could reflect the inflation of the times, or they might reflect John Peters's grandiose notions of the book's worth." Mann, *Republic of Debtors*, notes, "By the end of the war, Congress had issued some $200,000,000 in Continental currency, which had fallen in value from near par with specie to considerably less than a hundredth of the value of specie. The states had emitted a similar amount. . . . [Congress] compounded the distress—and doubled the debt—by appraising the state's wartime currency at par rather than revaluing it to reflect at least some of the depreciation that by early 1781 had reduced it to 75:1, as even the Continental Congress had" (170, 180).

26. Massachusetts Archives: Suffolk Files, Vol. 531, #93097.

27. *Boston Post-Boy*, 17 August 1772.

28. Massachusetts Archives: Suffolk Files, Vol. 531, #93027.

29. Massachusetts Archives: Suffolk Files, Vol. 531, #93097.

30. Odell, "Memoir," 20.

31. Greene and Harrington, *American Population before the Federal Census of 1790*, 33.

32. For help in locating town and Congregational Church records in Wilmington, I thank Andrea Houser, Adele Passmore, Caroline Harris, and Terry McDermott.

33. Appended to the pamphlet is William Billings (1746–1800), "Words for a funeral anthem. Taken from the following scriptures; and set to Musick by Mr. Billings. And performed at the Funeral of the Reverend Dr. Samuel Cooper, on Friday, Jan. 2, 1784." Mason notes that "Because of its use of 'performed at the funeral of' in the anthem's headnote, the pamphlet seems to have been printed after the funeral. It is possible that Wheatley's poem had been used at the funeral, as had the anthem. (Cooper died on Monday, December 29, but the funeral was not held until Friday.) The *Boston Magazine* for December 1783 reported in his obituary that Cooper 'had been confined to his chamber with a disorder of the lethargic kind for upwards of six weeks' before he died, so she may have even anticipated his death in her composition" (Mason, *Poems*, 173). Billings is often considered the father of American choral hymn music. His *New-England Psalm-Singer: or, American Chorister* was the first published collection of American music. Shields, *Phillis Wheatley and the Romantics*, 37, speculates that Wheatley may have "attended Billings's Singing School," and that Billings played a significant role in her development as a poet. Although Shields believes that

"Billings collaborated with Wheatley in their shared effort to commemorate the death of Samuel Cooper" (36), Billings's anthem was advertized separately before Ezekiel Russell published it and Wheatley's poem together after Cooper's funeral.

34. *Liberty and Peace, a Poem* is quite similar in subject matter and tone to Rev. John Lathrop's *A Discourse on the Peace*. Consequently, rather than having been published at the beginning of 1784, Phillis's poem may have been, as Lathrop's sermon was, occasioned by Governor John Hancock's *Proclamation*, published on 28 October 1784, calling for a day of thanksgiving on 25 November 1784.

35. Phillis and John Peters were unaffected by two consequential court rulings involving people of African descent made while they were out of Boston. Both were decided on generous applications of the statement in the preamble of Massachusetts state constitution that "All men are born free and equal." The first case was won by an enslaved woman named Elizabeth, nicknamed Bett or Mum Bett (ca. 1742–1829), who gained her freedom in 1781. She promptly appropriated a surname befitting her new legal status: Freeman. In the second case, which began simultaneously with Mum Bett's, Quok Walker finally won his freedom in 1783 in a ruling by Chief Justice William Cushing that undermined the institution of slavery in Massachusetts. Although the state had not outlawed slavery, Cushing's ruling that it was unconstitutional meant that any slave who sued for his or her freedom in court would win.

36. Massachusetts Archives: Suffolk County Court of Common Pleas, Record Books, Vol. 1784, 55; American Antiquarian Society: Massachusetts Court of Common Pleas, Record Book, Mss. Dept., Octavo vols. "M," 1783–1790, f. 56, 6 July 1784.

37. For a description of postwar Boston, see Carr, *After the Siege*.

38. Massachusetts Archives: Suffolk Files Collection, Vol. 679, #95576.

39. Ezell, *The New Democracy in America*, 119.

40. The manuscript is at the Schomburg Center for Research in Black Culture, The New York Public Library. I include it in my edition of Wheatley's writings. Mason does not consider the evidence for its attribution to Wheatley strong enough to justify inclusion in his edition.

41. Widow Sheaffe outlived Peters by ten years. Also living in ward eight in 1784 was "Prince Hall (Negro)," servant of the wealthy merchant "Isaac Smith Esqʳ."

42. Mann, *Republic of Debtors*, 176.

43. Ibid., 180.

44. Ibid. Mann notes, "Debtor-creditor relations had long been more hostile in Massachusetts than elsewhere."

45. On 15 July 1785 Deputy Sheriff Benjamin Hemans witnessed John Peters's signed testimony that the execution of the 6 October 1784 warrant against Joseph Scott had been "in no part satisfied" [Peters's signature looks the same as the one

on the 28 July 1784 petition for a liquor license]. Massachusetts Archives: Suffolk County Court of Common Pleas, Peters vs. Scott, Docket #244, July 1785 Session.

46. Nathaniel B. Shurtleff, "Phillis Wheatley, the Negro—Slave Poet," *Boston Daily Advertiser*, 21 December 1863.

47. Mason, *The Poems of Phillis Wheatley*, 179, very plausibly suggests that this poem is the "To P. N. S. & Lady on the Death of their Infant Son" advertized in the 1779 "Proposals."

48. Isani, "The Methodist Connection."

49. Wesley, *Thoughts upon Slavery*, 16–17.

50. Ibid., 18, 39.

51. Ibid., 31.

52. Ibid., 36. Compare Granville Sharp's opinion in *A Representation of the Injustice and Dangerous Tendency of Tolerating Slavery*, 73: "It were better for the English nation, that these American dominions had never existed, or even that they should have been sunk into the sea, than that the kingdom of Great Britain, should be loaded with the horrid guilt of tolerating such abominable wickedness!"

53. Massachusetts Historical Society, Ms. N-641: Robert Treat Paine (1731–1814), "Diary."

54. Eblen, "New Estimates of the Vital Rates of the United States Black Population during the Nineteenth Century," 306.

55. Melish, *Disowning Slavery*, 40.

56. Boston Public Library, Adlow J-S: Prisoner Lists A31.

57. Boston Public Library, Adlow J-S: Prisoner Lists A32.

58. Massachusetts Archives: Suffolk County Court of Common Pleas, Record Books, Vol. 1789, pp. 291–92. Suffolk Files, vol. 655, 105332.

59. "Names of the Inhabitants of the Town of Boston in 1790. Collected by Samuel Bradford. Printed from the original manuscript in the Library of the New England Historic-Genealogical Society," Saturday, 7 August 1790.

60. Pintles are the pins or bolts on which other parts, such as rudders or hinges, turn.

61. George E. Gifford, Jr. "Botanic Remedies in Colonial Massachusetts, 1620–1820, 276, 278.

62. Christianson, "The Medical Practitioners of Massachusetts, 1630–1800: Patterns of Change and Continuity," 52–53.

63. Richard D. Brown, 'The Healing Arts in Colonial and Revolutionary Massachusetts: the contexts for Scientific Medicine," 40.

64. Adams and Pleck, *Love of Freedom*, 34.

65. Cohen, "Legal Literature in colonial Massachusetts," 254. The full title of *Conductor Generalis* is *Conductor Generalis, or The Office, Duty and Authority of Jus-*

tices of the Peace, High Sheriffs, Under-Sheriffs, Goalers, Coroners, Constables, Jury Men, Over-seers of the Poor, and also The Office of Clerks of Assiza And of the Peace &c. Collected out of all the Books hitherto written on those Subjects, whether of Common or Statute Law. To which is added, A Collection out of Sir Matthew Hales concerning The Descent of Lands. The Whole Alphabetically Digested Under the Several Titles, With a Table Directing to the Ready finding out Proper Matter under those Titles.

66. Shurtleff, *Proceedings*, 279.

67. Boston Public Library Ms. Adl. w E309: Suffolk County Court of Common Pleas Writs of Attachment Issued by Samuel Barrett.

68. Massachusetts Archives: Suffolk Files 106682.

69. *Boston Record Commissioners' Reports*, Vol. 35, *Boston Town Records, 1796–1813*, 73.

70. Odell, "Memoir," 29.

71. Robinson, *Phillis Wheatley and Her Writings*, 65, mistakes the "Peters John, labourer, Belknap's lane" in *The Boston Directory* (Boston: John West, 1800) for Phillis's husband, who lived in a different ward.

72. Massachusetts Archives: Middlesex County Probate Court File Papers 17255.

73. Massachusetts Archives: Middlesex County Probate Court File Papers 17255, "The Inventory of sundry Effects Belonging to the Estate of John Peters late of Charlestown dec^d tak^n the 6 day of augs^t 1801 by the apprisers."

74. His administrators were "Josiah Wellington, gentleman, & Micah Brigden blacksmith, principals, John Nutting gentleman & Jabez Frothingham, gentleman." Jabez Frothingham (d. 1801), a wheelwright, was the cousin of Benjamin Frothingham (d. 1809), the cabinetmaker thought to have designed the writing desk in the Massachusetts Historical Society. See Wyman, *The Genealogies and Estates of Charlestown*.

75 Sancho, *Letters*, 112. Brooks, "Our Phillis, Ourselves," 16–17, especially indicts the white women who had supported Phillis earlier in her career for abandoning her during the last years of her life.

Afterword

1. Ladd, *The Poems of Arouet*, 22.

2. Crawford, *Observations upon Negro-Slavery (1784)*, 5–7. He quotes from the version of "To the Rev. Mr. Pitkin, on the Death of his Lady" revised for inclusion in *Poems*.

3. Crawford, *Observations upon Negro-Slavery. A New Edition* (1790), 20, 24–26.

4. Gregory, *Essays*, 300.

5. Nikolls, *Letter to the Treasurer of the Society Instituted for the Purpose of Effecting the Abolition of the Slave Trade*, 46.

6. Clarkson, *An Essay on the Slavery and Commerce of the Human Species, Particularly the African*, 175.

7. Stedman, *Narrative* 2: 259–60.

8. Jefferson, *Notes*, 147. Rather than intentionally misspelling Wheatley's name, Jefferson was probably correctly spelling it phonetically from memory: during the eighteenth century the words *eat* and *ate* were both pronounced as we now pronounce *ate*, and when Jefferson was writing *Notes* in France, he most likely did not have with him his copy of Wheatley's *Poems*, now in the Library of Congress. The "heroes" of Alexander Pope's satiric mock-epic *Dunciad*, published in London initially in 1728 and expanded in 1743, are the bad writers he targets. Unlike Hercules, Pope was hunchbacked, very thin, and less than five feet tall.

9. Imlay, *A Topographical Description* 1: 185–86. Verhoeven, *Gilbert Imlay*, 84–85, reveals that Imlay had participated in the transatlantic slave trade as recently as 1786.

10. *The Portfolio*, ed. Joseph Dennie (1768–1812), vol. 2 (30 October 1802), quoted in Basker, *Amazing Grace*, 577–78.

11. Gates, *The Trials*, 50.

12. *Ibid.*, 74.

13. Eleanor Smith, "Phillis Wheatley: A Black Perspective," 403. For surveys of the reception history of Phillis Wheatley and her writings, in addition to Gates, *Trials*, see Robinson, *Phillis Wheatley*, and Mason, *The Poems of Phillis Wheatley*, 23–34. Although often tendentious, Shields, *Phillis Wheatley's Poetics of Liberation* is the most thorough and up-to-date survey.

14. Huddleston, "Matilda's 'On Reading the Poems of Phillis Wheatley, the African Poetess.'"

Bibliography

MANUSCRIPT SOURCES

Cheshunt Foundation, Westminster College, Cambridge, United Kingdom
Countess of Huntingdon Correspondence.

Connecticut Historical Society
Samson Occom Papers.

Boston Public Library
Adlow Manuscripts.
Taking Books (tax lists), 1780–1820.

Cambridge University Library
Thornton Family Papers.

Dr. Williams's Library, London
"The Diary of Rev. Dr. Thomas Gibbons, 1749–1785."

Harvard University, Houghton Library
MS Hyde 25, Series: I Correspondence.

John Carter Brown Library
Brown Family Business Records.

Library Company of Philadelphia
Manuscripts of Hannah Griffitts: Poems, Essays, Extracts, on deposit at
    Historical Society of Pennsylvania.
Benjamin Rush Correspondence.
Rush Manuscripts on deposit at Historical Society of Pennsylvania.

Massachusetts Archives
Middlesex County Probate Court File Papers.
Suffolk County Court of Common Pleas.
Suffolk County Probate Record Books.
Suffolk (County, Massachusetts) Deeds.
Suffolk (County, Massachusetts) Files.

Massachusetts Historical Society
Andrews-Eliot Manuscripts.
Jeremy Belknap Papers.
Cushing Family Papers II.

John Lathrop Sermons 1758–1816, Miscellaneous papers.
Robert Treat Paine, "Diary."
John Tudor Papers.
Thomas Wallcut Papers, 1671–1866.
Second Church (Boston, Mass.) records.

Medford Historical Society
The Medford Slave Trade Letters—1759–1765.

New England Historic Genealogical Society
Crocker, Hannah Mather. "Reminiscences and Traditions of Boston: Being An
    Account of the Original Proprietors of that Town, & the Manners and Cus-
    toms of Its People" (ca. 1829).
"Names of the Inhabitants of the Town of Boston in 1790. Collected by Samuel
    Bradford. Printed from the original manuscript in the Library of the New En-
    gland Historic-Genealogical Society."

Newport Historical Society, Rhode Island
First Congregational Church, Newport, Rhode Island, Church record books.

Pierpont Morgan Library
Collection of Letters of John Paul Jones.

Rhode Island Historical Society
Moses Brown Papers.
Theodore Foster's diary, interleaved in his copy of *The New-England Almanack, or
    Lady's and Gentleman's Diary . . . 1776, by Benjamin West* (Providence, 1775).
Providence Town Papers, Manuscripts.

NEWSPAPERS AND PERIODICALS

Anti-Slavery Record.
Athenian Mercury.
Boston Chronicle.
Boston Evening Post.
Boston Gazette, and Country Journal.
Boston Magazine.
Boston News-Letter and New-England Chronicle.
Boston Post Boy.
Boston Weekly News-Letter.
Connecticut Courant.
Connecticut Gazette; and the Universal Intelligencer.
Connecticut Journal and New-Haven Post-Boy.

Critical Review.

Essex Gazette.

Essex Journal and Merrimack Packet.

General Evening Post.

Gentleman's Magazine.

Georgia Gazette.

Independent Chronicle and Advertiser (Boston).

Independent Chronicle and Universal Advertiser.

Lloyd's Evening Post.

Lloyd's Register.

London Chronicle or Universal Evening Post.

London Magazine.

The Massachusetts Gazette and Boston Post-Boy and Advertiser.

Massachusetts Gazette and the Boston Weekly News-Letter.

Massachusetts Spy or, Thomas's Boston Journal.

Monthly Review.

Morning Post and Daily Advertiser.

New Hampshire Gazette.

New London Gazette.

Newport Mercury.

New York Gazette and Weekly Post-Boy.

New York Magazine.

Nova Scotia Gazette and Weekly Chronicle.

Pennsylvania Chronicle.

Pennsylvania Journal and Weekly Advertiser.

Pennsylvania Magazine or American Monthly Museum.

Pennsylvania Packet.

The Prompter.

Providence Gazette, and Country Journal.

Public Advertiser.

Rivington's New York Gazeteer.

Scots Magazine (Edinburgh).

Sentimental Magazine, or, General Assemblage of Science, Taste, and Entertainment (London).

Virginia Gazette (Williamsburg).

DATABASES AND ONLINE SOURCES

The Trans-Atlantic Slave Trade Database, http://www.slavevoyages.org/tast/database/search.faces.

Wheatley to Tanner, 14 February 1776, published by National Public Radio, 21 November 2005: http://www.npr.org/templates/story/story.php?storyId= 5021077.n.p. Conrad Edick Wright, ed. CD-ROM *Colonial Collegians: Biographies of Those Who Attended Colonial Colleges before the War of Independence*. Boston: Published for the Massachusetts Historical Society by the New England Historic Genealogical Society, 2005.

Thwing, Annie. New England Historic Genealogical Society CD-ROM of Annie Thwing, *Inhabitants and Estates of the Town of Boston 1630–1800 and The Crooked and Narrow Streets of Boston, 1630–1822*. Boston: The Massachusetts Historical Society and the New England Historic Genealogical Society, 2001.

PUBLISHED SOURCES

An Abridgement of Burn's Justice of the Peace and Parish Officer. Boston, 1773.

Adams, Catherine, and Elizabeth H. Pleck. *Love of Freedom: Black Women in Colonial and Revolutionary New England*. New York: Oxford University Press, 2010.

Adams, Samuel. *Writings of Samuel Adams*. Ed. Harry Alonzo Cushing. New York: G. P. Putnam's Sons, 1904–08.

Adanson, Michel. *A Voyage to Senegal, the Isle of Goree, and the River Gambia. By M. Adanson, . . . Translated from the French. With Notes by an English Gentleman, who Resided some Time in that Country*. London, 1759.

Akers, Charles W. "'Our Modern Egyptians': Phillis Wheatley and the Whig Campaign against Slavery in Revolutionary Boston." *Journal of Negro History* 60 (1975): 397–410.

Altick, Robert D. *The Shows of London*. Cambridge, Mass.: Harvard University Press, 1978.

Amory, Thomas. *Daily Devotion Assisted and Recommended, in Four Sermons*. London, 1770; reprinted Boston, 1772.

Andrew, Donna, and Norma Landau, eds. *Law, Crime and English Society 1660–1840*. Cambridge: Cambridge University Press, 2002.

Appleton, Nathaniel. *Considerations on Slavery. In a Letter to a Friend*. Boston: 1767.

Aravamudan, Srinivas. *Tropicopolitans: Colonialism and Agency, 1688–1804*. Durham, N.C.: Duke University Press, 1999.

B., A. *The Memoirs of Miss Williams. A History Founded on Facts. In Two Volumes. By A. B.* London, 1773.

Bailyn, Bernard, and Philip D. Morgan, eds. *Strangers within the Realm: Cultural Margins of the First British Empire*. Chapel Hill: University of North Carolina Press, 1991.

Balkun, Mary McAleer. "Phillis Wheatley's Construction of Otherness and the Rhetoric of Performed Ideology." *African American Review* 36 (2002): 121–35.

Barbé-Marbois, François, Marquis de. *Letters.* In Chase, *Our Revolutionary Forefathers.*

Basker, James G., ed., *Amazing Grace: An Anthology of Poems about Slavery, 1660– 1810.* New Haven: Yale University Press, 2002. ✓

Bassard, Katherine Clay. *Spiritual Interrogations: Culture, Gender, and Community in Early African American Women's Writing.* Princeton, N.J.: Princeton University Press, 1999.

Benezet, Anthony. *Some Historical Account of Guinea.* Philadelphia, 1771.

Bennet, John. *Poems on Several Occasions. By John Bennet, a Journeyman Shoemaker.* London, 1774.

Benton, Josiah Henry. *Early Census Making in Massachusetts, 1643–1765: With a Reproduction of the Lost Census of 1765.* Boston: C. E. Goodspeed, 1905.

Bennett, Paula Bennett. "Phillis Wheatley's Vocation and the Paradox of the 'Afric Muse.'" *PMLA* 113 (1998): 64–76.

Berlin, Ira. *Many Thousands Gone: The First Two Centuries of Slavery in North America.* Cambridge, Mass.: Harvard University Press, 1998.

———. *The Making of African America: The Four Great Migrations.* New York: Viking, 2010.

Berlin Ira, and Ronald Hoffman, eds. *Slavery and Freedom in the Age of Revolution.* Charlottesville: University of Virginia Press, 1983.

Berthold, Arthur Benedict. *American Colonial Printing as Determined by Contemporary Cultural Forces, 1639–1763.* New York: Burt Franklin, 1934.

Bickerstaff's Boston Almanack. For the Year of Our Lord, 1773. Boston, 1772.

Bickerstaff's Boston Almanack. For the Year of Our Lord, 1782. Boston, 1781.

Billings, William. *New-England Psalm-Singer: or, American Chorister.* Boston, 1770.

Blackstone, William. *Commentaries on the Laws of England.* Oxford, 1765–69; reprinted Chicago: University of Chicago Press, 1979.

Blake, John B. *Public Health in the Town of Boston, 1630–1822.* Cambridge, Mass.: Harvard University Press, 1959.

Bly, Antonio T. "Wheatley's 'On the Affray in King Street.'" *Explicator* 56 (1998): 177–80.

Bollan, William. *Britannia Libera, or a Defence of the Free State of Man in England, against the Claim of any Man there as a Slave. Inscribed and Submitted to the Jurisconsulti, and the Free People of England.* London, 1772.

The Boston Directory. Boston: John West, 1796.

The Boston Directory. Boston: John West, 1800.

Boston Record Commissioners' Reports. Boston: Boston Registry Department, 1876–1909).

Boswell, James. *Life of Samuel Johnson*. Ed. Pat Rogers. Oxford: Oxford University Press, 1980.

Botting, Eileen Hunt, and Sarah L. Houser. "'Drawing the Line of Equality': Hannah Mather Crocker on Women's Rights." *American Political Science Review* 100 (May 2006): 265–78.

Boulukos, George. *The Grateful Slave: The Emergence of Race in Eighteenth-Century British and American Culture*. Cambridge: Cambridge University Press, 2008.

Bourn, Samuel. *Lectures to Children and Young People in a Catechetical Method, Consisting of Three Catechisms*. London, 1738.

Bradley, Patricia. *Slavery, Propaganda, and the American Revolution*. Jackson: University Press of Mississippi, 1998.

Breen, T. H. "Making History: The Force of Public Opinion and the Last Years of Slavery in Revolutionary Massachusetts." In Hoffman, Sobel, and Teute, *Through a Glass Darkly*, 67–95.

Bridenbaugh, Carl. *Mitre and Sceptre: Transatlantic Faiths, Ideas, Personalities, and Politics, 1689–1775*. New York: Oxford University Press, 1962.

Brooks, Joanna. *American Lazarus: Religion and the Rise of African-American and Native American Literatures*. New York: Oxford University Press, 2003.

———, ed. *The Collected Writings of Samson Occom, Mohegan*. New York: Oxford University Press, 2006.

———. "Our Phillis, Ourselves." *American Literature* 82 (2010): 1–28.

Brown, Christopher L. "The Empire without Slaves: British Concepts of Emancipation in the Age of the American Revolution." *William and Mary Quarterly* 3rd ser., 55 (1999): 273–306.

Brown, Richard D. "The Healing Arts in Colonial and Revolutionary Massachusetts: the Contexts for Scientific Medicine." In Estes, *Publications of the Colonial Society of Massachusetts* 57: 35–47.

Brown, Vincent. "Social Death and Political Life in the Study of Slavery." *American Historical Review* 114 (2009): 1231–49.

Brown, Wallace, ed. "An Englishman's Views of the American Revolution: The Letters of Henry Hulton, 1769–1776." *Huntington Library Quarterly* (1973): 1–26.

Bruce, Dickson D., Jr. *The Origins of African American Literature, 1680–1865*. Charlottesville: University Press of Virginia, 2001.

Buchan, William. *Domestic Medicine*. London, 1769.

Burke, Edmund. *The Writings and Speeches of Edmund Burke*, vol. 3: *Party, Parlia-*

ment, and the American War, 1774–1780. Eds. Warren M. Elofson and John A. Woods. Oxford: Oxford University Press, 1996.

Burke, Helen. "Problematizing American Dissent: The Subject of Phillis Wheatley." In Colatrella and Alkana, *Cohesion and Dissent in America*, 193–209.

Butterfield, L. H., Wendell D. Garrett, Marjorie E. Sprague, eds. *The Adams Papers, Series II, Adams Family Correspondence.* Cambridge, Mass.: Harvard University Press, 1963–93.

Byles, Mather. *Poems on Several Occasions.* Boston, 1744.

Cameron, Christopher Alain. "Freeing Themselves: Puritanism, Slavery, and Black Abolitionists in Massachusetts, 1641–1788." Diss. University of North Carolina at Chapel Hill, 2008.

Capitein, Jacobus Elisa Joannes. *The Agony of Asar: A Thesis on Slavery by the Former Slave, Jacobus Elisa Joannes Capitein, 1717–47.* Trans. and ed. Grant Parker. Princeton, N.J.: Markus Wiener, 2001.

Carey, Brycchan. *British Abolitionism and the Rhetoric of Sensibility: Writing, Sentiment, and Slavery, 1760–1807.* Houndmills, Basingstoke, Hampshire: Palgrave Macmillan, 2005.

Carr, Jacqueline Barbara. *After the Siege: A Social History of Boston, 1775–1800.* Boston: Northeastern University Press, 2005.

Carretta, Vincent. *Equiano, the African: Biography of a Self-Made Man.* New York: Penguin, 2007.

———. "Equiano's Paradise Lost: The Limits of Allusion in Chapter Five of *The Interesting Narrative*." In Kaplan and Oldfield, *Imagining Transatlantic Slavery*, 79–95.

———. "Francis Williams: An Eighteenth-Century Black Jamaican Man of Letters." *Early American Literature* 38 (2003): 213–37.

———, ed. *Letters of the Late Ignatius Sancho, an African.* New York: Penguin Putnam, 1998.

———, ed. *Olaudah Equiano, The Interesting Narrative and Other Writings.* New York: Penguin Putnam, rev. ed. 2003.

———. "Phillis Wheatley, the Mansfield Decision of 1772, and the Choice of Identity." In Schmidt and Fleischmann, *Early America Re-Explored*, 201–23.

———, ed. *Quobna Ottobah Cugoano, Thoughts and Sentiments on the Evil of Slavery and Other Writings.* New York: Penguin, 1999.

———, ed. *Unchained Voices: An Anthology of Black Authors in the English-Speaking World of the Eighteenth Century.* Lexington: University Press of Kentucky, 1997; rev. ed. 2004.

Carretta, Vincent, and Philip Gould, eds. *Genius in Bondage: Literature of the Early Black Atlantic.* Lexington: University Press of Kentucky, 2001.

Carter, Elizabeth. *Poems on Several Occasions.* London, 1762.

Cavendish, Margaret. *Philosophical and Physical Opinions.* London, 1655.

Cavitch, Max. *American Elegy: The Poetry of Mourning from the Puritans to Whitman.* Minneapolis: University of Minnesota Press, 2007.

Chapone, Hester. *Letters on the Improvement of the Mind, Addressed to a Young Lady.* London, 1773.

Chase, Eugene P., ed. and trans. *Our Revolutionary Forefathers: The Letters of François, Marquis de Barbé-Marbois [1745–1837], During His Residence in the United States as Secretary of the French Legation, 1779–1785.* New York: Duffield & Company, 1929.

Chater, Kathleen. *Untold Histories: Black People in England and Wales during the Period of the British Slave Trade, c. 1660–1807.* Manchester: Manchester University Press, 2009.

Christianson, Eric H. "The Medical Practitioners of Massachusetts, 1630–1800: Patterns of Change and Continuity." In Estes, *Publications of the Colonial Society of Massachusetts* 57: 49–67.

Christopher, Emma. *Slave Ship Sailors and their Captive Cargoes, 1730–1807.* Cambridge: Cambridge University Press, 2006.

Church, Benjamin (attrib.). *The Times: A Poem. By an American.* Boston, 1765.

The Church-Member's Directory, or Every Christian's Companion. London, 1773.

Cohen, Morris L. "Legal Literature in Colonial Massachusetts." In Coquillette, *Publications of the Colonial Society of Massachusetts* 62: 243–72.

Clarkson, Thomas. *An Essay on the Slavery and Commerce of the Human Species, Particularly the African.* London, 1786.

Colatrella, Carol, and Joseph Alkana, eds. *Cohesion and Dissent in America.* Albany: State University of New York Press, 1994.

Coldham, Peter Wilson. *Emigrants in Chains: A Social History of Forced Emigration to the Americas of Felons, Destitute Children, Political and Religious Nonconformists, Vagabonds, and Other Undesirables, 1607–1776.* Baltimore: Genealogical Publishing Company, 1992, 2nd ed. 2007.

Coleridge, Samuel Taylor. *Poems on Various Subjects.* London, 1796.

The Commissioned Sea Officers of the Royal Navy, 1660–1815. Aldershot: Scolar Press for the Navy Records Society, 1994.

A Companion to Every Place of Curiosity and Entertainment in and about London and Westminster. London, 1767; 3rd ed. 1772.

Cook, William W., and James Tatum. *African American Writers and Classical Tradition.* Chicago: University of Chicago Press, 2010.

Coquillette, Daniel R., ed. *Publications of the Colonial Society of Massachusetts* 62 (1984).

Cotter, William R. "The Somerset Case and the Abolition of Slavery in England." *History* 79 (1994): 31–56.

Coviello, Peter. "Agonizing Affection: Affect and Nation in Early America." *Early American Literature* 37 (2002): 439–68.

Craton, Michael. *Sinews of Empire: A Short History of British Slavery.* Garden City, N.Y.: Anchor Press, 1974.

Crawford, Charles. *Observations upon Negro-Slavery.* Philadelphia, 1784, 1790.

Cray, Robert E. "Memorialization and Enshrinement: George Whitefield and Popular Religious Culture, 1770–1850." *Journal of the Early Republic* 10 (1990): 339–61.

Crocker, Hannah Mather. *A Series of Letters on Free Masonry. By a Lady of Boston.* Boston: Printed by John Eliot, 1815.

Cugoano, Quobna Ottobah. *Thoughts and Sentiments on the Evil and Wicked Traffic of the Slavery and Commerce of the Human Species, Humbly Submitted to the Inhabitants of Great-Britain, by Ottobah Cugoano, a Native of Africa.* London, 1787. In Carretta, *Thoughts and Sentiments on the Evil of Slavery and Other Writings,* 1–111.

———. *Thoughts and Sentiments on the Evil of Slavery; Or, the Nature of Servitude as Admitted by the Law of God, Compared to the Modern Slavery of the Africans in the West-Indies; In an Answer to the Advocates for Slavery and Oppression. Addressed to the Sons of Africa, by a Native.* London, 1791. In Carretta, *Thoughts and Sentiments on the Evil of Slavery and Other Writings,* 113–50.

Cushing, John D. "The Cushing Court and the Abolition of Slavery in Massachusetts: More Notes on the 'Quock Walker Case.'" *American Journal of Legal History* 5 (1961): 118–44.

Dabydeen, David. *Hogarth's Blacks: Images of Blacks in Eighteenth Century English Art.* Athens: University of Georgia Press, 1987.

Darwall, Mary [Whateley]. *Original Poems on Several Occasions.* London, 1764.

Davis, Thomas J. "Emancipation Rhetoric, Natural Rights, and Revolutionary New England: A Note on Four Black Petitions in Massachusetts, 1773–177." *New England Quarterly* 62 (1989): 248–63.

Day, Thomas. *Fragment of an Original Letter on the Slavery of the Negroes.* London, 1784.

———. *The History of Sandford and Merton, A Work Intended for the Use of Children.* London, 1783, 1786, and 1789.

Day, Thomas, and John Bicknell. *The Dying Negro.* London, 1773.

Desrochers, Robert E., Jr., "Slave-for-Sale Advertisements and Slavery in Massachusetts, 1704–1781." *The William and Mary Quarterly,* 3rd series 59 (2002): 623–64.

———. "'Surprizing Deliverance': Slavery and Freedom, Language and Identity in the Narrative of Briton Hammon." In Carretta and Gould, *Genius in Bondage*, 153–74.

Deverell, Mary. *Miscellanies in Prose and Verse.* London, 1781.

Dickinson, John. *Letters from a Farmer in Pennsylvania.* Philadelphia, 1768.

Dorsey, Peter A. *Common Bondage: Slavery as Metaphor in Revolutionary America.* Knoxville: University of Tennessee Press, 2010.

Downs, Harry. "Unlikely Abolitionist: William Cushing and the Struggle against Slavery." *Journal of Supreme Court History* 29 (2004): 123–35.

Drescher, Seymour. *Capitalism and Antislavery: British Mobilization in Comparative Perspective.* London: Macmillan, 1986.

Duffy, John. *Epidemics in Colonial America.* Baton Rouge: Louisiana State University Press, 1953.

Dunkle, Robert J., and Ann S. Lainhart. *Inscriptions and Records of the Old Cemeteries of Boston.* Boston: New England Historic Genealogical Society, 2000.

Dunlap, Jane. *Poems Upon Several Sermons Preached by the Rev'd and Renowned George Whitefield While in Boston. . . . A New Year's Gift from a Daughter of Liberty and Lover of Truth.* Boston, 1771.

Eblen, Jack Ericson. "New Estimates of the Vital Rates of the United States Black Population during the Nineteenth Century." *Demography* 11 (1974): 301–19.

Egerton, Douglas R. *Death or Liberty: African Americans and Revolutionary America.* New York: Oxford University Press, 2009.

An Elegiac Poem Sacred to the Memory of the Rev. George Whitefield. Boston, 1770.

Elrod, Eileen Razzari. "Moses and the Egyptian: Religious Authority in Olaudah Equiano's *Interesting Narrative.*" *African American Review* 35 (2001): 409–25.

———. "Phillis Wheatley's Abolitionist Text: The 1834 Edition." In Kaplan and Oldfield, *Imagining Transatlantic Slavery*, 96–109.

———. *Piety and Dissent: Race, Gender, and Biblical Rhetoric in Early American Autobiography.* Amherst: University of Massachusetts Press, 2008.

Eltis, David. "The U.S. Transatlantic Slave Trade, 1644–1867: An Assessment." *Civil War History* 54 (2008): 347–78.

———. "The Volume and Structure of the Transatlantic Slave Trade: A Reassessment." *The William and Mary Quarterly*, 3rd Series 58 (2001): 17–46.

Ennis, Daniel J. "Poetry and American Revolutionary Identity: The Case of Phillis Wheatley and John Paul Jones." *Studies in Eighteenth-century Culture* 31 (2002): 85–98.

Equiano, Olaudah. *The Interesting Narrative of the Life of Olaudah Equiano, or Gustavus Vassa, the African. Written by Himself.* London, 1789. In Carretta, *The Interesting Narrative.*

Erkilla, Betsy. *Mixed Bloods and Other Crosses: Rethinking American Literature from the Revolution to the Culture Wars.* Philadelphia: University of Pennsylvania Press, 2005.

———. "Phillis Wheatley and the Black American Revolution." In Shuffleton, *A Mixed Race*, 225–40.

Estes, J. Worth, Philip Cash, and Eric H. Christianson, eds. *Publications of the Colonial Society of Massachusetts* 57 (1980).

Estwick, Samuel. *Considerations on the Negroe Cause Commonly So Called, Addressed to the Right Honourable Lord Mansfield . . . . By a West Indian.* London, 1772.

Ezell, John S., ed. *The New Democracy in America: Travels of Francisco de Miranda in the United States, 1783–84.* Trans. Judson P. Wood. Norman: University of Oklahoma Press, 1963.

Feiler, Bruce. *America's Prophet: Moses and the American Story.* New York: William Morrow, 2010.

Fielding, John. *Extracts from Such of the Laws, as Particularly Relate to the Peace and Good Order of this Metropolis.* London, 1768.

Fithian, Philip Vickers. *Journal & Letters of Philip Vickers Fithian [1747–1776], 1773–1774: A Plantation Tutor of the Old Dominion.* Ed. Hunter Dickinson Farish. Charlottesville: University of Virginia Press, 1943; rpt. 1968.

Flavell, Julie. *When London Was Capital of America.* New Haven: Yale University Press, 2010.

Foster, Frances Smith. "Narrative of the Interesting Origins and (Somewhat) Surprising Developments of African-American Print Culture." *American Literary History* 22 (2005): 714–40.

———. *Written by Herself: Literary Production by African American Women, 1746–1892.* Bloomington: Indiana University Press, 1993.

Fox, George. *Gospel Family-Order, Being a Short Discourse Concerning the Ordering of Families, Both of Whites, Blacks, and Indians.* London, 1676.

Franklin, Benjamin. *"Autobiography." Benjamin Franklin: Writings.* Ed. J. A. Leo Lemay. New York: Library of America, 1987.

———. *The Papers of Benjamin Franklin.* Ed. Leonard W. Labaree. 38 vols. New Haven: Yale University Press, 1959–2006.

Fryer, Peter. *Staying Power: The History of Black People in Britain.* London: Pluto Press, 1984.

Gates, Henry Louis, Jr. *The Trials of Phillis Wheatley: America's First Black Poet and Her Encounters with the Founding Fathers.* New York: Basic Books, 2003.

———. "Writing 'Race' and the Difference It Makes." *Critical Inquiry* 12 (1985): 1–20.

Gerzina, Gretchen Holbrook. *Black London.* London: John Murray, 1995.

————. *Mr. and Mrs. Prince: How an Extraordinary Eighteenth-Century Family Moved out of Slavery and into Legend.* New York: Amistad, 2008.

Gibbons, Thomas. *Juvenalia: Poems on Various Subjects of Devotion and Virtue.* London, 1750.

Gifford, George E., Jr. "Botanic Remedies in Colonial Massachusetts, 1620–1820." In Estes, *Publications of the Colonial Society of Massachusetts* 57: 263–88.

Gillies, John. "Memoirs of the Life of the Reverend George Whitefield." In Gillies, *Works* 7: 17–357.

————, ed. *The Works of the Rev. George Whitefield, M.A. Late of Pembroke College, Oxford, and Chaplain to the Rt. Hon. The Countess of Huntingdon, Containing All his Sermons and Tracts Which Have Been Already Published with a Selected Collection of Letters.* 7 vols. London and Edinburgh, 1771–72.

Glasson, Travis. "'Baptism doth not bestow Freedom': Missionary Anglicanism, Slavery, and the Yorke-Talbot Opinion, 1701–30," *William and Mary Quarterly,* 3rd series 67 (2010): 297–318.

Gomez, Michael A. Gomez. *Exchanging Our Country Marks: The Transformation of African Identities in the Colonial and Antebellum South.* Chapel Hill: University of North Carolina Press, 1998.

Gordon, William. *The History of the Rise, Progress, and Establishment, of the Independence of the United States of America.* London, 1788.

Grant, Douglas. *The Fortunate Slave: An Illustration of African Slavery in the Early Eighteenth Century.* Oxford: Oxford University Press, 1968.

[Great Britain], Anno Regni Georgii III. Regis Magnae Britanniae, Franciae, & Hiberniae, quinto. At the Parliament begun and holden at Westminster, the nineteenth day of May, anno Dom. 1761, in the first year of the reign of our Sovereign Lord George the Third, by the grace of God, of Great-Britain, France, and Ireland, King, Defender of the Faith, &c. And from thence continued by several prorogations to the tenth day of January, 1765, being the fourth session of the twelfth Parliament of Great Britain. London; New-London,Conn., 1765.

Green, James. "The Publishing History of Olaudah Equiano's *Interesting Narrative.*" *Slavery and Abolition* 16 (1995): 362–75.

Greene, Evarts B., and Virginia D. Harrington. *American Population before the Federal Census of 1790.* New York: Columbia University Press, 1932.

Greene, Jack P., and Philip D. Morgan, eds. *Atlantic History: A Critical Appraisal.* New York: Oxford University Press, 2009.

Greene, Lorenzo Johnston. *The Negro in Colonial New England 1620–1776.* New York: Columbia University Press, 1942.

Gregory, George. *Essays Historical and Moral*. London, 1785.

Grimsted, David. "Anglo-American Racism and Phillis Wheatley's 'Sable Veil,' 'Length'ned Chain,' and 'Knitted Heart.'" In Hoffman and Albert, *Women in the Age of the American Revolution*, 340–444.

Gronniosaw, James Albert Ukawsaw. *A Narrative of the Most Remarkable Particulars in the Life of James Albert Ukawsaw Gronniosaw, an African Prince, as Related by Himself.* Bath, 1772.

Hall, Kim F. *Things of Darkness: Economies of Race and Gender in Early Modern England*. Ithaca, N.Y.: Cornell University Press, 1996.

Hammon, Briton. *Narrative of the Most Uncommon Sufferings and Surprizing Deliverance of Briton Hammon, a Negro Man*. Boston, 1760.

Hammon, Jupiter. *An Address to Miss Phillis Wheatley, Ethiopian Poetess, in Boston, Who Came from Africa at Eight Years of Age, and Soon Became Acquainted with the Gospel of Jesus Christ*. Hartford, Conn., 1778.

———. *An Address to the Negroes in the State of New York*. New York and reprinted in Philadelphia, 1787.

———. *An Evening Thought. Salvation, by Christ, with Penitential Cries: Composed by Jupiter Hammon, a Negro Belonging to Mr. Lloyd*. New York, 1760.

Hancock, John. *Proclamation*. Boston, 1784.

Handler, Jerome S. "The Middle Passage and the Material Culture of Captive Africans." *Slavery and Abolition* 30 (2009): 1–6.

Haywood, Eliza. *Secret Histories, Novels, and Poems*. London: 1742.

———. *Works*. London: 1724.

Hoare, Prince. *Memoirs of Granville Sharp*. London, 1820.

Hoffman, Ronald, and Peter J. Albert, eds. *Women in the Age of the American Revolution*. Charlottesville: University Press of Virginia, 1989.

Hoffman, Ronald, Mechal Sobel, and Fredrika J. Teute, eds. *Through a Glass Darkly: Reflections on Personal Identity in Early America*. Chapel Hill: University of North Carolina Press, 1997.

Hopkins, Samuel, and Ezra Stiles. *To the Public*. Newport, R.I., 1776.

Hopkins, Stephen. *The Rights of Colonies Examined. Published by Authority*. Providence, R.I.: 1764.

Huddleston, Eugene L. "Matilda's 'On Reading the Poems of Phillis Wheatley, the African Poetess.'" *Early American Literature* 5 (1970–71): 57–67.

Hughes, Langston. *Famous American Negroes*. New York: Dodd, Mead and Co., 1954.

Hume, David. *Essays and Treatises on Several Subjects*. London and Edinburgh, 1764.

Hutchinson, Thomas. *The Diary and Letters of His Excellency Thomas Hutchinson, Esq*. Ed. Peter Orlando Hutchinson. Boston, 1886.

The Ill Policy and Inhumanity of Imprisoning Insolvent Debtors, Fairly Stated and Discussed. Newport, R.I., 1754.

Imlay, Gilbert. *A Topographical Description of the Western Territory of North America.* 2 vols. New York, 1793.

Inikori, Joseph E., and Stanley L. Engerman, eds. *The Atlantic Slave Trade: Effects on Economies, Societies and Peoples in Africa, the Americas, and Europe.* Durham: Duke University Press, 1992.

Isani, Mukhtar Ali. "The British Reception of Wheatley's *Poems on Various Subjects.*" *Journal of Negro History* 66 (1981): 144–49.

———. "The Contemporaneous Reception of Phillis Wheatley: Newspaper and Magazine Notices during the Years of Fame, 1765–1774." *Journal of Negro History* 85 (2000): 260–73.

———. "The Methodist Connection: New Variants of Some of Phillis Wheatley's Poems." *Early American Literature* 22 (1987): 108–13.

———. "'On the Death of General Wooster'; An Unpublished Poem by Phillis Wheatley." *Modern Philology* 77 (1980): 306–09.

———. "Wheatley's Departure for London and her 'Farewel to America.'" *South Atlantic Bulletin* 42 (1979): 123–29.

Jefferson, Thomas. *Notes on the Sate of Virginia.* Ed. Frank Shuffelton. New York: Penguin, 1999.

Johnson, Samuel. *Taxation No Tyranny.* London, 1775. In *Samuel Johnson: Political Writings. Yale Edition of the Works of Samuel Johnson.* Vol. 10. Edited by Donald J. Greene. New Haven: Yale University Press, 1977.

Jones, E. Alfred. *The Loyalists of Massachusetts: Their Memorials, Petitions and Claims.* London: The Saint Catherine Press, 1930.

Kaplan, Cora, and John Oldfield, eds. *Imagining Transatlantic Slavery.* Houndmills, U.K.: Palgrave Macmillan, 2010.

Kaplan, Sidney, and Emma Nogrady Kaplan. *The Black Presence in the Era of the American Revolution, 1777–1800.* Rev. ed. Amherst: University of Massachusetts Press, 1989.

Kelley, Mary. "'A More Glorious Revolution': Women's Antebellum Reading Circles and the Pursuit of Public Influence." *New England Quarterly* 76 (June 2003): 163–96.

———. *Learning to Stand and Speak: Women, Education, and Public Life in America's Republic.* Chapel Hill: University of North Carolina Press, 2006.

———. "Reading Women/Women Reading: The Making of Learned Women in Antebellum America." *Journal of American History* 83 (September 1996): 401–24.

Kendrick, Robert. "Re-Membering America: Phillis Wheatley's Intertextual Epic." *African American Review* 30 (1996): 71–88.

Kidd, Thomas S. *The Great Awakening: The Roots of Evangelical Christianity in Colonial America*. New Haven: Yale University Press, 2009.

Kiple, Kenneth F., and Brian T. Higgins. "Mortality Caused by Dehydration during the Middle Passage." In Inikori and Engerman, *The Atlantic Slave Trade*, 321–37.

Klein, Herbert S. *The Middle Passage: Comparative studies in the Atlantic Slave Trade*. Princeton, N.J.: Princeton University Press, 1978.

Klein, Herbert S., and Stanley L. Engerman. "Long-Term Trends in African Mortality in the Transatlantic Slave Trade." *Slavery and Abolition* 18 (1997): 36–48.

Klein, Herbert S., Stanley L. Engerman, Robin Haines, and Ralph Shlomowitz. "Transoceanic Mortality: The Slave Trade in Comparative Perspective." *William and Mary Quarterly* 58 (2001): 93–117.

Kuncio, Robert. "Some Unpublished Poems of Phillis Wheatley." *New England Quarterly* 43 (1970): 287–97.

Ladd, Joseph Brown. *The Poems of Arouet*. Charleston, 1786.

Lambert, Frank. *Pedlar in Divinity: George Whitefield and the Transatlantic Revivals, 1737–1770*. Princeton, N.J.: Princeton University Press, 2002.

Landry, Donna. *The Muses of Resistance: Laboring-Class Women's Poetry in Britain, 1739–1796*. Cambridge: Cambridge University Press, 1990.

Lathrop, John. *Consolation for mourners, from the doctrine of a resurrection, and the future happiness of believers. A discourse occasioned by the death of Mrs. Mary Lathrop, who departed this life 24th September, 1778. Aged 35. Delivered the Lord's Day after the funeral. By her afflicted consort, John Lathrop. A.M. Pastor of the Second Church in Boston. Published at the desire of many who heard it, and the particular acquaintance of the deceased*. Boston, 1778.

———. *A Discourse on the Peace; Preached on the Day of Public Thanksgiving, November 25, 1784. By John Lathrop, A.M. Pastor of the Second Church in Boston*. Boston, 1784.

———. *The Importance of Early Piety*. Boston, 1771.

Leonard, Keith D. *Fettered Genius: the African American Bardic Poet from Slavery to Civil Rights*. Charlottesville: University of Virginia Press, 2005.

Levernier, James A. "Phillis Wheatley and the New England Clergy." *Early American Literature* 26 (1991): 21–38.

———. "Style as Protest in the Poetry of Phillis Wheatley." *Style* 27 (1993): 172–93.

Long, Edward. *Candid Reflections upon the Judgement Lately Awarded by the Court of King's Bench, in Westminster-Hall, On What Is Commonly Called The Negroe-Cause*. London, 1772.

———. *The History of Jamaica. Or, General Survey of the Antient and Modern State of that Island: with Reflections on its Situation, Settlements, Inhabitants, Climate, Products, Commerce, Laws, and Government.* London: 1774.

Lorimer, Douglas A. "Black Slaves and English Liberty: A Re-examination of Racial Slavery in England." *Immigrants and Minorities* 3 (1984): 121–50.

MacEacheren, Elaine. "Emancipation of Slavery in Massachusetts: A Reexamination, 1770–1790." *Journal of Negro History* 55 (1970): 289–306.

Maitland, F. W. *Selected Historical Essays.* Ed. Helen M. Cam. Boston: Beacon Press, 1957.

Mann, Bruce H. *Republic of Debtors: Bankruptcy in the Age of American Independence.* Cambridge, Mass.: Harvard University Press, 2002.

Marshall, P. J., ed. *The Eighteenth Century.* Vol. 2 in *The Oxford History of the British Empire.* Oxford: Oxford University Press, 1998.

Mason, Julian D., Jr. "Examples of Classical Myth in the Poems of Phillis Wheatley." In *American Women and Classical Myth*, edited by Gregory Staley, 23–33. Waco: Baylor University Press, 2009.

————. *The Poems of Phillis Wheatley: Revised and Enlarged Edition with an Additional Poem.* Chapel Hill: University of North Carolina Press, 1966, 1989.

Mason, William. *The Best Improvement of the Much Lamented Death of that Eminent and Faithful Minister of the Gospel, The Rev^d Mr. George Whitefield, Chaplain to the Countess of Huntingdon.* London, 1771.

The Massachusetts Tax Valuation List of 1771. Ed. Bettye Hobbs Pruitt. Facsimile reprint. Boston: G. K. Hall & Co., 1978.

Mauduit, Israel. *The Case of the Dissenting Ministers.* London, 1772; rpt. Boston, 1773.

————. *Considerations on the American War. Addressed to the People of England.* London, 1776.

————. *A Short View of the History of the Colony of Massachusetts.* London, 1769.

————. *A Short View of the History of the New England Colonies.* London, 1769.

May, Cedrick. *Evangelism and Resistance in the Black Atlantic, 1760–1835.* Athens: University of Georgia Press, 2008.

McBride, Dwight A. *Impossible Witnesses: Truth, Abolitionism, and Slave Testimony.* New York: New York University Press, 2001.

Melish, Joanne Pope. *Disowning Slavery: Gradual Emancipation and "Race" in New England, 1780–1860.* Ithaca, N.Y.: Cornell University Press, 1998.

Meyers, Norma. *Reconstructing the Black Past: Blacks in Britain c. 1780–1830.* London: Frank Cass, 1996.

Miller, Joseph. *African Way of Death: Merchant Capitalism and the Angolan Slave Trade, 1730–1830.* Madison: University of Wisconsin, 1988.

————. "Mortality in the Atlantic Slave Trade: Statistical Evidence on Causality." *Journal of Interdisciplinary History* 2 (1981): 385-424.

Minardi, Margo. *Making Slavery History: Abolitionism and the Politics of Memory in Massachusetts.* New York: Oxford University Press, 2010.

Miranda y Rodríguez, Sebastián Francisco de. "Diary." In Ezell, *The New Democracy in America.*

Monaghan, E. Jennifer. *Learning to Read and Write in Colonial America.* Amherst: University of Massachusetts Press, 2005.

Morgan, Philip D. "Africa and the Atlantic, c. 1450 to c.1820." In Greene and Morgan, *Atlantic History,* 223–48.

———. "British Encounters with Africans and African-Americans, circa 1600–1780." In Bailyn and Morgan, *Strangers within the Realm,* 157–219.

———. "'To Be Quit of Negroes': George Washington and Slavery." *Journal of American Studies* 39 (2005): 403–29.

Nash, Gary B. *The Forgotten Fifth: African Americans in the Age of Revolution.* Cambridge, Mass.: Harvard University Press, 2006.

The New-England Almanack, or Lady's and Gentleman's Diary . . . 1776, by Benjamin West. Providence, 1775.

Nielsen, A. L. "Patterns of Subversion in the Works of Phillis Wheatley and Jupiter Hammon." *The Western Journal of Black Studies* 6 (1982): 212–19.

Nikolls [Nichols], Robert Boucher. *Letter to the Treasurer of the Treasurer of the Society Instituted for the Purpose of Effecting the Abolition of the Slave Trade.* London, 1788.

Nisbet, Richard. *The Capacity of Negroes for Religious and Moral Improvement.* London, 1789.

———. *Slavery not Forbidden by Scripture. Or a Defence of the West-India Planters, From the Aspersions Thrown out against them, by the Author of a Pamphlet, Entitled, "An Address to the Inhabitants of the British Settlements in America, upon Slave-Keeping."* By a West-Indian. Philadelphia, 1773.

Norton, Mary Beth. *Liberty's Daughters: The Revolutionary Experience of American Women, 1750–1800.* Boston, Toronto: Little, Brown and Co., 1980.

O'Brien, William. "Did the Jennison Case Outlaw Slavery in Massachusetts?" *William and Mary Quarterly* 17 (1960): 219–41.

Occom, Samson. *A Choice Collection of Hymns and Sacred Songs.* New London, 1774.

———. *The Collected Writings of Samson Occom, Mohegan.* Ed. Joanna Brooks. New York: Oxford University Press, 2006.

———. *A Sermon Preached at the Execution of Moses Paul, an Indian.* New Haven, 1772.

Odell, Margaret Matilda. "Memoir." In *Memoir and Poems of Phillis Wheatley, A Native African and a Slave. Dedicated to the Friends of the Africans.* Boston: Geo. W. Light, 1834.

O'Neale, Sondra. *Jupiter Hammon and the Biblical Beginnings of African-American Literature*. Metuchen, New Jersey: Scarecrow Press, 1993.

———. "A Slave's Subtle War: Phillis Wheatley's Use of Biblical Myth and Symbol." *Early American Literature* 21 (1986): 144–65.

Otis, James. *The Rights of the British Colonies Asserted and Proved*. Boston, 1764.

Paine, Thomas. *Common Sense*. Philadelphia, 1776.

Paley, Ruth. "After Somerset: Mansfield, Slavery and the Law in England." In Andrew and Landau, *Law, Crime and English Society 1660–1840*, 165–84.

Parker, James. *Conductor Generalis, or The Office, Duty and Authority of Justices of the Peace, High Sheriffs, Under-Sheriffs, Goalers, Coroners, Constables, Jury Men, Over-seers of the Poor, and also The Office of Clerks of Assiza And of the Peace &c. Collected out of all the Books hitherto written on those Subjects, whether of Common or Statute Law. To which is added, A Collection out of Sir Matthew Hales concerning The Descent of Lands. The Whole Alphabetically Digested Under the Several Titles, With a Table Directing to the Ready finding out Proper Matter under those Titles*. Philadelphia, 1722.

Patterson, Orlando. *Slavery and Social Death: A Comparative Study*. Cambridge, Mass.: Harvard University Press, 1982.

Pemberton, Ebenezer. *Heaven the Residence of the Saints*. London, 1771.

Personal Slavery Established, By the Suffrages of Common and Right Reason. Being a Full Answer to the Gloomy and Visionary Reveries, of all the Fanatical and Enthusiastical Writers on that Subject. Philadelphia, 1773.

Piersen, William D. *Black Yankees: The Development of an Afro-American Subculture in Eighteenth-Century New England*. Amherst: University of Massachusetts Press, 1988.

Pope, Alexander. *Poems on Several Occasions*. London, 1717.

Price, Ezekiel. "Diary of Ezekiel Price." In *Massachusetts Historical Society Proceedings 1863–1864*. Boston, 1864.

Quaque, Philip. *The Life and Letters of Philip Quaque, the First African Anglican Missionary*. Eds. Vincent Carretta and Ty M. Reese. Athens: University Press of Georgia, 2010.

Quarles, Benjamin. *The Negro in the American Revolution*. Chapel Hill: University of North Carolina Press, 1961.

———. "The Revolutionary War as a Black Declaration of Independence." In Berlin and Hoffman, *Slavery and Freedom in the Age of Revolution*, 283–305.

Rawley, James A. "The World of Phillis Wheatley." *New England Quarterly* 50 (1977): 666–77.

Rediker, Marcus. *The Slave Ship: A Human History*. New York: Viking, 2007.

Richards, Phillip M. "Phillis Wheatley, Americanization, the Sublime, and the Romance of America." *Style* 27 (1993):194–221.

———. "Phillis Wheatley and Literary Americanization." *American Quarterly* 44 (1992): 163–91.

Richardson, David. "The British Empire and the Atlantic Slave Trade, 1660–1807." In Marshall, *The Eighteenth Century*, 440–64.

Roberts, George. *Juvenile Poems on Various Subjects*. Limerick, 1763.

Robertson, Robert. *The Speech of Mr. John Talbot Campo-Bell, a Free Christian Negro, to his Countrymen in the Mountains of Jamaica*. London, 1736.

Robinson, William H. *Phillis Wheatley: A Bio-Bibliography*. Boston: G. K. Hall, 1981.

———. *Phillis Wheatley and Her Writings*. New York: Garland, 1984.

———. "Phillis Wheatley in London." *CLA Journal* 21 (1977): 187–201.

Rogal, Samuel J. "Phillis Wheatley's Methodist Connection." *Black American Literary Forum* 21 (1987): 85–97.

Romans, Bernard. *A Concise Natural History of East and West Florida*. New York: Printed for the Author, 1775.

Rowe, Elizabeth Singer. *Poems on Several Occasions. Written by Philomela*. London, 1696.

Rozbicki, Michal J. "To Save Them from Themselves: Proposals to Enslave the British Poor, 1698–1755." *Slavery and Abolition* 22 (2001): 29–50.

Rush, Benjamin. *An Address to the Inhabitants of the British Settlements in America, on the Slavery of Negroes in America*. Philadelphia, 1773.

———. *A Dissertation on the Spasmodic Asthma of Children*. London, 1770.

Russell, Ezekiel. *The Appendix. Or some Observations of the Expediency of the Petition of the Africans, Living in Boston, etc., lately Presented to the General Assembly of this Province. To which Is Annexed, the Petition Referred to Likewise, Thoughts on Slavery with a useful Extract from the Massachusetts Spy, of January 28, 1773, by Way of an Address to the Members of the Assembly. By a Lover of Constitutional Liberty*. Boston, 1773.

Sabine, Lorenzo. *Biographical Sketches of the American Revolution with an Historical Essay*. 1864; reprinted, Port Washington, N.Y.: Kennikat Press, 1966.

Sancho, Ignatius. *Letters of the Late Ignatius Sancho, an African*. London, 1782. In Carretta, *Letters of the Late Ignatius Sancho*.

Saunders, Richard H., and Ellen G. Miles. *American Colonial Portraits 1700–1776*. Washington, D.C.: Smithsonian Institution Press, 1987.

Scheick, William J. *Authority and Female Authorship in Colonial America*. Lexington: University Press of Kentucky, 1998.

———. "Subjection and Prophecy in Phillis Wheatley's Verse Paraphrases of Scripture." *College Literature* 22 (1995): 122–30.

Schmidt, Klaus H., and Fritz Fleischmann, eds. *Early America Re-Explored: New Readings in Colonial, Early National and Antebellum Culture*. New York: Peter Lang, 2000.

Scott (Taylor), Mary. *The Female Advocate*. London, 1774.

Seeber, Edward Derbyshire. *Anti-Slavery Opinion in France during the Second Half of the Eighteenth Century*. Baltimore: Johns Hopkins Press, 1937.

Segal, Ronald. *Islam's Black Slaves: the Other Black Diaspora*. New York: Farrar, Straus and Giroux, 2001.

Sewall, Samuel. *The Selling of Joseph*. Boston, 1700.

Sharp, Granville. *An Essay on Slavery*. Burlington, 1773.

———. *Remarks on Several Very Important Prophecies, in Five Parts*. London, 1768.

———. *A Representation of the Injustice and Dangerous Tendency of Tolerating Slavery; or of Admitting the Least Claim of Private Property of Men, in England*. London, 1769.

Shaw, Gwendolyn DuBois. "'On Deathless Glories Fix Thine Ardent View': Scipio Moorhead, Phillis Wheatley, and the Mythic Origins of Anglo-African Portraiture in New England." In Shaw, *Portraits*, 26–43.

———, ed. *Portraits of a People: Picturing African Americans in the Nineteenth Century*. Seattle: University of Washington Press, 2006.

Shenstone, William. *Poems on Various Occasions, Written for the Entertainment of the Author*. London, 1737.

———. *The Works in Verse and Prose of William Shenstone, Esq*. London, 1744.

Shields, John C. *The American Aeneas: Classical Origins of the American Self*. Knoxville: University of Tennessee Press, 2001.

———, ed. *The Collected Works of Phillis Wheatley*. New York: Oxford University Press, 1988.

———. "Phillis Wheatley and Mather Byles: A Study in Literary Relationships." *CLA Journal* 23 (1980): 377–90.

———. *Phillis Wheatley and the Romantic Age*. Knoxville: University of Tennessee Press, 2010.

———. *Phillis Wheatley's Poetics of Liberation: Backgrounds and Contexts*. Knoxville: University of Tennessee Press, 2008.

———. "Phillis Wheatley's Use of Classicism." *American Literature* 52 (1980): 97–111.

Shuffleton, Frank, ed. *A Mixed Race: Ethnicity in Early America*. New York: Oxford University Press, 1993.

———. "Phillis Wheatley, the Aesthetic, and the Form of Life." In *Studies in Eighteenth-Century Culture* 26, edited by Syndy M. Conger and Julie C. Hayes, 74–85. Baltimore: Johns Hopkins University Press, 1998.

Shurtleff, Nathaniel B. *Proceedings of the Massachusetts Historical Society* 7 (1863–1864): 270–72.

Shyllon, F. O., *Black People in Britain, 1555–1832*. Oxford: Oxford University Press, 1977.

Sidbury, James. *Becoming African in America: Race and Nation in the Early Black Atlantic.* New York: Oxford University Press, 2007.

Singleton, John. *A General Description of the West-Indian Islands.* Barbados, 1766.

Slauter, Eric. "Neoclassical Culture in a Society with Slaves: Race and Rights in the Age of Wheatley." *Early American Studies* (2004): 81–122.

———. *The State as a Work of Art: The Cultural Origins of the Constitution.* Chicago: University of Chicago Press, 2009.

Smith, Cynthia J. "'To Maecenas': Phillis Wheatley's Invocation of an Idealized Reader." *Black American Literature Forum* 23 (1989): 579–92.

Smith, Eleanor. "Phillis Wheatley: A Black Perspective." *Journal of Negro Education* 43 (1974): 401–7.

Society Instituted for the Purpose of Effecting the Abolition of the Slave Trade. London, 1788.

Spear, Chloe. *Memoir of Mrs. Chloe Spear, A Native of Africa, Who was Enslaved in Childhood, and Died in Boston, January 3, 1815. . . . Aged 65 Years. By a Lady of Boston.* Boston: Published by James Loring, 1832.

Spector, Robert M. "The Quock Walker Cases (1781–1783)—Slavery, Its Abolition, and Negro Citizenship in Early Massachusetts." *Journal of Negro History* 53 (1968): 12–32.

Stedman, John Gabriel. *Narrative of a Five Years Expedition against the Revolted Negroes of Surinam.* London, 1796.

Swaminathan, Srividhya. "Developing the West Indian Proslavery Position after the *Somerset* Decision." *Slavery and Abolition* 24 (2003): 40–60.

Swan, James. *A Dissuasion to Great-Britain and the Colonies from the Slave Trade to Africa. Shewing the Contradiction this Trade Bears, both to Laws Divine and Provincial.* Boston, 1772.

Sweet, John Wood. *Negotiating Race in the American North, 1730–1830.* Baltimore: Johns Hopkins Press, 2003.

Sword, Kirsten. "Remembering Dinah Nevil: Strategic Deceptions in Eighteenth-Century Antislavery." *Journal of American History* 97 (2010): 315–43.

Thacher, Oxenbridge. *Sentiments of a British American.* Boston, 1764.

Thorn, Jennnifer. "'All beautiful in woe': Gender, Nation, and Phillis Wheatley's 'Niobe.'" *Studies in Eighteenth-Century Culture* 37 (2008): 233–58.

Tobin, Beth Fowkes. *Picturing Imperial Power: Colonial Subjects in Eighteenth-Century British Painting.* Durham: Duke University Press, 1999.

Tobin, James. *Cursory Remarks upon Mr. Ramsay's Essay.* London, 1785.

Tolman, George. *John Jack, the Slave, and Daniel Bliss, the Tory: The Story of Two Men of Concord, Massachusetts who Lived before the Revolution: A Paper Prepared and Presented before the Concord Antiquarian Society.* Concord. Mass.: T. Todd Company, 1939.

Van Cleve, George. "The Somerset Case and its Antecedents in Imperial Perspective," with responses by Daniel J. Hulsebosch and Ruth Paley. *Law and History Review* 24 (2006): 601–71.

Verhoeven, Wil. *Gilbert Imlay: Citizen of the World*. London: Pickering & Chatto, 2008).

Waldstreicher, David. *Runaway America: Benjamin Franklin, Slavery, and the American Revolution*. New York, 2004.

Wallcut, Robert F. "Memoir of Thomas Wallcut." *Proceedings of the Massachusetts Historical Society* 2 (1841): 193–208.

Walters, Tracey L. *African American Literature and the Classicist Tradition: Black Women Writers from Wheatley to Morrison*. New York: Palgrave MacMillan, 2007.

Walvin, James. *Black Ivory: A History of British Slavery*. New York: HarperCollins, 1992.

Watson, Marcia. "A Classic Case: Phillis Wheatley and Her Poetry." *Early American Literature* 31 (1996): 103–32.

Wesley, John. *Primitive Physic*. London, 1747.

———. *Thoughts upon Slavery*. London, 1774.

Wheatley, Phillis. *Complete Writings*. Ed. Vincent Carretta. New York: Penguin, 2001.

———. *Poems on Various Subjects, Religious and Moral*. London: Archibald Bell, 1773.

Whitefield, George. *Eighteen Sermons Preached by the Late Rev. George Whitefield*. London, 1771.

———. *Three Letters from the Reverend Mr. G. Whitefield . . . Letter III. To the Inhabitants of Maryland, Virginia, North and South-Carolina*. Philadelphia, 1740.

———. *The Works of the Rev. George Whitefield, M.A. Late of Pembroke College, Oxford, and Chaplain to the Rt. Hon. The Countess of Huntingdon, Containing All his Sermons and Tracts Which Have Been Already Published with a Selected Collection of Letters*. Ed. John Gillies. 7 vols. London and Edinburgh, 1771–72.

Whyte, Laurence. *Original Poems on Various Subjects, Serious, Moral, and Diverting*. Dublin, 1742.

Wiecek, William M. "*Somerset*: Lord Mansfield and the Legitimacy of Slavery in the Anglo-American World." *The University of Chicago Law Review* 42 (1974): 86–146.

Wilcox, Kirstin. "The Body into Print: Marketing Phillis Wheatley," *American Literature* 71 (1999): 1–29.

Willard, Carla. "Wheatley's Turns of Praise: Heroic Entrapment and the Paradox of Revolution." *American Literature* 67 (1995): 233–56.

Williams, Francis. "To That most upright and valiant Man, GEORGE HALDANE, Esq; Governor of the Island of *Jamaica*; Upon whom All military and moral Endowments are accumulated. An Ode." In Long, *The History of Jamaica* 2: 478–83.

Winslow, Anna Green. *Diary of Anna Green Winslow: A Boston School Girl of 1771.* Ed. Alice Morse Earle. Boston and New York: Houghton Mifflin Company, 1894.

Winterer, Caroline. *The Mirror of Antiquity: American Women and the Classical Tradition, 1750–1900.* Ithaca, N.Y.: Cornell University Press, 2007.

Wise, Steven M. *Though the Heavens May Fall: The Landmark Trial that Led to the End of Human Slavery.* Cambridge, Mass.: Da Capo Press, 2005.

Wood, Betty. *The Origins of American Slavery.* New York: Hill and Wang, 1997.

Wrigley, E. A. "A Simple Model of London's Importance in Changing English Society and Economy, 1650–1750." In *People, Cities and Wealth: The Transformation of Traditional Society,* edited by E. A. Wrigley, 133–56. Oxford: Oxford University Press, 1987.

Wyman, Thomas Bellows. *The Genealogies and Estates of Charlestown, in the County of Middlesex and Commonwealth of Massachusetts, 1629–1818.* 2 vols. Boston, 1879.

Young, Jeffrey Robert, ed. *Proslavery and Sectional Thought in the Early South, 1740–1829: An Anthology.* Columbia: University of South Carolina Press, 2006.

Zachs, William. *The First John Murray and the Late Eighteenth-Century Book Trade.* Oxford: Oxford University Press, 1998.

Zafar, Rafia Zafar. *We Wear the Mask: African Americans Write American Literature, 1760–1870.* New York: Columbia University Press, 1997.

Zagarri, Rosemarie. *Revolutionary Backlash: Women and Politics in the Early American Republic.* Philadelphia: University of Pennsylvania Press, 2008.

Zilversmit, Arthur. *The First Emancipation: The Abolition of Slavery in the North.* Chicago: University of Chicago Press, 1967.

———. "Quock Walker, Mumbet, and the Abolition of Slavery in Massachusetts." *William and Mary Quarterly* 25 (1968): 614–24.

Index

abolitionist movement, 153, 161, 207n2; and revolutionary rhetoric, 139–40; and Wheatley, 195–96, 198–99

Abridgement of Burn's Justice of the Peace and Parish Officer, 193

"Act to prevent the Importation of Negro Slaves into this Province," 139

Adams, Abigail, 157, 226–27n32

Adams, John, 47, 70, 157, 226–27n32

Adams, John Quincy, 201

Adams, Samuel, 74

Adams, Thomas, 181

Adanson, Michel, 188; *A Voyage to Senegal*, 152

Addison, Joseph, *Cato. A Tragedy*, 51; *Rosamund. An Opera*, 51

Address to Miss Phillis Wheatley, Ethopian Poetess (Hammon), 54, 170

"Address to the Atheist, by P. Wheatley at the Age of 14 Years—1767—" (Wheatley), 54–56, 211n15

"Address to the Deist—1767—" (Wheatley), 56–57, 58

Address to the Inhabitants of the British Settlements in America (Rush), 89–91, 127

Address to the Negroes in the State of New York (Hammon), 53

Adkins, Dilly, 193

Africa, 1, 4; Gold Coast, 151, 206n38, 226n18; idealized descriptions of, 151, 152

African descent, people of: arguments on intelligence of, 198–201; in Boston 1761, 1; and education, 38–39; eighteenth-century prejudices and stereotypes about, 5–6; free, and compulsory labor, 20; and identity, 4; life expectancy of, 190; participating in the slave trade, 1, 2; and portraits, 100

Alexis (pseud.), "Wrote after reading some Poems composed by PHILLIS WHEATLLY," 166

"Amazing Grace" (Newton), 195

"America" (Wheatley), 70–71

American colonies: commercial transactions in, 177–78; enslaved Africans in, 3–4; hypocrisy of, regarding slavery, 126–27, 132; law practiced in, 193; and the Mansfield ruling, 125–26, 129–30, 222–23n45; medicine practiced in, 192–93; and revolutionary rhetoric, 132; tensions between Britain and, 67–72, 104, 126, 148, 213n41

American Revolution, 126; currency during, 16; depression following, 184, 186; and Wheatley, 171

American South, 15, 18

Amory, Thomas, *Daily Devotion Assisted and Recommended*, 88

Andrews, John, 85, 87, 93, 146, 147

Anglican Church of England, 24, 25

Annis, John, 124–25

"Answer" (Rochfort), 149–51

Appleton, Nathaniel, 140

apprenticeship, 21

"A REBUS. BY I.B." (Bowdoin), 103

Arminianism, 28

Arminian Magazine, 172, 188, 195

Arminius, Jacobus, 28